Medievalism
in American Culture

medieval & renaissance
texts & studies

VOLUME 55

Medievalism
in American Culture

Papers of the Eighteenth Annual Conference
of the Center for Medieval and Early Renaissance Studies

Edited by

Bernard Rosenthal
Paul E. Szarmach

meɒɪeval & ʀenaɪssance texts & stuɒɪes
Binghamton, New York
1989

Library of Congress Cataloging-in-Publication Data

State University of New York at Binghamton. Center for
  Medieval and Early Renaissance Studies. Conference
  (18th : 1984 : State University of New York at
  Binghamton)
  Medievalism in American culture.

  (Medieval & Renaissance texts & studies ; v. 55)
  Includes index.
  1. United States—Civilization—Medieval influences—
Congresses. I. Rosenthal, Bernard, 1934–
II. Szarmach, Paul E. III. Title. IV. Series: Medieval
& Renaissance texts & studies ; v. 55.
E169.1.S7685   1984a   973   89–8923
ISBN 0–86698–039–3 (alk. paper)

This book is made to last.
It is set in Bodoni, smythe-sewn,
and printed on acid-free paper
to library specifications.

Printed in the United States of America

In Memoriam

Morton W. Bloomfield   John Gardner

Contents

Part Three: Architecture

Medievalism
in American Culture

Introduction

THE EIGHTEENTH ANNUAL CONFERENCE OF THE CENTER FOR MEDIEVAL AND Early Renaissance Studies at SUNY-Binghamton (October 19–20, 1984) departed radically from the Center's traditional topics of exploration. Rather than focus directly on the Medieval or Renaissance periods, the Eighteenth Conference addressed itself to the idea of "Medievalism in American Culture." Two basic concepts defined the concerns of the conference. One sought to explore the ways in which medieval culture affected the shaping of American society. The other searched for the ways in which American culture constructed its own ideas of the Middle Ages. The first sought to find a historical line of influence; the second looked for the way imagination constructed a past that did not necessarily exist but that nevertheless converged with the present of America. Certainly, separating the two ways in which Medievalism bears on American culture does not always lend itself to neat divisions, and the history and the fiction of a medieval world in America sometimes have inextricably converged. But the presence of that Medievalism, however one divides it, has emerged as a significant one in American culture, even if this presence has been obscured by the dominant concern of intellectual historians in seeing our culture as an outgrowth of America's Puritan roots.[1]

The subject of American Medievalism itself has been often noted, but it has not received the kind of systematic inquiry that British Medievalism has in Alice Chandler's *A Dream of Order* or Mark Girouard's *The Return to Camelot*.[2] Probably the major scholarly attempts to examine the subject have appeared in the journal *Studies in Medievalism* edited by Leslie H. Workman and in portions of T. J. Jackson Lears's *No Place of Grace*.[3] While numerous other distinguished scholars have commented in one way or another on the subject, its analysis has generally been peripheral to other considerations. Specialized aspects of Medievalism have, of course, been examined, as, for example, Angelina La Piana's *Dante's American Pilgrimage: A Historical Survey of Dante Studies in the United States, 1800–1944* and A. Bartlett Giamatti's *Dante in America*.[4] Other studies of the medieval period from a myriad of perspectives abound. But broad inquiries into American Medievalism remain far less extensive. Although this volume will not offer an integrated thesis to account for the relative absence of scholarly inquiries into American Medievalism, the essays in it represent the considered reflections of a group of scholars who convened together to examine different facets of this topic, one that finds its way into American history, literature, art, architecture, theology, and other disciplines. This volume purports neither to be conclusive nor exhaustive. It does seek to focus attention on the subject and to look at American culture as in part something other than an extension of the Puritan search for a city on the hill. As in the Conference, we have made no attempt to force this volume into the development of a particular thesis. We have followed the model of the Conference, however, dividing this book into three general sections: Culture and History, Literature, and Architecture. Here we offer by way of introduction some observations on the general subject of Medievalism in America and suggest how the contributors to this volume illuminate it in their discussions.

Our central premise is that no scholar approaches the history of American culture without recognizing its imaginative roots in European perceptions. That is, as Morton Bloomfield reminds us in his essay, America was "invented" in Europe. Few scholars dealing with the history of ideas in America fail to note this imaginative relationship between the two continents. Over and over, Shakespeare's *Tempest* has been cited as a vision of the possibilities and limits of a "brave new world." Scholars, however, have given less attention to the converse side of this story, which is the American "invention" of Europe, or more specifically, of a medieval world on the other side of the ocean that resides in the realm of fantasy. Arthur returns from Avalon every time we invoke this image.

This is the medieval land of beautiful ladies and noble knights, of pervasive ignorance and degradation, of spectacle and magic, of splendor and chaos. It is a world where one of America's earliest novelists, Charles Brockden Brown, located a significant portion of his "History of the Carrils," Brown's most ambitious and extensive piece of fiction: this history of an imaginary family, published in magazine form, to this day has never appeared as a book. It is the world where Thoreau, inspired by the Old English translation of Bede's *Historia Ecclesiastica*, writes the poem "Speech of a Saxon Ealderman,"[5] where Lowell conjures Sir Launfal, where Cooper locates his *The Bravo* and *The Heidenmauer*, where writers through our history such as Adams, Cabell, Robinson, Steinbeck, White, and Malamud have found a world of make-believe to explore contemporary social problems or to escape from them, a world of best selling fiction created by Marion Zimmer Bradley and lesser known writers. Nor is this evocation confined to literature. In architecture, e.g. Ralph Adams Cram, H. H. Richardson, Louis Sullivan, and even Phillip Johnson have re-created medieval structures or alluded to them in buildings sacred and profane: The Cloisters, the Cathedral of St. John the Divine, the Woolworth Building, the Crystal Cathedral, and most recently the PPG Building in Pittsburgh are clear and present examples. To list all who have invented a medieval past would be to compile a long list indeed including writers, musicians, architects, graphic artists, and others. Some of the essays in this collection offer suggestions as to why this Europe has been invented in the various arts and disciplines.

Other essays look to the history recoverable through fact rather than fantasy, to the line of influence and interplay between a past we can apprehend and a present we seek to understand. Eugene Genovese, for example, explores the ways in which the medieval world was appropriated by Southern slave holders, and Susan Mosher Stuard examines the interplay of feminism and historiography as they pertain to America and the medieval world. Thus, the writers who have contributed to this collection explore both the myth and history of medievalism in our culture, even as the very term existing as the object of this exploration remains slippery and persists in resisting an easy definition.

"Medievalism," as is inevitable with labels, exists in the way we define it rather than as some fixed Platonic reality. Thus, whether those aspects of culture broadly defined as "medieval" reflect an accurate past becomes a separate issue. More immediately germane for those seeking "Medievalism in American Culture" is the matter of contemporary imaginings that evoke another order of reality. That kind of reality, as it applies to Medievalism in American culture, has taken two antithetical forms, a past wallowing in its dark ignorance and an age of spectacle, hope, and romance. This is the ambivalent world of Mark Twain's *A Connecticut Yankee in King Arthur's Court*, where on one side stands a realm of disease, theological tyranny, oppression; on the other shines Camelot. The symbiosis between America and the medieval world grows from the central fact that each has been invented and that neither in its mythic form corresponds very closely to historical scrutiny. In D. R. Castleton's now obscure novel, *Salem: A Tale of the Seventeenth Century*, published in 1874, one of the characters remarks, "Our fathers left England to enjoy freedom of conscience, and the liberty of thought and speech, and we have been taught to honor them for it."[6] To this day that myth of the Puritan settlement governs popular imagination, even though historians of the period know and teach that those early settlers would have looked in utter bewilderment at such a notion. But the texture of a culture cannot be so easily ignored through the simple matter of denying its sense of historical accuracy. The question of history subordinates itself to one of fable, as Emerson noted in his essay "History," where he recited Napoleon's rhetorical question, "What is history ... but a fable agreed upon?"[7]

The accuracy of this observation is a matter for resolution elsewhere. For our popular imagination, it is the agreed upon fable that gives Medievalism its texture in America. When Morton Bloomfield offers his account of Medievalism, he invokes many of the myriad and unsystematic ways in which Medievalism has taken hold in our culture. To systematize this myth into a tightly constructed structure would devastatingly falsify what Medievalism has meant in America. At its root is its diversity, its capacity to conform to whatever imperatives myth makers shape about Medievalism. When Reverend Schuller, as described by Jane Welch Williams, builds a crystal cathedral, the point is not to duplicate icon for icon the structure of Chartres. The task for Schuller, rather, is to transform the resplendent myth into a contemporary edifice that pays homage to the necessities of today, as it draws upon the magic created not in the High Middle Ages by obscure artisans but by nineteenth-century Americans such as Henry Adams and Ralph Adams Cram, who in their imaginations helped construct a terrain for Schuller and others to occupy. When Peter Williams or Richard Wilson follow the bizarre life of Cram and delineate that version of history created by a nineteenth-century devotee of never-never land, the issue does not center on Cram's misunderstanding of a medieval past. Instead, we learn how through one man's imaginings a world of "medieval" architecture arises. And the eccentricity of Cram frequently governs our perception of the medieval world.

Less bizarre, though broader in its political implications, is the Medievalism of the antebellum South to which Eugene Genovese directs his attention. How well the defenders of the South's social order understood or even manipulated medieval culture in purely historical terms varied among individuals, but the significance of Medievalism's connection with the pro-slavery forces in the antebellum South stems from their power to shape versions of the past into conformity with political requirements of the present, synthesizing and articulating an intellectual defense of the morally indefensible. In the service of that cause, Medievalism worked its magic.

But if this Medievalism served the oppressors of the South, it also gave the icons of liberty that would condemn the horrors of oppression. In weaving the story of the transforming image of the female icon, Marina Warner along the way shows the medieval roots of icons of liberty, traditionally considered classical, such as the *Apotheosis of Washington*. And in showing us the falsifications of the greatest of female heroines in American imagination (inevitably from Europe), Joan of Arc, she shows us also how relentlessly a myth of Joan persists, the always lovely female, the vulnerable woman of myth, who stands ready in America's imagination to come to freedom's rescue when needed, as Arthur from Avalon will come when the time is right.

Arthur and Joan, the god-king and the peasant girl chosen by God, lie in our culture as two mystic points, one from the fairytale world of castles and wizards, the other from the fairytale world of the common person. Yet Joan presented America with paradoxes from which Arthur is free. Heroes can be strong, handsome, and fearless, but heroines must be models of purity and submission. How then were we able to get Joan past the American "cult of domesticity"? In part, of course, our myths never allowed it. But a counter myth, invented or exploited by Whitman — and we may fairly quarrel over which applies — saw the potentialities of American women transcending the limited vision that consigned them to keeper's of the hearth. Thus, Whitman prophesies an America populated by "fierce and athletic girls," and perhaps in part from his imagination comes an America prepared for the Joan who will slay dragons.[8] Paradoxically, from these strong women comes the mystical Phoebe Palmer and the "cult of domesticity" explored by Theodore Hovet in his examination of the medieval roots of an American mysticism of the nineteenth-century that within an evangelical movement sought to exalt the female, to return her to a proper place in mystical unity with the male counterpart in a spiritual merger where neither could be whole without the other.

Are Joan, or Whitman's fierce girls, or Phoebe Palmer the same woman? Do they grow from the common cultural origins where Whitman found his "fierce and athletic girls"? Probably they do. The existence of Whitman's girls or Phoebe Palmer, or the myth of Joan no doubt will not obviate concerns about how women have been depicted in American imagination, but they may temper them for some, shape the contexts, and remind us that the archetypal common man of America who could rise against the invading oppressor was after all a medieval woman. By what else but through the power of such a myth could Mark Twain have thought so well of his *Joan of Arc*, a work heavily faulted by literary critics. But Twain may have remembered something we tend to forget. It was not the glory that was Rome that America's imagination has coveted. It is the glory of a Joan or an Arthur. If we have few Joans celebrated in America's past, the absence points to our cultural tension between competing myths of women as saviors, whether on the battlefield or as guardians of morals by the hearth, and a culture that has denigrated the physical and intellectual capacities of women. But our mythic allegiance to Joan, even as it often incorporates the ambiguities of her myth, nevertheless survives.

So also with Arthur. His history in America, as indicated by Valerie Lagorio, has been broad and deep. Nor has he merely consorted with Presidents. Arthur finds his way into our deepest yearnings. Binghamton's local newspaper dropped at its peril the comic strip "Prince Valiant," but in response to an outraged public soon capitulated and restored it. In comic strips, in games such as Dungeons and Dragons, in printed stories, in movie theatres, on television screens, and on the Broadway stage his tale repeats itself, embellished many ways, but rooted always in the central core of another order of experience that our culture has designated as medieval. This strange world of make-believe lures to it those most hostile to its ornate impulses, as Peter Williams shows in connection with America's Puritans, and those most caught in the mixed web of rationality and fantasy, as Kathleen Verduin reveals, particularly in connection with Emerson. Even when our artists turn away from Medievalism, as Narciso Menocal demonstrates in showing the interplay of Louis Sullivan and the tradition of the Gothic, the thrust of that Medievalism in our culture remains a powerful one. Indeed, Susan Mosher Stuard demonstrates how contemporary feminists, in part to escape the make-believe of America's imagination, seek to find in the medieval world a truer history of women than that which our American culture has misleadingly passed on to us. Thus, we have the paradox of finding in our medieval roots a counter to an invented world inhabited by invented women.

Medievalism, of course, has invited other kinds of inventions, particularly those of fiction writers. Herman Melville, Washington Irving, Edward Arlington

Robinson, and John Gardner as well as numerous other writers mentioned and unmentioned in these pages plundered the medieval world for literary material; yet it is only in the shared plundering grounds that commonality emerges. Their tales differ radically, not merely in the nature of their story, but in the agenda they follow. Writers seeking material in medieval terrain often have little in common, and in this very diversity one sees the essential chaos of Medievalism in American culture. That it lacks a coherent and organizing principle diminishes in no way its force in our culture. Its only synthesizing point rests in the evocation of another land, where the artist has free reign to shape it to contemporary needs. For this very reason it flirts often with the literature of pure fantasy, whether in comic strips or in the once lionized novel *Jurgen* by James Branch Cabell. But the fantasy of a world where middle-aged pawn brokers and dryads cavort, as in Cabell's tale, where brave women come from the village to repel invading armies, where Excalibur awaits the man strong enough to free and unleash its magic powers, runs head on into another American myth. For Medievalism has generally embraced the myth of a magic past even though from time to time, it invokes a vision of the future.[9]

The brief introductory comments to this volume cannot explore adequately the broad implications of this paradox for American Studies. But some brief comment does appear required regarding America's capacity to juggle at the same time its medieval nostalgia with its myth of progress and the future. It is, of course, a commonplace of American scholarship to note that from the time Europe invented America, the last frontier (as it was then believed), the new land became the place where imagination could create infinitely the possibilities of material, political, and spiritual gain in a temporal world. This vision has for the most part been a masculine one, populated with heroes who conquered the West. The archetypal American heroine of America's early fiction of the nineteenth century emerged from or had an affinity with the "female," to use Cooper's word, who populates the stories of the Leatherstocking tales. In these stories the creator of America's great frontiersman perpetuated and in some way fixed the image in our mind of the helpless woman forever rescued by the sexually disinterested hero, our American Sir Gawain (not the medieval ladies' man) who rescues fair ladies and struggles to distance himself sexually from them. Here is our tradition of the lone American cowboy riding into the sunset with the woman left behind, each ultimately too pure for any other outcome. Here also is the juggling of America's paradoxical attractions for a country at once free from Europe and at the same time wedded to an Old World Medievalism. For Cooper has done more than create an American myth. He has transformed the virtues of Sir Gawain to Natty Bumppo. He has made Medievalism an integral if unobtrusive aspect of a myth that has powerfully influenced our popular culture.

We may also suggest that Medievalism has served an even broader function than the transformation of Gawain into the lone hero, whether as Natty Bumppo or John Wayne. It has offered one of the major imaginative alternatives to America's promise of material success. If most Americans have done well enough in this world of material dreams first dreamed in Europe, they have not done so well as to find the El Dorado of the Conquistadors or the Emersonian divinity within the self. For such prizes they have looked away from their land, and even away from Europe's land. They have looked to the world of Harlequin romances and competing fantasies. And of all these fantasies, none has matched the capacity to provide escape from an American dream unfulfilled as has that constructed from Camelot. So in seeking its dream of the future, America has wanted the soothing memory of the land that never was, its own particular vision of a medieval world, an alternative to the hard vision of every individual having the possibility of being Horatio Alger and having only the self to blame in failing, an idea running from Ralph Waldo Emerson to Ayn Rand and Ronald Reagan.

It does not, however, follow that all escapist imaginings of Medievalism are false. No doubt many are true. But the crux resides in the selectivity of them. We have found varieties of culture that appeal to us, that truly or falsely answer our questions and fulfill our yearnings. This process has no order, and to impose one is to falsify the image. The medieval past, thus, remains an aggregate of private domains, chaotically suffusing American culture, having in common an appeal of escape, as old as American Puritanism, which had its own medieval affinities, as Harrison Meserole so cogently shows. When Bernard Malamud in *The Natural* wrote his sad parable of a fall from grace, the relatively few people who read it saw the medieval connections structuring the context for a private, or perhaps univeral loss. When the movie of the novel came to a broader public, huge audiences thrilled to the medieval tale of redemption set on the playing fields of America and personified by "Jack Armstrong" transformed into Robert Redford. The people's myth of Medievalism crushed the horrifying image Malamud had evoked. Medieval heroes were appropriated to prevail over those forces that impede our private dreams.

In a sense this contrast between the Medievalism of Malamud's novel and the Medievalism of the film, parallels another kind of opposition in the context of a broader assessment of the whole topic of Medievalism in America. Stated in its crudest form, the issue reduces itself to the question of whether Medievalism in America belongs as an academic discipline to the Medievalists or to the Americanists. The question raises a broader concern than simply one of Linnaean classification. For the fact is that since neither group has made any significant attempt to appropriate the topic, the vast field has for the most part remained unexplored. For the Medievalist, the topic has had little to do with the conventional areas of inquiry related to such a scholar's field. The medieval scholar has worried more about whether, for example, courtly love represented a social convention or a literary creation than what Mark Twain, perhaps via Walter Scott, did with the concept. Inevitably, the subject of Medievalism has had a greater attraction for the Americanist, to pursue the same example, who has to render Twain's world coherent. Thus, the Twain scholar inevitably must deal with Medievalism just as the student of Ralph Adams Cram must face the same question. But to do so successfully, the Americanist in either case must in some sense become a Medievalist. That the transition can be made is demonstrated by the examples in this collection. Yet, quite a gulf exists between the ability of an Americanist to explore a medieval issue in connection with one or two people being studied and the ability to offer an overview of America and Medievalism.

It was partly with that problem in mind that we felt particularly fortunate at the outset of this project to have anticipated an important role in the Eighteenth Conference for John Gardner, our friend and colleague who had lived an extensive literary and scholarly life in the American and medieval worlds. Brilliant and controversial in much of his life's work, his contribution promised to cross both fields, to help focus the problem of defining the field of Medievalism in America, and to stimulate the kind of healthy debate that the subject required. It was not to be, of course, since he tragically and unexpectedly died in a motorcycle accident in September of 1982.

Although we cannot know what John Gardner might have said at the Conference, we can speculate from his fiction, however, as to how he might have regarded the confrontation of the medieval with the modern world. In his novel *Grendel* Gardner heavily exploited his medieval subject even as he powerfully and wittily demythologized it. Perhaps the paradigmatic episode that illustrates the complexities for the scholar-artist straddling the medieval and American worlds occurs in the attempt by Unferth to pose a heroic threat to Grendel. Rather than meet Unferth in some noble contest and destroy him, Grendel punishes the brash would-be-hero more severely by ridiculing his pretenses and letting him posture until Unferth falls asleep. Grendel completes the humiliation of his adversary by gently carrying him home, and Unferth lives out his life in humiliation. Among other things *Grendel* presents a world as seen from a culture whose literature mocks the heroism of Unferth in conflict with a world that remains fascinated by that heroism.

It may be that we force the analogy in proposing that the task of reconciling the texture of the medieval world with that of modern America rests in an approach that has no allegiance to one or the other. As with John Gardner, we cannot insist on merely defining Grendel as monstrous and Unferth as ridiculous. Similarly, we cannot say that the province of Medievalism in America belongs either to the Americanist or to the Medievalist. The field belongs to those who can see the plight of Grendel as well as Unferth, and if alternative visions have not let this new field mature, we need alternative ones not yet considered. It is our hope that the essays in this collection argue against the notion that we have forced the analogy and that in their rich and manifold ways they further the explorations in specific contexts of the strange and tenacious hold that the medieval world has held in American imagination.

There were more than forty papers at the Eighteenth Conference. As we began the process of selection for this volume, it became clear that our participants were offering us many different ways to organize the Proceedings. The conference coordinators, now editors, made their choices along the lines of the genres of scholarship, thus offering two volumes to readers. This volume contains wide-ranging studies that, while perhaps focussing on specific authors or artists or works initially, nevertheless entertain the larger perspectives and implications of "Medievalism in American Culture." The other volume, which has appeared as the inaugural number in a new series of conference volumes sponsored by *Studies in Medievalism*, focusses specifically on works or objects, seeking to explain or interpret them.[10] Readers who study both volumes may not agree with the editors on choices here and there, of course, but it is hoped that this general plan for organizing two volumes successfully forces all to acknowledge the essentially interdisciplinary nature of Medievalism. Two or more volumes organized along disciplinary lines would certainly diminish the pervasive range and complexity of the topic. Thus, in the overall organization of the Proceedings of the Eighteenth Conference we imitate in another mode altogether the doubling of American Culture and the Middle Ages with its attraction and repulsion, its convergence and divergence, its tension and resolution, and its final complementarity.

The co-editors gratefully acknowledge the help and assistance of many friends and colleagues in the publication of this book as well as in the general work of the Conference. The contributors to this collection, coming from diverse fields and interests, have demonstrated both cooperation and patience in the entire process. We owe a special debt of thanks to Mrs. Dorothy Huber, the Center's secretary, who was most efficient and helpful in the administration of the Conference during a time of family tragedy. Leslie Workman, Pete and Linda Forcey, J. A. Leo Lemay, Sacvan Bercovitch, Rosalind Rosenthal, among many others gave us timely advice and many suggestions. Our thanks also go out to Nicholas Delbanco who, as executor of the John Gardner estate, granted permission for a production of the radio play *The Temptation Game*, admirably performed by the Susquehanna Choral Society, to whom we offer our gratitude. For assistance in proofreading a portion of the manuscript we express our appreciation to Helen Rosenthal. Mario Di Cesare, Director of Medieval and Renaissance Texts and Studies, expedited the production of this volume with his usual energy and commitment. The co-editors, who were also co-coordinators of the Conference, share equally in the achievements and shortcomings of both the conference and its proceedings volume. The order of names indicates only obedience to the rules of alphabetical order. The co-editors are happy, as it were, to have only each other to blame.

It is an unhappy postscript that we now add at the pre-proof stage. Morton W. Bloomfield, old friend and mentor to one of us and new friend and mentor to the other, died before he was able to add the final touches to his essay. We hope that we have been true to his intentions in preparing his essay for publication and indeed to his larger vision of humane scholarship that serves broad ends.

Bernard Rosenthal
Paul E. Szarmach

SUNY-Binghamton

NOTES

1. If scholars of American history have sometimes overstated the influence of Puritanism on American culture, the reality of that influence nevertheless remains. Ever since Perry Miller turned his formidable intellectual powers to studying the American Puritans, the connection between the Puritans and Augustinianism in America has become broadly accepted. But Miller, though ultimately seeking a broad understanding of American culture, had inquiries to make other than the general question of Medievalism in American culture.

2. The complete citations are: Alice Chandler, *A Dream of Order* (Lincoln, NB:

University of Nebraska Press, 1970; London: Routledge & Kegan Paul, 1971); Mark Girouard, *The Return to Camelot* (New Haven and London: Yale University Press, 1981).

3. *Studies in Medievalism* issued its first volume in 1979. The complete citation for Lears's book is: T. J. Jackson Lears, *No Place of Grace* (New York: Pantheon Books, 1981).

4. The complete citations are: Angelina La Piana, *Dante's Pilgrimage; A Historical Survey of Dante Studies in the United States, 1800–1944* (New Haven: Yale University Press, 1948); A. Bartlett Giamatti, ed. and trans., *Dante in America*, Medieval and Renaissance Texts and Studies. vol. 23 (Binghamton, 1983).

5. See *Collected Poems of Henry Thoreau*, ed. Carl Bode (Baltimore: The Johns Hopkins Press, 1966), 213–14 and Bode's explanatory notes.

6. D. R. Castleton [Caroline Rosina Derby], *Salem: A Tale of the Seventeenth Century* (New York: Harper and Brothers, 1874), 184.

7. *The Collected Works of Ralph Waldo Emerson*, text established by Alfred R. Ferguson and Jean Ferguson Carr with introduction and notes by Joseph Clark (Cambridge, MA: Harvard University Press, 1979), II: 6.

8. Walt Whitman, "A Woman Waits for Me," in *Leaves of Grass*, ed. Harold W. Blodgett and Sculley Bradley (New York: New York University Press, 1965), 101–03, esp. 103.

9. For an excellent example see Walter M. Miller Jr.'s *A Canticle for Leibowitz* (1959; repr. New York: Bantam Books, 1961).

10. The complete citation is: Bernard Rosenthal and Paul E. Szarmach, eds., *Medievalism in American Culture: Special Studies*, Studies in Medievalism Conference Papers, vol. 1 (Binghamton, NY, 1987).

Part One: History and Culture

Reflections of a Medievalist: America, Medievalism, and the Middle Ages

Morton W. Bloomfield

A S HAS BEEN NOTED MORE THAN ONCE THE GREATEST ACHIEVEMENTS OF THE Middle Ages were the discovery of America and the Renaissance, even if the latter can be traced back to the twelfth century. The Renaissance may have done much to awaken Europe to Greek (with, for example, Robert Grosseteste and Roger Bacon in the thirteenth century) and classical Latin and its culture. Its artistic achievements are great, although not greater than those of the Middle Ages. On the other hand, to the Middle Ages we owe parliamentary government, Romanesque and Gothic cathedrals and churches, universities, the modern library, the revival of learning, and many other achievements.

The continuing influence of the Middle Ages on subsequent history has been great even down to today. The Middle Ages as an ideal and as a rich store of realistic and exciting literature, art, architecture, government and so forth has persisted in Western and indeed in Arabic and Persian culture to a great degree. It has manifested itself in various ways, but we can classify this influence into three categories: medieval achievements that often reached their full flower in modern times (since 1525) as listed above, Medievalism that provided an idealistic picture of the Middle Ages, which was imitated in various ways even down to today, and finally, the serious study of the Middle Ages, an activity begun in the late seventeenth century, which still continues in the present. At no time, however, was the Middle Ages ever forgotten, and its study was never totally neglected. There were chronicles between 1525 and 1660, and medieval history was used by various groups to justify their actions. A good example is provided by the bishops of the English Church in the sixteenth century, who attempted to prove that the Anglo-Saxon Church was separate from Rome (a tough thing to prove, I should say). The Middle Ages continued to be a subject of serious study from the mid-seventeenth century on.

Alongside the continuation of medieval institutions and ideas and the serious study of the Middle Ages, we also find what has been called Medievalism: the idealization of medieval life and culture, with an emphasis upon a rich, mysterious and imaginary world of nobility, honor, class-consciousness, defenders of women, battles and so forth that, it was believed, flourished in the Middle Ages. It put great emphasis, but not exclusively, on the Arthurian tradition as interpreted by late medieval, Renaissance, and later writers. Malory, Spenser, Tasso, Shakespeare, Du Bellay, and others invented this golden Middle Ages and were the fathers of modern Medievalism. Milton, we must remember, had originally planned to write a great epic on Arthur, and only substituted *Paradise Lost* for it later in life. To England and America, Walter Scott was the great father of later Medievalism.

In spite of this indebtedness to medieval culture, which has never died, there still persists in America a strong anti-medieval bias. As Peter W. Williams put it, "Even though medieval themes and elements have become more acceptable in both popular and academic culture during the present century, it is clear that our everyday vocabulary is still 'loaded' against that epoch which many Europeans have traditionally regarded as the time of the grandest flowering of Western culture."[1]

Yet Williams points out that Medievalism is still alive and healthy in the U.S.A., thanks largely to the growth of Catholicism in this country. Certainly, Catholicism played a major part in American Medievalism, but I doubt whether it is the only force for its growth in America. In spite of their hatred towards Catholicism, the early American Protestants were also brought up in an atmosphere of medieval culture and a knightly tradition that must not be ignored. The life of Captain John Smith and the attitude towards the Indians may be taken as examples. The early Puritans were country men and women for the most part, especially in New England; and Puritans except for their religious deviance were still medieval men and women. As Ernst Robert Curtius put it in his address on July 3, 1949 at the Goethe Bicentennial Convocation at Aspen, Colorado,[2] "... medieval forms of life subsist until about 1750."[3]

This statement has its truth, but not the whole truth. The medieval tradition has never been broken, unlike the classical tradition. Around 1750, an important change in that medieval tradition in Europe and to a lesser extent in America took place, but it by no means disappeared. In fact, it took up new forms of Medievalism after that date, thanks to the Romantic movement and to American interest in its missing Middle Ages[4] as reflected in an attraction to writers such as Dante and Walter Scott as well as in a recovery of medieval customs and ideas. America succeeded in putting new life into medieval common law, parliamentary establishments, universities, libraries, and so forth. The very architecture of its buildings, Gothic and Romanesque, particularly in the 1840s and after, offered signs of America's attraction to Medievalism.

There are then, as we have said, three major medieval legacies in America in the nineteenth century: medieval institutions and buildings; Medievalism, which is an idealized picture of medieval life; and finally, the re-creation or study of the history, literature and arts of the Middle Ages. In this essay I am concerned with the last two — Medievalism and the Middle Ages. As time goes on and new ages appear, we may decide that the "middle" idea, a creation of the early modern period, may become unsuitable. The middle will no longer be the middle. It is well to keep this in mind.

We can divide thinking humans into roughly two groups in relation to our topic. One group thinks that history has been a long story of decline. There was once a golden age, perhaps followed by silver and bronze ones, and then misery and evil became rampant. These humans tend to honor the past and deplore the present. The future is unspeakable. These are our conservatives and reactionaries (by no means the same). The second group, influenced perhaps by evolution, not to speak of their own natures, believes that we are steadily moving upward towards a golden age — perhaps Marxist, perhaps not. The future holds a glorious age. We shall have climbed out of our muck and mire, and we or our descendants will see the ushering in of an ideal world. These are our liberals or radicals (by no means the same) united by the dream of a happier if not ideal world.

When we talk about Medievalism, we are of course talking about a subdivision of the first group. These are those who believe our golden age did exist in the past. Love, decency, balance have disappeared or are disappearing. To the second group, Medievalism is anathema. The age we are to admire lies in the future when poverty, crime, brutality, inequality, nastiness will have vanished and only love will endure.

Needless to say, there are various intermediate grades, but in general thinking humans tend to veer to one end or the other of human history—to believe in a lost Eden, a lost paradise, or to believe in a coming golden age where each human will sit under his tree and enjoy the pleasures of life. Some, however, more religious, believe that the future will, like the past, offer a golden age, but usually put it into another age or even world—the messianic age or millenium as the ancient prophets envisioned. Most conservatives, if they believe in any redemption at all, put it into the world to come or into heaven. Most liberals believe that the world to come will be in this world, on this planet.

Another factor that must be considered is the apocalyptic element that embraces both groups in various degrees. The end of the world has been and is now again in the minds of most humans. In the West this attitude is largely influenced by Jewish and Christian speculation preserved in the Bible, in the Apocrypha and Pseudepigrapha. The invention and use of the atom bomb has contributed to the modern revivification of the apocalyptic tradition, which had never completely died out. Further, the voyage to the moon and the satellite explosion of the seventies also stimulated the apocalyptic tradition. However, the tradition had never vanished completely since its origin in the Old Testament, probably borrowed from Zoroastrianism. The Medievalism of the postmedieval world was fueled to some extent by this tradition, especially the destructive side of Medievalism. This tradition supported a pessimism that found consolation in a kind of worship of a happier, earlier age and even more important, a conviction that the modern world is going to the dogs.

Another minor but still potent element in Medievalism is the fact that our Western culture was strongly affected by the destruction of the Roman Empire out of which our culture arose. The decline of the Western Empire in the fifth and sixth centuries was reinforced by the fact that in the late Middle Ages the Eastern Empire had also met its doom. The blow to Byzantium and the rise and incursions of the Turks stimulated fear of the future. The memory of destruction of whole cultures was indeed deeply embedded in Western culture. Medievalism was a major by-product of apocalypticism and a sense of the fall of the Roman Empire and Byzantium. It fostered a desire to hold back the forces of destruction by imitating the Middle Ages and preserving what Western man believed was its social ideals and noble aspirations.

The birth of Medievalism was largely due to an attempt to create a happier present and to avoid a disastrous destruction by imitating a past (as it was understood) that was happier than the present misery. Other factors, of course, were involved—some were social and economic, some were aesthetic, and some were simply fear of the future. No doubt, an attempt to keep the world from a feared future made the upper and even part of the middle classes conservative and imitative of the past. Of all the pasts, the ideal Middle Ages were the best for Europeans to imitate. The lower classes, who had little to lose, could look towards a better future. For them, no attempt to stop the clock and turn to the past was desirable. The past to them was a long history of misery. Medievalism, for those who loved it, was a social ideal which had little justification in reality.

When did Medievalism begin? In one sense it began in the Middle Ages itself. The earliest extant literature gave a heroic and, no doubt, inaccurate picture of the past. It created out of dim memories and tradition a largely imaginary past. *Beowulf* presented a world that never existed, and the *Chanson de Roland* celebrated a heroic but false past. The family sagas from Iceland, later in time, had more history than most heroic tales (possibly because the gap in time between the historical facts and the written presentation was shorter than was the case with earlier literature such as *Beowulf*). Yet they also idealized to some degree the past. The Edda and the early extant poems, including the Norse praise poems or Skaldic poetry, were exaggerated and raised to a mythical height.

In English-speaking lands, the Arthurian dream has perhaps been the most persistent and important of all medieval revivals. From the time of Malory on, we find Arthur and his court a subject of greatest interest in England — with many Elizabethans, Milton, the Gothic revival with Hurd, Wharton and others who embraced and went beyond the Arthurian tradition and, above all, in the nineteenth century with the Romantics and Victorians, notably Tennyson, Ruskin and William Morris.[5] The notion of knighthood particularly attracted the nineteenth century, both in England and America. The Arthurian stories were made pure by the elimination of most of the adulterous and sexual episodes. The knights were presented as idealized fifteenth and sixteenth century noblemen. The barbaric fighters of the Arthurian age (if there was such an age) were clothed in late medieval armor and given to high and late medieval jousting, and portrayed as rescuers of damsels in distress instead of the crude rapists that they probably were. The damsels of the fifth and sixth centuries of our era in Britain were more frequently violated than rescued. This Arthurian mania has persisted down to today — in the Society for Creative Anachronism, musicals and movies, and numerous books and stories.

The history of post-sixteenth-century tournaments gives us another example of the persistence of Medievalism. The Eglinton Tournament of 1839 is only one of a group which were to be found in England and America, but

it has a book[6] devoted to its rather comic story. Earlier in the century in
Massachusetts, a native of that state wanted to fight any challenger to prove
his innocence of some charge. This act led to the formal cancellation in Massachusetts of trial by combat, which was still then nominally on the books.[7]

Next to the Arthurian mania in popularity was probably the Gothic revival
and the rise of the so-called Gothic novel or story. Continuing the eighteenth-
century Gothic novel and influenced by E. T. A. Hoffman, the German Gothic
artist, in America were Charles Brockden Brown, Edgar Allan Poe, and
Nathaniel Hawthorne. The revival is perhaps more easily seen in the popularity
of Gothic architecture that appeared in England and the United States in the
nineteenth century. In America, and to some extent in England, a Romanesque
revival (which is mainly associated with the name of H. H. Richardson) and
a Byzantine revival also occurred.[8] All these revivals are convincing proof
of the widespread appeal of Medievalism.

The new energies displayed in the Medievalism of the nineteenth century
reveal the increasing importance of the medieval in that century and, to some
extent, in ours. Its revival (and it was never totally dead) began in slight fashion
in the seventeenth century and more strongly in the eighteenth century, in
part in opposition to the Enlightenment and in part due to the Enlightenment
itself, which led to scientific and rational study of the past based on a strong
dependence on documents.[9] The Enlightenment is, however, more the explanation of the rise of modern medieval history than it is of Medievalism.

The most interesting center of Medievalism is America, and it is to it that
I now turn. The conquest and discovery of America is an extraordinary story. It was, along with the Renaissance, the greatest invention and discovery
of the Middle Ages. As has been pointed out by Edmundo O'Gorman in his
Invention of America,[10] America had to be invented before it was discovered, and the Middle Ages did both. It was discovered after its invention
and developed by medieval men and women, many of whom were adven-
turers of various sorts. Columbus, who was the predecessor of the discoverers
(except for the Vikings who explored America out of Greenland and the earlier
Asians who probably crossed the Bering Strait to settle America), was to some
extent apocalyptically minded. The letter to the sovereigns of Spain, written
concerning his fourth voyage, refers to the Abbot Joachim who wrote that
the rebuilder of Jerusalem and Mount Sion would be a Spaniard,[11] with the
implication that Columbus would be he. Columbus at that time thought he
had touched Asia somewhere. All the great discoverers of America were
medieval men. As Hugh Honour writes, "the conquest of Mexico was readily
absorbed into the late medieval view of the world."[12]

Captain John Smith (1579–1631) was a real medieval adventurer, if not a knight, before his arrival in America in 1605.[13] He embodied late medieval dash and boldness as well as nastiness. So too were Cortez and Pizarro, not to speak of others. They loved violence and honor (but not to the extent of avoiding trickery), fighting in armor and single combat when necessary. They were all travelling warriors. In England we find Anthony Woodville (d. 1483), Sir Philip Sidney (d. 1586), and Sir Henry Lee (d. 1610). This spirit was more present in Virginia and, later, the rest of the South than in New England, New York, and Pennsylvania, especially Philadelphia, regions that saw by the late seventeenth and early eighteenth century more mercantilism and less medieval influence.

Later in the eighteenth century, the American Revolution brought a new spirit of independence and freedom, especially present in the expanding West. Subsequently, the Louisiana Purchase, the opening of the prairie states, and the ultimate step in the progress – the annexation of California, all presented new and exciting vistas repeating on a new level the exhilaration of the discovery of America. The Indians were still bothersome, and Mexico provided another bone to chew on, all of which stimulated militaristic and expansionist aims. These spirits, predominantly of America's West, remain alive to the present day.

The West is partially, as a friend once pointed out to me, both the twenty-first century and the eighteenth century. It is still the area of openness, drive, manliness, movement, and dream. Paradoxically, it offered a continuation of the Middle Ages, nicely presented in Professor Lynn White, Jr.'s fine article of 1965.[14] The West is, however, partly a continuation of the real Middle Ages and partly a new Medievalism with cowboys taking the role of the good knights and the crooks and hangers-on assuming the role of the bad knights.

White's article mainly, though not exclusively, concentrates on the various devices, activities and objects, including log cabins, various coaches, revolvers, and hangings invented in the Middle Ages, which found their home in the U.S.A., especially in the West. White, however, also touches on other aspects, especially the continuity with the European Middle Ages as opposed to the development of Europe since the sixteenth century. He finds the West's hatred of centralization, its deep religiosity, its tendency to take the law into its own hands, its love of whiskey, its use of barbed wire, as inheritances from the Middle Ages. He also points to Latin America and its Medievalism, uninfluenced by Protestantism and the Reformation, and hence even easier to link with the Middle Ages than the U.S.A.

One element did escape Lynn White's keen eye—the cowboy and his "chivalric code." He ideally is the one who fights against foes who aim to steal the cattle in his care; he is a Paladin either unarmed, or more frequently, bearing a pistol or rifle. He is the "good guy" against the "bad guy." He aims at expelling the "bad guys" from the town or area, at defending the ladies, at fighting the Indians, and he emerges as the man of justice. John Ford's *Stage Coach* (1939) with its apocalyptic journey to Lordsburg and its hero John Wayne magnificently captures the "chivalry" of America's imaginative West.

Yet, Medievalism was by no means confined to this region. We find a plethora of medievalistic literature in nineteenth- (and indeed even twentieth-) century novels and poetry. Walter Scott's romantic pictures of the Middle Ages, for example, had great influence upon America just as he had had on Europe. In America, his chivalric figures and attitudes especially impressed themselves on the South.[15]

Other writers similarly were stongly influenced by the romantic notion of the Middle Ages, which produced—more than any other dominant mood of the four centuries since the Middle Ages themselves—the most powerful notion of Medievalism. Literary medievalists include, among others, Henry Adams, Henry Wadsworth Longfellow, Orestes Brownson, Washington Irving, Nathaniel Hawthorne, Charles Eliot Norton, Mark Twain, James Russell Lowell, Francis Parkman, Edwin Arlington Robinson, James Branch Cabell, and Ezra Pound.

Although there is little need to list these writers' medievalistic works, a few may be mentioned. Adams, whose *Mont St. Michel and Chartres* with its Hymn to the Virgin and his *Education of Henry Adams*, especially his chapter on "The Virgin and the Dynamo," is a major figure in both Medievalism and the study of the Middle Ages. With Longfellow, we have several medievalistic poems like "The Golden Legend" and "In the Cathedral," which is a part of "The Golden Legend," with both belonging to the larger "Christus." We also have his translation of *The Divine Comedy*. With Hawthorne, we may especially associate *The Marble Faun* and some of his short stories. With Lowell, we note particularly his poem, "The Cathedral."

Washington Irving has a number of essays on medieval buildings and their mystique, the one on Westminster Abbey being perhaps the most notable. Mark Twain, who was highly aware of Medievalism, discusses it in *Life on the Mississippi* and plunges into it in *A Connecticut Yankee in King Arthur's Court, The Prince and the Pauper, Joan of Arc* (incidentally, his favorite among the books he wrote), and many minor references in his other works, especially *Huckleberry Finn* (which also gives an amusing and not unrealistic picture of Southern chivalry). Francis Parkman shows admiration for medieval-like figures and episodes in *Jesuits in North America, LaSalle and the Discovery of the Great West,* and parts of *Pioneers of France in the New World.*

James Fenimore Cooper's books betray signs of Medievalism, especially in their chivalric action, a subject frequently explored in the nineteenth century. Sidney Lanier wrote a number of stories for young people on Arthur and his court and on Froissart, while others wrote biographies of the Black Prince, Henry V, Sir Walter Raleigh, and Philip Sidney.[16]

Twentieth-century America has continued the motif of chivalry, particularly in the form of the detective who appears frequently in books. Yet another is the manly "tough guy" of whom the best known is probably Ernest Hemingway, who acted as if he were crude masculinity personified. Clint Eastwood, John Wayne, and earlier Hoot Gibson and William S. Hart evoke the macho cowboys whose names bring to mind myths of their boldness, toughness, and chivalric spirit.

The South in particular, with its code of honor and gentlemanliness, adopted "chivalric" models of dominant masculinity and submissive femininity along with punishment for those who violated the new "Medievalism," an Arthurian model that glorified battle. The dueling, pistol shooting, tar and feathering, and hanging in the South are notorious. Here the lash and other instruments of torture prevailed, as well as a polite formalism in most human relations. In the midst of slavery the antebellum South enjoyed ring tournaments, some of which were knightly tournaments as they were then conceived.

Art and architecture were not untouched by the popularity of Medievalism. This led to the revival of Gothic and Romanesque buildings. American painters loved to paint gloomy, mysterious, and medievalistic scenes as they were imagined. Hawthorne, in his preface to *The Marble Faun,* wrote: "No author without a trial can conceive of writing a romance about a country where there is no shadow, no antiquity, no mystery, no picturesque and gloomy wrong, nor anything but a commonplace prosperity, in broad and simple daylight, as is happily the case with my dear native land." That he could write this, even though he knew that America had over two hundred years of antiquity and gloomy wrong, some of which he had used for his best fiction, reflects the powerful hold that the supposed characteristics of the Middle Ages held on his imagination.

Washington Allston (1779–1843) is a remarkable medievalist painter, carrying on some of the later eighteenth-century strands and bringing in new nineteenth-century ones wherein contemporary German art was a great stimulus, especially the Nazarene painters. The English Sarah Tytler wrote of him that he "shared with the writers Hawthorne and Wendell Holmes, not merely the love of the supernatural, but the predilection for what is abnormal and weird, which strikes us dwellers in the mother country as something in itself abnormal, when it springs up in the sons of a fresh young world, but which is notably the reaction from the very fresh materialism of their surroundings."[17] Allston was raised in South Carolina where he developed a love for the marvelous and the mad. He used subjects from Schiller's *The Robbers* and Mrs. Radcliffe's *The Mysteries of Udolpho*. He loved mysterious and misty landscapes, as many of his canvases show.[18]

Albert Pinkham Ryder (1847–1907) recalls the medieval romanticism of Allston and Frederick Remington. He painted the well-known *The Last of the Cowboys*, which is a most medievalistic work featuring Western "chivalric" cowboys and aspects of their lives.

This medievalistic mood is also to be found on the Continent, in France and Germany particularly, and above all in England.[19] America was, as might be expected, influenced especially by England in this matter. The nineteenth-century English love of Gothic was repeated in America. The New York Church of St. John the Divine is a still unfinished monument to American Gothic. Harvard's Memorial Hall of the 1870s is another Gothic monument which is at least completed. Its red-brick form clashes strongly in the mind with the popular image of white stone associated with most Gothic cathedrals, churches, and buildings.

The roots of this Medievalism in literature and architecture lie, of course, in the Middle Ages themselves, but the movement already idealized outlived the age of its birth and childhood and continued to live and grow from the sixteenth century down to today, especially in the late eighteenth century. Medievalism had its greatest period of growth in the nineteenth and twentieth centuries, leaning farther and farther away from the facts and the true medieval world. The continuing popularity of Arthur and his knights in film and on the stage, and in an organization like the Society for Creative Anachronism, has insured Medievalism's modern survival.

The serious study of the Middle Ages began in the Middle Ages themselves, with the chroniclers, some of whom approximated modern historians. The idealization of the Middle Ages which explains Medievalism began, as I have indicated above, during the Middle Ages themselves, especially with those humans, who are always with us, who look to the past for spiritual nourishment. Besides those medieval people who idealized the past, were those who wished to record the past both for legal reasons (that is, to make sure that claims could be made) and for the purpose of remembrance to provide exemplars and to indulge their idealistic side as well. Medieval chroniclers began with a desire to celebrate and keep straight the religious calendar so that religious remembrance would be accurate and kept alive. The notable events of weather, of elections and elevations of crops, of activities, of days on which notable local (and sometimes national) figures died, were gradually added to these rather empty early chronological calendars.

Earlier, of course, in the days of Rome and Greece in their hey-day, histories more or less as we regard them were written. This procedure continued all through the Middle Ages, although in the early centuries of that period not many were written, but religious calendars came in to keep the scriptorium busy. These later grew into annals, a procedure still to be found in the history of our newspapers. As pointed out, histories such as those of Gregory of Tours and Bede, as well as saints' lives, never ceased to be written, but in the early Middle Ages they were few. The annotated calendars were the source of most annals and histories from the fifth to the tenth centuries. After that they took off for themselves, although in some cultures such as the Anglo-Saxon, annals and histories are found early. Law also demanded recording, and we find early laws of many of the Germanic peoples, including those of the Anglo-Saxons. There are also early Irish and Old Norse legal documents, as well as some histories.

The history of the Middle Ages has always accompanied Medievalism as a corrective and at times intermingling companion. I shall briefly concentrate on the historiography of the Middle Ages, that is, the factual and interpretative writings of that age and, even more important, of the later writings on the same subject. Medievalism is, as we know, different, although we shall return briefly to that subject at the end.

Judaism, Christianity, and Islam are historical religions that not only depend on the past but are also concerned with the future. The coming of the Messiah or the return of the Messiah in the future forces Judaism and Christianity to be historically oriented in a way that is not normally found in religions of non-Semitic origin, such as Hinduism or purely pagan religions of the past and present. Other religions such as Buddhism pay some attention to history, but do not belong to the category of historical religions. History is largely illusion to Buddhism and Hinduism. Confucianism is, to some extent, historical. If we had earlier Germanic records we might find a role for history in these religions, but our main source of pagan Germanic religion is the Old Norse records, which may have been influenced by Christianity as we now have them.

Monotheism is the chief characteristic of the Semitic religions. This makes history extremely important, for their God is a god who creates humans and who has a divine plan for them. Medieval history is thus different from Roman and Greek histories. There is a divine plan at work in it, and it has a beginning and an end. Orosius, St. Augustine, and Cassiodorus raised the Christian story to history, for which the Old Testament provided a model. St. Augustine in the *City of God* provided Christianity with a philosophy of history. Orosius, his disciple, focused his master's theories into a history of Christianity that he called *Against the Pagans*. He made use of the four world-monarchies, taken from the Book of Daniel in the Old Testament. From this Orosian work, we get the notion of the *translatio regni*, the transfer of world power from one kingdom to another, after which the return of Jesus may be expected. This idea was supposed to be fulfilled and to have reached its end in the Holy Roman Empire as applied to the Germanic peoples' empire, which lasted at least until Napoleon's time.

Besides Gregory of Tours and Bede, Otto of Freising and Guibert of Nogent wrote genuine histories. There were also, as the Middle Ages developed, other chroniclers who wrote in the vernacular such as Villani (d. 1348) and Froissart.

The Renaissance had its great historians like Laurentius Valla and Ulrich von Hutten. The seventeenth century saw the rise of critical history that paid much attention to sources. It saw the appearance of the *Acta Sanctorum* (by the Bollandists), Jean Mabillon's *De Re Diplomata* (1681), Ducange's medieval Latin glossary, and other histories that graced the century. In Italy, L. A. Muratori (1672–1750) was another critical historian who is rightly famed for his *Rerum Italicarum Scriptores*. Earlier we have Cardinal Baronius's *Annales Ecclesiastici* (1588–1607), which used the annals form and was a genuine historical work. In spite of its errors due to inadequate available sources, it is a valuable piece of work. In England we find in the seventeenth century William Dugdale's *Monasticon*, Wilkin's *Concilia*, and Thomas Rymer's *Foedera* (treaties). The eighteenth and early nineteenth centuries produced some great historians such as Gibbon and Guizot (who translated Gibbon into French as well as writing books on French and English history). This brief consideration of historiography brings us to modern historiography, which begins with Ranke and the other pioneers who in the 1840s and 50s used primary sources and valued accuracy.

In spite of a fairly long list of American scholars who went to Germany to study the new scientific history, it was not until 1870 that the first American professor of medieval history was appointed. He was Henry Adams, whom

President Charles W. Eliot of Harvard appointed to the position. Henry Charles Lea had begun before 1870 to write some or parts of his numerous works on the Middle Ages even before his great work on the Inquisition was finished. He was, however, a private scholar. In the years from 1877 (when Adams left Harvard) to 1921, the number of medievalists in American universities increased extensively. Ephraim Emerton, a pupil of Adams and a Ph.D. from Leipzig, continued the tradition at Harvard until 1918. In 1876, Francis Child retired from teaching rhetoric at Harvard to turn to medieval English philology and the medieval ballads. Edward Sheldon in 1877 became a professor at Harvard in Romance philology. Slightly later, Johns Hopkins, Yale, Cornell and Columbia appointed medievalists to their faculties. Medieval literature as philology was the most popular of all the fields in medieval subjects. The Dante tradition at Harvard was even older, for Longfellow gave his lectures on Dante there in the early 1840s. He had visited Europe from 1826–29 and then later from 1835 to 1836, but he was rather outside the scholarly stream and was certainly not a pupil of Ranke. In 1867, Longfellow's translation of the *Divine Comedy* appeared, a translation begun some thirty years before. His work and Longfellow himself proved to be a great stimulus to Dante studies in America, leading to the foundation of the Dante Society, which still flourishes and that had its annual meeting until recently in Longfellow's house on Brattle Street in Cambridge.

The appearance of professors of medieval history and literature in American universities attracted large numbers of students, partly out of interest in medieval subjects and Medievalism, and partly because of required courses. Others came because of their interest in common law. Those were the heydays of historicism, when a good lawyer had to know his Bracton and the other distinguished legalists of the past. Quite a number of medieval scholars in the last part of the nineteenth and early days of the twentieth century were themselves private persons. We have already mentioned Lea above. There were also Henry Osborn Taylor, Ralph Adams Cram, and, in his early days, Arthur Kingsley Porter.

Gradually, medieval history became more and more important in American academic life. Great scholars appeared, men like Charles Homer Haskins, Alfred Todd, James Harvey Robinson, Lynn Thorndike, and George Sellery. Philology continued to be popular and based on the historical method. The Medieval Academy was founded in America in 1925. The influx of scholars from central Europe in the 1930s brought new medieval art and music studies to that which already existed in America. Although there had been some art and music departments in a few American university departments, these subjects were not to be found in every university as today. Names like Erwin Panofsky, Ernst Kitzinger, Richard Krautheimer, Adolph Katzenellenbogen, and Willi Apel spring to mind. These two fields which had been much neglected before this influx were not, however, the only departments to benefit from the European immigration, as names like Spitzer, Ladner, Lopez, Baron, Kantorowicz, Cassirer, and Kristeller clearly indicate.[20]

Enough of names. I think I have made my point. I skip the various institutes and research centers devoted to the study of the Middle Ages. The important point for me of this long discussion of Medievalism and the study of the Middle Ages is the relation between the two.

Medieval scholars have always tended to look down on Medievalism. They labor in the vineyard while they perceive medievalists as having been toying with pseudo-tournaments, reading about knights and their ladies and dreams of questing. Perhaps to some extent this is true, but fundamentally it is unfair. We cannot expect the world to be scholarly. What are we as medieval scholars aiming at? We are aiming at an accurate knowledge of the Middle Ages. Medieval people lived in the Middle Ages and loved and fought; helped and hindered; enjoyed and hated as, *mutatis mutandis*, we also live if we can. They dreamed of and hoped for joy and satisfaction for themselves and prayed that misfortune not strike them and theirs.

The people who lived in the Middle Ages had dreams, hopes, victories, and defeats, just as we have, and will continue to have. The ideal with their religious faith was the stuff of their internal life, and in the love of Medievalism some people are reliving dreams, even if they do not have exactly the same content. One of our persistent dreams is the ideal Middle Ages with noble knights, lovely ladies and manly men, honest and decent human beings who defeat or punish the evil ones. It is, as I have suggested, the soil out of which Medievalism grew and still grows.

The success of medieval story and legend in our present-day art and literature and their manifestations in organizations such as the Society for Creative Anachronism all show that Medievalism is not dead. Many of our excellent scholars were, when young, driven to explore their delight in Arthur, knights, ladies in distress, lovely women, honest laborers, beautiful castles and paintings in greater detail by taking our courses. Medievalism is the seed-bed of medieval scholarship. It is, of course, other things as well, but it is because of Medievalism that many of us go to conferences like those at Binghamton and Kalamazoo to learn more exactly what the Middle Ages were.

We should all be grateful to Medievalism, and we should hope that it will continue to bring young men and women to swell our ranks, even if at present many cannot make their living by teaching others about medieval history, literature, art, and music. We shall not lose our love of the Middle Ages whether real or idealized. The study of the Middle Ages grew out of Medievalism just as Medievalism is stimulated by increased knowledge of the Middle Ages. Our deepest dreams and hopes are often clothed in medieval garments. Let us hope that they continue to lead us to a study of the true Middle Ages, which combines fact and meaning. The history of the Middle Ages will continue to stimulate lovers of Medievalism just as Medievalism stimulates study of the Middle Ages. They both need each other. No other period of our history has had such a persistent and profound existence as the medieval period. Even in its most romanticized garb, it echoes the deepest hopes and beliefs of mankind. This relationship is not duplicated in any other period. The Renaissance, Reformation, Restoration, the Augustan age, Romanticism, Victorianism, the Edwardian age, and our present unhappy world—none of them—have had the influence the Middle Ages has had upon the mind of modern man, nor has persisted with such tenacity and believers as the history of the Middle Ages and Medievalism. So may it continue.

NOTES

1. "The Varieties of American Medievalism," *Studies in Medievalism* 1, no. 2 (1982): 7.

2. Published in English as an appendix to the English translation of his *Europäische Literatur und lateinisches Mittelalter* (Berne: M. Francke AG, 1948), which appeared as *European Literature and the Latin Middle Ages*, trans. Willard R. Trask (London: Routledge & Kegan Paul, 1953).

3. Ibid., 589.

4. Ibid., 587–88, where Curtius emphasizes the American need for a Middle Age and its quest for one as for a mother. He also here discusses the important role of Dante in America in the nineteenth and twentieth centuries.

5. See David Staines, *Tennyson's Camelot: The "Idylls of the King" and Its Medieval Sources* (Waterloo, Ontario: Wilfrid Laurier University Press, 1982), wherein Tennyson's use of Malory is carefully delineated. See also, for the bowdlerization of Malory in the Victorian era, Yuri Fuwa, "The Globe Edition of Malory as a Bowdlerized Text in the Victorian Age," *Studies in English Literature* 61 (1984): 3–17.

6. See Ian Anstruther, *The Knight and the Umbrella: An Account of the Eglinton Tournament 1839* (London: Geoffrey Bles, 1963). In its appendix I (246–48), a list of some 18th- and 19th-century tournaments (1750–1839) covering Western

Europe, Britain, and the USA is given. In 1778 one was held in Philadelphia, and in June 1839 another was held in New Orleans. See also, for other American (the Southern states mainly) tournaments, R. G. Osterweis, *Romanticism and Nationalism in the Old South*, Yale Historical Publications, vol. 49 (New Haven, 1949).

7. See Morton W. Bloomfield, "Beowulf, Byrhtnoth, and the Judgment of God: Trial by Combat in Anglo-Saxon England," *Speculum* 44 (1969): 555 and note 37. It was legally repealed in England in 1819.

8. For works of these Gothic, Romanesque, and Byzantine revivals, see the excellent text and illustrations from English sources available in Mark Girouard, *The Return to Camelot: Chivalry and the English Gentleman* (New Haven and London: Yale University Press, 1981) and M. Charles Dellheim, *The Face of the Past: The Preservation of the Medieval Inheritance in Victorian England* (Cambridge: Cambridge University Press, 1982) (although the latter has fewer illustrations). These give one a good idea of how deeply Medievalism in all its forms had penetrated English life. As far as I am aware, no comparable book on America has been written.

9. On the rise of medievalism (and Medieval Studies) in France in the eighteenth century, see Lionel Gossman, *Medievalism and the Ideologies of the Enlightenment: The World and Work of La Curne de Sainte-Palaye* (Baltimore: The Johns Hopkins Press, 1968).

10. (Bloomington: Indiana University Press, 1961). See also, Richard Konetzke, "Der weltgeschichtliche Moment des Entdeckung Americas," *Historische Zeitschrift* 182 (1956): 267–89, and Percy G. Adams, "The Discovery of America and European Renaissance Literature," *Comparative Literature Studies* 13 (1976): 100–15. O'Gorman's insightful book furthers an idea well understood by Americanist scholars. See for example Howard Mumford Jones, *O Strange New World* (New York: The Viking Press, 1952).

11. See the translation of this letter in *The Four Voyages of Christopher Columbus*, ed. and trans., J. M. Cohen (Baltimore, 1969), 300. For a recent clarification of this reference, see an article on the subject by Robert E. Lerner, which will appear soon in the *American Historical Review*.

12. See Hugh Honour, *The New Golden Land: European Images of America from the Discoveries to the Present Time* (New York: Pantheon Books, 1975), 21.

13. On his pre-Virginian life, see Jennifer Goodman, "The Captain's Self-Portrait: John Smith as Chivalric Biography," *Virginia Magazine of History and Biography* 89 (1981): 27–38.

14. "The Legacy of the Middle Ages in the American Wild West," *Speculum* 40 (1965): 191–202.

15. On the notion of Southern chivalry and honor, see Bertram Wyatt-Brown, *Southern Honor: Ethics and Behavior in the Old South* (New York and Oxford: Oxford: Oxford University Press, 1982), especially Chapters 16 and 17. See also Wilbur J. Cash, *The Mind of the South* (New York: Knopf, 1941), *passim*.

16. See John Fraser, *America and the Patterns of Chivalry* (Cambridge: Cambridge

University Press, 1982), 9. In spite of its valuable references, this book attacks almost everyone of any distinction for their love of violence. Fraser seems to think that only America is violent and that all violence is the work of reactionaries.

17. *Modern Painters and Their Paintings*, 5th ed. (London, 1886), 336. Quoted from Barbara Novak, *American Painting of the Nineteenth Century: Realism, Idealism and the American Experience* (New York, Washington, and London: Praeger Publishers, 1969), 45.

18. Novak, 45.

19. A good introduction to English Medievalism may be found in Alice Chandler, *A Dream of Order: The Medieval Ideal in Nineteenth-Century English Literature* (Lincoln: University of Nebraska Press, 1970). There is an especially good chapter (6) on Ruskin and Morris.

20. For a number of essays on the study of the Middle Ages in North America, see Francis G. Gentry and Christopher Kleinhenz, *Medieval Studies in North America: Past, Present and Future* (Kalamazoo, Michigan: Medieval Institute Publications, 1982), especially the articles of William J. Courtenay, Luke Wenger, Paul E. Szarmach, and Carl T. Berkhout.

The Southern Slaveholders' View of the Middle Ages

Eugene D. Genovese

A S THE FABLED "EVERY SCHOOLBOY" KNOWS, THE OLD SOUTH LOVED SIR Walter Scott. In consequence, the slaveholders who dominated society are supposed to have been in love with the Middle Ages and with feudalism, and to have equated the manors with their own plantations. Since Scott wrote for the modern world and read the Middle Ages through other than medieval eyes, the deduction startles and invites a broad reinterpretation of what Scott and his southern admirers were in fact all about. And since he appears to have been no less popular in the North, other questions arise. Be that as it may, the Old South was hardly a refurbished medieval society, and few southerners ever pretended that it was. Slaves were not serfs; slaveholders were not feudal lords; and plantations were not manors. Occasionally, as in Francis Pendleton Gaines's valuable book, *The Southern Plantation: A Study in the Development and the Accuracy of a Tradition*, the slaveholders' fascination with the Middle Ages is taken seriously as an indication of their special circumstances and mentality.[1] More often, we are treated to studies that end by finding the slaveholders to have been garden-variety capitalists with bourgeois values, and their intellectuals to have been either men of bad faith who were creating a silly legend to defend slavery or men driven to schizophrenia by their isolation from the larger Atlantic bourgeois world of letters in consequence of the opprobrium attached to slavery.

Those who denigrate the pro-slavery intellectuals in this way fail to do justice to a remarkable collection of good brains, but people who lose wars, especially wars in a bad cause, cannot expect justice or even mercy. Those who do not denigrate the pro-slavery intellectuals have an important point to make, which has recently reappeared with special force in the work of Michael O'Brien, who treats them with the respect they deserve.[2] The slaveholders as a class, and their intellectuals in particular, were "modern" men who accepted the world of the nineteenth century, with its idea of Progress, its railroads, telegraph, steamships, and with the rest of what the industrial revolution was making possible. They were consciously looking toward a bright future, not toward the past and toward some restoration of a lost world. In consequence, with few exceptions, they regarded the Middle Ages as backward, superstitious, static, and on balance as unattractive.[3]

Yet, we remain stuck with the Cavalier myth, with the repeated expression of respect for some things medieval, and above all with the insistence upon a historical and indeed divinely sanctioned continuity between the medieval world and the world of modern slavery. Indeed, thoughtful Southerners typically perceived a disastrous rupture between the Middle Ages and the bourgeois world of the North. We are stuck, that is, with a discernible element of a kind of "medievalism" in their sensibility. For despite a commitment to "modernity," Southerners could not dismiss the Middle Ages with a sigh of good riddance. At issue was not their appreciation of Gothic cathedrals or, in contrast, their revulsion at dirt and ignorance, but their concern with God's will as revealed through history. They did fall into serious contradictions in their effort to evaluate the Middle Ages in a manner appropriate to their position as slaveholders, and those contradictions arose less from a failure of individual talent than from the impossibility of reconciling slavery to the modern world. But their ablest intellectuals, including those who most strongly influenced public opinion, made an impressive effort to forge a coherent world view. Their attempt to identify the divinely inspired, the permanent, the admirable in the medieval experience proved both intellectually powerful and politically significant.

Their effort was quintessentially political. The South, with a broad pro-slavery consensus, had been slowly developing as a slave society—not merely a society that tolerated slavery, but a society in which slavery provided the social basis for the morality, ideology, and sensibility of modern Christians. Such a society was an anachronism in the modern world. It lacked models and precedents. The ancient world had had slave societies, and throughout history societies had included slavery in their social relations. But a slave society in the modern world of expanding capitalism, industrialization, bourgeois individualism, and Enlightenment liberalism presented something new. And since this something new was emerging in the most democratic republic the world had ever seen, and since a majority of white Southerners were not only non-slaveholders but active citizens, the elitist politics and ideology that might appear natural and appropriate to a society based on slaveholding would not easily serve. The South, in consequence, remained rent throughout its history among competing visions of the good society—the good slave society. Those slaveholders who saw most clearly that their class was in fact building a new world of sorts also saw that it rested on the master-slave relation. But non-slaveholders who accepted slavery in principle could not readily accept such a view, and even a substantial number of slaveholders resisted some of the implications, especially those which rejected the Jeffersonian democratic values on which they had been brought up. In this many-sided ideological struggle, the most conservative and, simultaneously, the most revolutionary spirits—those who were fighting for the recognition of a separate southern cultural as well as political future—saw themselves as heirs of the ages and defenders of Western Civilization. However critical they were of the Middle Ages and however much they looked toward the future, they claimed historical and spiritual continuity with the European past.

The planters of Virginia took their aristocratic origins in England for granted, and their fellow Southerners readily conceded their claims. Even such men of the world as Daniel Hundley of Alabama—and Chicago—and T. C. De Leon of South Carolina proved no more critical of the legend than the most vain of Virginians.[4] Hundley, De Leon, and their like were also quick to provide an aristocratic pedigree for the Huguenot planters of South Carolina and the Spanish and French planters of Louisiana. Notwithstanding a measure of illusion and even some silliness in normally sober men, they might not have been surprised to hear from twentieth-century social historians that the overwhelming majority of southern planters, including the Virginians, had plebeian origins.

For if the antebellum supporters of the legend of aristocratic origins took some liberties with the truth, they could fairly plead *se non é vero, é ben trovato*. As men who appreciated tradition, they risked exaggeration for two reasons: first, Virginia probably could claim a higher proportion of old-world aristocratic families than other states; and second and more important, the planter elite among the slaveholders actively sought identification with the aristocratic tradition. The planters thereby provided an excellent illustration of the distinction made by Jaroslav Pelikan in his recent Jefferson lectures on "The

Vindication of Tradition": they eschewed the "traditionalism" of later lost-cause romantics as the dead faith of the living, while they warmly embraced "tradition" as the living faith of the dead.[5]

The haughty planters of the South Carolina low country collectively styled themselves "The Chivalry," and Southerners everywhere invoked the word "chivalrous" as the mark of the special kind of gentlemen they claimed to be. Among innumerable examples, let us settle for a speech by Parson William G. Brownlow of Tennessee, a plebeian to the core who spoke not for the planters but for the largely non-slaveholding if nonetheless pro-slavery yeomen. In a debate with an abolitionist minister, held in Philadelphia in 1858, he defiantly proclaimed, "Yes, gentlemen, ours is the land of chivalry, the land of the muse, the abode of statesmen, the home of oratory; the dwelling place of the historian and the hero...."[6] And T. C. De Leon invoked common language in his eulogy of Turner Ashby, who fell during the War for Southern Independence: "True knight—doughty leader—high-hearted gentleman.... Chivalric—lion-hearted—strong armed."[7]

In speaking this way, the slaveholders no doubt meant to draw attention to such presumed aristocratic virtues as gallantry, contempt for money-grubbing—although not for money—classical education, polished manners, and a high sense of personal and family honor. These themes appeared frequently in, among other places, commencement addresses at the universities, at which "The Middle Ages" surfaced as a favorite topic. And never mind that many of these virtues and ideals probably arose, in the forms then appreciated, with the commercial, urban *grande bourgeoisie* and the courtiers of the Renaissance and the early-modern national states. They were widely perceived and cherished as products of the High Middle Ages and, specifically, of feudal and manorial life. Modern historians, not all of them damned Yankees, have had great sport in ridiculing these pretensions.

No doubt much pretense did go into the making. The assertion of the gentlemanly ideal as a standard of conduct was not thereby rendered unworthy, and, among other advantages, it encouraged a measure of decency toward slaves in a world that badly needed every such measure. The slaves, for their part, notwithstanding a burning desire for freedom and critical distance on their masters, often spoke highly of that gentlemanly ideal and referred to those who lived up to it as "de quality."[8]

Pretense or no, posturing or no, the gentlemanly ideal, with its presumed roots in medieval feudalism and the seigneurial manor, provided invaluable support for the paternalism that mediated master-slave relations. It encouraged acceptance by the masters of duties, responsibilities, and a code of conduct that made the ultimate test of a gentleman the humane and Christian treatment of his slaves.

A cult of medievalism, strictly speaking, did not spread far and wide in the South, not even among those much maligned southern ladies who supposedly had nothing to do with their time except read romantic novels. Hundley, in *Social Relations in Our Southern States*, published on the eve of secession, charged that the sons of those he called "cotton Snobs" – parvenu planters who may have been aspirant aristocrats but could hardly pass for Southern Gentlemen – ostentatiously played at being knights-errant, parading like peacocks in front of their ladies at pseudo-medieval tournaments. Genuine Southern Gentlemen dressed a bit carelessly, lived unostentatiously, and carried quietly their claims to being a kind of New World version of the European nobility – claims Hundley respected and considered historically valid.[9]

Yet, while Hundley suggested that the genuine Southern Gentlemen put on no such airs, he attributed to them a deeply ingrained attitude that implied its own version of aristocratic continuity with the ages: "No matter what may be the Southern Gentleman's avocation, his dearest affections usually centre in the country. He longs to live as his fathers lived before him, in both the Old World and the New; and he turns with unfeigned delight ... to the quiet and peaceful scenes of country life."[10]

Hundley, in his attack on the tournaments, had, as he often did, a private axe to grind. Many of the young men who flocked to the summer vacation resorts to play at knight-errantry qualified as the finest products of their class, even if many others did not. Turner Ashby, for example, had earned widespread praise for a life that was widely hailed as representative of the highest chivalric ideals. He lived, if his contemporaries may be believed, *sans peur et sans reproche*, taxed with no youthful excesses, admired for his piety, morality, temperance, gallantry, and honor. A veritable modern knight. A legend in his own time.[11]

Whether Ashby and the others who tried to approach his high standards actually qualified as saints may be left to God to judge. That they appeared to represent the hopes for a great southern future cannot be questioned. Why else would Thomas Roderick Dew and Nathaniel Beverley Tucker, among other luminaries, have appeared at Fauquier White Springs, which especially featured the tournaments, to deliver the ceremonial orations? Dew, as was his wont, spoke seriously to the young men and their ladies and spelled out the significance of the medieval ritual for modern Southerners. Dew charged the southern "knights" to remember that knighthood had grown out of the

Dark Ages, which failed to recognize the rights of womanhood, and that it
was created "to arrest the downward progress of civilization; that all true knights
must be honorable, courteous, liberal, clement, loyal, devoted to woman,
to arms, to religion."[12]

As Dew well knew, the slave plantation, no matter how closely its social
relations approximated the ideal, was no latter-day medieval manor.[13]
Medieval manors were not autarchic, wholly outside the world of commerce
and even trade, but there was a vast qualitative difference between them and
the slave plantations that produced staples for a world market. Manors and
other kinds of seigneurial estates could enter into the process of international commodity production, as the Second Serfdom in Eastern Europe forcefully demonstrated, but they had long existed without it. In contrast, the slave
plantations were creatures of the early phase of the rise of a world market
and had no economic or social rationale without it. Every slaveholder necessarily became something of a modern businessman, whose ability to survive,
not to mention prosper, depended upon the supply of and demand for human labor and the commodities it produced. The great cultural and political
struggle for the soul of the Old South raged between the South and the capitalist
world in which it was enmeshed, but more tellingly, it also raged between
irreconcilable tendencies within the plantation world itself.[14]

Southern conservatives, then and now, have understood that slaves are
not serfs and that an identification can be made only for limited and carefully specified purposes. They have also understood, as most historians have
not, that the common denominator of slavery and serfdom—unfree labor in
a stratified social system—provides a social basis for the rejection of the
market and its cash-nexus as an adequate standard of human relations. No
matter how much greed, brutality, and acquisitiveness went into the making
of the southern slaveholders, they could not justify their economic activity
by a straightforward appeal to the profit motive and some version of the trickle-
down theory. To be sure, even a Southern Gentleman needed money to
provide for his "family, white and black," but the reigning spirit was the age-
less one of acquisitiveness, of the desire for wealth and power, not the historically specific one of capital accumulation, of making money to make more
money.

The slaveholders no doubt slighted the extent to which their dependence
upon commodity production compromised their highest values and turned
them into heartless exploiters of human beings, but they did not collectively
slip into bad faith when they sought to link themselves to the older European
aristocracies. Feudal lords exploited, oppressed, abused, and bashed their

serfs and dependent peasants a great deal more than they ever protected them. Indeed, since the lords usually offered their vaunted protection against other lords, they were in effect treating their peasants to a medieval version of the modern Mafia's "protection racket." The much celebrated security and traditional rights of serfs and dependent peasants arose more from their overt and covert resistance than from lordly largesse. The same could be said for the black slaves of the South, who also had rights, however few and hedged in. In both cases those struggles and mutual accommodations, notwithstanding much violence and violation of norms, contributed to a process in which human relations emerged as organic, with mutual if unequal rights, responsibilities, and duties. In both cases men related to men directly, not through the mechanism of the market.

The more worldly of the slaveholders, especially the pro-slavery intellectuals, betrayed increasing fascination with the Catholic Church's great work of social mediation during the Middle Ages. In the Protestant South that fascination had to be curbed and expressed cautiously, although it did not, contrary to facile assumption, confront the harsh anti-Catholicism prevalent in the Northeast. The slaveholders had strong feelings about individual liberties, especially in matters of faith. Southern slave society proved remarkably tolerant of religious, political, and intellectual diversity, always provided that the heterodox did not challenge slavery.[15]

The grudging respect for medieval Catholicism that emerged in the work of leading southern intellectuals, including, most significantly, those educators who shaped the minds of the sons of the planter elite, rested firmly on an appreciation of the Church's stabilizing influence on medieval social relations. We might not be surprised to find it expressed by the deeply conservative George Frederick Holmes of Virginia, who flirted with personal conversion. We may well be surprised to find it expressed by Thomas Cooper and Thomas Roderick Dew, who espoused Progress and what is now tendentiously called "modernization," even while they defended slavery. These men, unlike George Frederick Holmes, admired Adam Smith and the new political economy and much else that had come out of the Enlightenment.[16] Indeed, Cooper, who had been an English radical and Jeffersonian democrat in earlier incarnations, was an unabashed materialist who was widely perceived as an unbeliever despite his politically wise decision to attend church regularly while president of the University of South Carolina. Cooper hated the clergy, especially the intellectually prestigious and powerful Presbyterians, and had no fondness for Rome. But in his lectures on political economy, subsequently published, he gave the devil his due:

During this period, Europe was governed politically by the maxims of the feudal law, which was expressly invented and digested to regulate the distribution of conquered territory—and by monkish Christianity, which was adverse to the accumulation of wealth, unless in the hands of the clergy: and I think it must be acknowledged, that this powerful body of men, with all their faults, made a far more liberal and disinterested use of their accumulated riches, during the dark and middle ages, than we have since witnessed, in times when knowledge has been more extended.[17]

Dew had even less patience with the reactionary effects of Catholicism and declared the introduction of Protestantism to be one of the four principle causes of English prosperity. For good measure he denounced Catholicism as an enemy of free government, which he ranked as the first of those four principle causes. These themes appeared forcefully in his own lectures on political economy, but they reappear only with heavy qualification in his lectures on history. There he swallowed hard and praised the medieval Church warmly for its contribution to the humanity and stability of pre-capitalist social relations.[18]

It remained for the irrepressible George Fitzhugh of Virginia, writing in the 1850s, to go as far as a Protestant could in a staunchly Protestant country. He judged the Reformation necessary and good, for the old church had become corrupt and rigid. But he condemned such "excesses" as the right of private judgment, which he held responsible for the flourishing of the bourgeois individualism he fiercely hated.[19] Long before Allen Tate, he knew that Protestantism left much to be desired as the religion of an organic slaveholding society.[20]

The most self-consciously "modernizing" of the slaveholding intellectuals contradicted themselves long enough to join their more romantically inclined, not to say reactionary, colleagues in insisting upon the continuity of their class and its civilization with medieval institutions and values. The slaveholders, like those who spoke in the name of the medieval lords, proclaimed themselves protectors of their slaves as well as guardians of social order. They spoke frequently of "our family, white and black," within which they included both field hands and house servants. They described their ownership of slaves as a "duty" and a "burden" and were convinced that without the protection they offered the blacks would, literally, be exterminated in a marketplace in which they could not compete. When, therefore, they referred to themselves as The Chivalry and as functional equivalents of the European nobility, they were speaking not only of the graces, accomplishments, and aristocratic virtues they claimed for themselves, but of their commitment to the organic social relations on which their civilization was based.

The slaveholders' professed link to medieval lordship marked a fateful turn in the maturation of their class and its ideological rationale. It flowered especially during the nineteenth century and contributed to the transformation of a narrowly economic and racial defense of slavery as a necessity for a society in which the labor force was recruited from a racially inferior people into a militant defense of slavery, abstracted from race, as an extreme form of the subordination to which all labor ought to be subjected and to which it in fact has been subjected throughout history. The insistence upon continuity from the medieval enserfment and even enslavement of white Europeans to the modern enslavement of black Africans thereby projected a solution to the modern social question according to principles that rejected free labor as an ideal for whites as well as blacks.[21]

As the slavery question waxed hotter after 1831, abolitionist attacks and the shock of Nat Turner's rebellion forced the southern intellectuals—poets and novelists as well as theologians and social theorists—to take high ground in defense of slavery. The defenders of slavery began by asserting that their slaves were well and humanely cared for and that, as an inferior race, they could not care for themselves in a rapidly developing modern world. But virtually at the first moment the defenders of slavery counter-attacked by questioning whether industrial free workers and European peasants lived any better. They quickly answered their own question in the negative and proceeded to argue that the insecurity imposed by market relations, combined with the whip of outright hunger, actually left most free workers immeasurably worse off than southern slaves. Now, if those who commanded capital were Christians and therefore responsible for their fellow men as well as to their God, and if slavery offered labor a more secure, bountiful, and peaceful life than capitalist wage relations, then it followed that Christians should advocate the enslavement of all labor, white as well as black. By the 1850s George Fitzhugh of Virginia and, in slightly veiled form, Henry Hughes of Mississippi were saying just that, and their viewpoint was echoing throughout the South, albeit with hesitations, qualifications, and much gnashing of teeth.[22]

As a prime corollary of this defense of slavery in the abstract, as Fitzhugh called it, the pro-slavery militants, who were assuming a commanding position in southern intellectual life, insisted that the maintenance of social order required some form of slavery. They pointed to the historical record, which, in their reading, showed slavery to have been ubiquitous in world history.

Throughout the South men of letters joined the political leaders in repudiating Mr. Jefferson's nonsense about equality—not merely racial equality, which Jefferson never believed in anyway, but equality in general—and in proclaiming their break with the Enlightenment liberalism they had inherited. Thus emerged a broadly accepted social theory and interpretation of history according to which all civilization, all culture, all social order, and, yes, all Progress have grown, indeed must grow, out of the subjugation of the laboring masses to the will of their social superiors. This bold new view, at once deeply reactionary and yet modernist in its commitment to material and cultural progress, increasingly stamped the work of the South's leading theologians, such as James Henley Thornwell and William Stringfellow, its leading men of letters, such as Nathaniel Beverley Tucker and William Gilmore Simms; its leading social theorists, such as Thomas Roderick Dew and George Frederick Holmes; and its leading political scientists and politicians, such as John C. Calhoun and James H. Hammond.

This view of the proper condition of labor and of what was called "the social question" lay at the heart of the positive view of the Middle Ages. For the insistence upon the historical and divinely sanctioned continuity of slavery from Biblical times to the present encouraged the assimilation of all unfree and dependent labor to slavery or, what came to the same thing, the assimilation of slavery to a general pattern of social subordination in which chattel slavery became merely the extreme form appropriate to time, place, and circumstance. The slaveholders could reasonably take for granted that the widely revered Greek and Roman civilizations supported their primary ideological case. They invoked Greece and Rome frequently but rarely paused to elaborate their claims to so obvious a historical continuity.

They paid more attention to ancient Israel, for Southerners were a genuinely religious people who read their Bible, listened attentively to their preachers, and had to have assurance of divine sanction for their institutions. The preachers were an extraordinarily powerful, if little studied, force for the dissemination of ruling-class values, and they provided an important, perhaps decisive, mediation across class lines. Thus, when the leading theologians and a growing army of ordinary preachers began to sound like Fitzhugh during the 1850s, often virtually paraphrasing his defense of the subordination of the laboring classes, they were carrying a message few others would have dared carry beyond the elite. They were also strategically placed to make the message a good deal more palatable by rendering it as an analogue to, or an outgrowth of, the strict subordination of women to men—a theme they rarely failed to hammer at.[23]

The southern theologians proved impressive when they met the abolitionists head-on on the question of the divine sanction for slavery and bested them on the critical terrain of biblical exegesis. In so doing, they offered a much sounder reading of Israelite history. For when the abolitionists demonstrated that many of the ancient Hebrew slaves had been indentured servants, the pro-slavery theologians countered that the Canaanites and other heathens had in fact been reduced to outright slavery and that Israel's social system included a wide variety of subordinate statuses, with free labor as exceptional.

When the pro-slavery theologians turned to the Middle Ages, they projected a continuity of class superordination and subordination and recognized the extent to which, as recent scholarship has demonstrated, chattel slavery continued to exist in Europe as the extreme form of unfree labor in a wider system of social stratification. Without attempting a fallacious equation of serfdom with slavery, they plausibly argued that the two were compatible and parallel in their reduction of the many to the direct control of the few. They needed to take only one short step to the interpretation of pre-Cromwellian or pre-Elizabethan England as a society in which the peasants, even when formally free, lived in secure, stable communities under the protection of paternalistic lords, and to the derivative interpretation of the rise of capitalism and "free" labor as a social catastrophe for the peasants and the poor, who were transformed into wage-slaves and left to shift for themselves and even to starve. The southern romance with the English aristocracy rested in no small part on the presumed sense of responsibility of the old landed classes toward their dependents.[24]

The pro-slavery ideologues in effect separated themselves from everything medieval that might appear obnoxious or opposed to material progress, while they identified themselves as heirs to everything that appeared morally superior in medieval social relations. Even Hundley, who had been enjoying life as a businessman in Chicago during the 1850s, could not resist filing the slaveholders' typical brief against the decline of seigneurialism. The peasants of Europe and the British Isles, he insisted, were not better off than the serfs from whom they had descended:

> It may be that the old order of things, the old relationship between landlord and villein, protected the latter from many hardships to which the nominal freemen of the nineteenth century are subjected by the blessed influences of free competition and the practical workings of the good old charitable and praiseworthy English maxim: "Every man for himself, and the devil take the hindmost."[25]

Hundley acknowledged that the end of primogeniture in Jeffersonian Virginia had brought fresh, vigorous, middle-class blood into the planter class and had, on balance, probably sustained its vitality, but, expressing the doubts that were rampant among the southern intellectuals, he dwelt on the negative effects of such leveling and on the dilution of the Cavalier blood of the early colonists. And like the great majority of southern intellectuals, he had no sympathy for the revolutionary overthrow of the Old Regime in France or, for that matter, for the challenges that were then being mounted to the remnants of the feudal order in Europe.[26]

Thus, a bright young graduate of the University of North Carolina, preparing himself for a career at law, could simultaneously condemn feudalism's restrictions on individual liberty and condemn all appeals to social revolution: "We read with pain the accounts of the feudal system. And we cannot but wonder how men who had within them the souls of freemen, and loved liberty—could live the slaves of corrupt and *hard* masters." But then, he wanted no part of the excesses of revolutionary France, which had banished religion and unleashed the Terror: "Men have learned to despise riot and revolution. . . . The past has taught men *caution*, and education has refined the feelings of the Multitude to such a degree that only palpable & gross oppression occasions open rebellion & disaffection."[27]

Dew, who regarded the progress of industrialization as irreversible, considered ominous the attendant progress of bourgeois social relations. He invoked both medieval serfdom and modern slavery as safer social systems that could provide the social peace capitalism could not. Class war had broken out with the severing of the organic ties of serfs to lords and the onset of liberty for the masses. The end of that road had been Wat Tyler's insurrection and the great peasant war in Germany in Luther's time. Similarly, so long as the dependence of black slaves on their masters remained complete, kindness would continue to mark social relations, but "when the law interposes and inspires [the] negro with notions of freedom, then there is insolence on one side and revenge and cruelty on the other."[28] Dew had written those words for his students, and southern students generally, in a textbook version of his historical lectures at The College of William and Mary in a course we would now call Western Civilization. He and others like him, then and after, were playing a big part in the shaping of the minds of the elite slaveholders, especially the political leaders. His theme became standard fare in the numerous academies and on the burgeoning college campuses, and it contributed immensely to the forging of a world view appropriate to a slaveholding class.

With increasing boldness the pro-slavery ideologues, especially the theologians, logically extended their critique of wage-labor into a denunciation
of the emancipation of the serfs. The able polemicist George Armstrong, pastor
of the Presbyterian Church of Norfolk, Virginia, began with an attack on Roman society for giving men the patriarchal power of life and death over wives,
children, and slaves—a common theme in the late antebellum South—and
he praised Christianity for introducing humane social relations into slave society. He thereupon extolled medieval social relations and denounced the
enclosures and similar measures for crushing, while supposedly emancipat-
ing, the laboring classes.[29] The fiery Parson Brownlow virtually equated serfdom with slavery and obliquely criticized the French Revolutionaries who
allegedly threw the peasants into the marketplace.[30] George Sawyer, a lawyer in Louisiana, denounced the enclosures for "removing the poor peasant-
ry from the homes of their fathers" and denounced the "immediate
emancipation" of the European peasants as in fact their brutalization.

Sawyer lumped as slaveholders the landed classes of Russia, Spain, and
the South, whom he praised for juridically mandating the proper care and
feeding of their bondmen. And he added a harsh condemnation of the English capitalists for their heartless attitude toward their workers.[31] Samuel Nott
of Massachusetts, who upheld the pro-slavery cause in the North, thought
France a mess since the Revolution and specifically criticized the emancipation of the serfs there and elsewhere as a withdrawal of protection and
security.[32]

This defense of medieval social relations was usually expressed negatively
as a criticism of post-medieval bourgeois social relations. Sometimes, it led
to a consideration of agrarian life in central and eastern Europe, where relations of dependency, including serfdom, still existed but were on the wane.
Here too, the pro-slavery ideologues trod carefully. They showed no special
fondness for the manifestations of social and economic backwardness that
marked those residually seigneurial societies, but they did maneuver to uphold the quasi-medieval patterns of social relations and either to lament their
passing or to praise their staying-power.

T. R. R. Cobb, Georgia's learned jurist who, although a secessionist, generally eschewed radical rhetoric and polemical excesses, came close to Fitzhugh
in arguing: "The present condition of the laboring classes in Great Britain
differs from personal bondage chiefly in the name. Necessity and hunger are
more relentless masters than the old Saxon lords. . . . When time and labor
of one person are by any means not purely voluntary, the property of another,
the former is a slave and the latter is a master." Cobb noted the existence

of outright slavery in Russia and Turkey and added that in Hungary and Translyvania "the serfs rise but little above the state of slavery." He concluded that slavery in fact, although not in name, existed throughout Europe and would continue to exist until Christian enlightenment purified the heart of man and rendered everyone content "to occupy that sphere for which his nature fits him."[33]

These polemics display considerable ambiguity in the slaveholders' attitude toward the Middle Ages and toward those nineteenth-century societies perceived as still feudal. Few went as far as Fitzhugh and invoked the words of Ecclesiastes, "There is no new thing under the sun," or flirted with a preference for the Middle Ages to the modern world, or ridiculed the idea of progress. Most probably thought of themselves as modernists or progressives of a kind, who sought only to purge the modern world of its heresies and errors. Yet, one by one, step by step, their commitment to plantation slavery compelled them to uphold medieval social relations, to view slavery as a modern variant of those relations, and, most ominously, to advocate a veritable worldwide revolution against the social relations of the marketplace. They thereby plunged into a contradiction from which they could not escape and which exposed them as men who were desperately fighting for a future based simultaneously upon some form of pre-capitalist social relations and on the material progress that had been effected by the overthrow of those very relations.

Any attempt to extol the civilization of medieval Europe, including or rather especially its seigneurialism, ran afoul of the non-slaveholding yeomen who constituted a majority of the white population and who both voted and carried guns.[34] No southern politician who valued his career, not to mention his life, was going to campaign on a platform that proclaimed some form of subordination as the natural and proper condition of labor, not even of industrial labor. Racism provided an obvious way out, and sensible politicians contented themselves with the argument that the presence of black slaves guaranteed the equality as well as the freedom of all whites. But as the proslavery ideologues, including many prominent politicians, turned to the Bible and to history for divine sanction and temporal legitimacy, they found that their arguments proved too much. The arguments led inexorably to a critique of bourgeois social relations and to one or another version, however qualified or disguised, of Fitzhugh's defense of slavery in the abstract. They could not, in consequence, master the South's own kind of social question; to the contrary, they writhed and fudged.

The yeomen generally faded out of the discussions of the historical evolution of social relations and out of the attempts to link the social relations of the medieval manor with those of the slave plantation. The critique of the emancipation of the serfs and their subsequent expulsion from the land ought to have raised the question of the proper relation of yeoman to slaveholding planters, for it explicitly argued that ordinary country folk needed the protection of paternalistic lords. But that question could not be made a subject for discussion. The yeomen prided themselves on their independence and asserted social as well as civic equality with the richest of planters. They were, after all, freeholders, and the racial defense of slavery reinforced their attitude and raised it to the status of official ideology.

The slaveholders, especially the big planters, did often extend their paternalism toward the slaves to local whites, but much of their effort could be assimilated by the recipients to a code of rural neighborliness that precluded dependence. In any case, the yeomen did not want to hear about the beauties of tenancy, although more antebellum southern whites were driven into tenancy, share-cropping, and part-time labor for planters than is generally appreciated. There is no evidence that the yeomen cared a whit about anything medieval, and much evidence that they despised planters who affected aristocratic airs.

Thus, the interest in the Middle Ages, unlike the religiously compelling interest in ancient Israel, was largely restricted to the slaveholding elite, primarily to its influential if numerically few intellectuals—a category that should be understood to include many prominent politicians as well as ordinary preachers and teachers. For them the yeomen could be idealized in a manner that fit, if awkwardly, into the projection of historical continuity. These sturdy freemen, tried and true, filled out a solid, stable, religiously grounded community. This romance has become even stronger among twentieth-century southern conservatives than it ever was among the antebellum planters, whose relations with the yeomen were by no means free of antagonism and tension. And it was a romance that confused the social relations of the Middle Ages with those of the post-medieval transition to capitalism. That confusion made a certain historical sense, for it implicitly and soundly divided history into two distinct epochs, the first of which was based on relations of dependency and the second on market relations. But it also masked the essential nature of southern society in a way that has plagued the modern conservative interpretations of the Old South. For just as slaves were not serfs, so the yeomen of a modern slaveholding society were neither tenants of lordly estates, nor formally free but dependent peasants, nor the equivalent of farmers in northern market society. The Old South was developing as a historically unique slave society, with historically unique class relations. Plantation slavery left room for a numerous yeomanry of a distinct social type—or, better, types—that occupied freeholds but remained marginal to the market. In this respect too, the world of the plantation ranged far from that of the manor while it sought an analagous social stability and tried to preserve a sense of being a "traditional" order.

The slaveholders' difficulties in coming to terms with the Middle Ages— their attraction and repulsion—have been recapitulated by southern conservatives in our century. The myth of the Old South as a feudal society received its primary, certainly its boldest and most challenging, support from Allen Tate, that brilliant man of letters whose imaginative if extravagant interpretations, unfortunately peppered with gross factual errors, continue to offer excellent insights. Tate regarded the southern plantation, with its cavaliers and ladies, its ties of kinship, its love of liberty, its combination of social grace and rustic simplicity, as the direct heir of the medieval manor. His reading was preposterous on all principal counts, including the quaint notion that the medieval manor ever boasted such characteristics. Among other problems, Tate was too learned not to know that those attributes of the aristocratic tradition were largely a product of merchant capital, urban life, and the Renaissance and early national courts.[35]

Tate revered the combination of feudal liberties with paternalism—of an extreme if pre-modern individualism with acceptance of the duty to protect subordinates in a properly ordered society. For Tate, the tragedy of the Old South was to have a feudal society without a feudal religion and therefore to be at war with itself. In the end Tate acknowledged that he sought not to restore the antebellum regime but to build on what, from his point of view, was best in it—what was dominant not in numbers of adherents but in the spirit and qualities of its finest products, who stood against the majority of their own section as well as against the Modern World, and who stood for an old way of life that retained vitality even in the South of the twentieth century.[36]

Tate criticized Protestantism in the context of an interpretation of the Old South as, above all, a religious society. He shared that interpretation with his fellow Agrarians, and it has recently been reasserted by the conservatives associated with *Why the South Will Survive*.[37] But unlike some of the Agrarians and unlike the recent conservatives, Tate was arguing that the South's inheritance of, as it were, the wrong kind of Christianity proved its undoing. For Protestantism, with its bourgeois rather than aristocratic and peasant individualism, proved inadequate to the cultural and ideological demands of a society that was in but not of the world market and that was struggling to overcome its bourgeois legacy. Tate ended in an impasse, for if the historic values he sought to maintain and spread proved too weak to withstand the onslaught of capitalism, industrialism, and urbanization during the middle of the nineteenth century, what chance does it have in the twentieth? For Tate, as for his contemporaries and for recent conservatives, a system of values, which he himself clearly rooted in a feudal past, can somehow be restored while abstracted from the seigneurial social relations on which they were based. Rarely has historical idealism created for itself so formidable a political task.

The most painful contradiction in the social thought of the Agrarians has largely been overcome by the neo-conservatives, but in a way that deepens the larger dilemma of southern conservatives. The Agrarians had trouble with free-market economics. In upholding good old-fashioned individual initiative against the onrushing welfare state, they stressed community solidarity and a kind of traditionalist cooperationism. In consequence, *I'll Take My Stand*, which some of the contributors wanted to call "Tracts Against Communism," reads more like tracts against liberalism. The book contains virtually nothing about political economy, and its successor, *Who Owns America?* repudiates market economics.[38] The neo-conservatives have overcome the contradiction by declaring for the free market, which, I suppose, has now been around long enough to quality as "traditional." But their choice merely reinforces the premise that, somehow, a modern capitalist economy – that astonishingly self-revolutionizing destroyer of traditional culture and values – can provide the social basis for the maintenance, indeed the restoration, of those very values.

Lewis P. Simpson, the distinguished literary critic and cultural historian, has criticized Tate for reading the Old South as a feudal society and has gently chided me for calling the slaveholders "prebourgeois" when my own principal argument defines them as a new and historically unique social class. Speaking of the world the slaveholders aspired to build, Simpson cogently observes: "Such a society ... would not have been prior to any other society. It would have required new modes of thinking and feeling and new modes of literary expression. A new kind of literary mind."[39]

Simpson here probes to the heart of the slaveholders' attitude toward the Middle Ages and the feudalism, seigneurialism, and Catholicism associated with it – an attitude marked by appreciation and fondness but not by a loving quest for intimacy. For not many could, like Fitzhugh, look backward and proclaim, "We want no new world!" And even he understood that if things were to remain the same, things would have to change, that an unlovely new world was a-borning and would have to be strangled. The pro-slavery intellectuals sought to master that new world, for they did not share Fitzhugh's expressed hope that it could in fact be strangled. With reason, they hated and feared the abolitionists, whom they regarded not merely as enemies of slavery but of religion, the family, and all social order. And if they misunderstood the abolitionists, if they overestimated the strength of anarchism among them and woefully underestimated the extent of bourgeois solidity, they nonetheless had a point. For whatever the intentions of the abolitionists, who were hardly a monolithic group, their desired end of slavery represented not only the emancipation of the blacks but the final triumph of bourgeois social relations—the final triumph of the market and the cash-nexus over organic social order. What place would be left for tradition, for stable and family-based community, for religion as a living world view in daily action, for everything the slaveholders held dear?

The pro-slavery ideologues responded in several ways, but their responses betrayed two principal variants of an attempt to master modernity and shape the future. In the first variant, enunciated with special force by the prominent journalist, statistician, and political economist, J. D. B. DeBow, the South would retain slavery but somehow overcome its impediments to material progress. The South would beat the North at its own game by developing an advanced industrial economy while it miraculously avoided the social costs. Those who espoused this variant had no special interest in the Middle Ages, which they regarded as static, backward, and unenlightened, although even they could wax eloquent over the charms of the rustic medieval gallantry to which the South was proudly heir.

Those who espoused the second variant sought to shape the future with the weapons of a different kind of modernity. They sought to project southern social relations, most notably the master-slave relation, as the standard for the whole world. The world would continue to progress materially as well as morally, but the rate and content of material progress would be determined by the exigencies of organic, not market, relations. Thus, if the first variant sought to accommodate a modernized slavery to the bourgeois world, the second sought to reform, not to say revolutionize, the world through the moral, ideological, and material extension of slavery and related forms of social subordination.[40] Those who espoused the second variant, which largely captured the hearts of the intellectuals, thus looked back to the Middle Ages not as a Golden Age but as a valued way station on the road to a corporatist future.

The assertion of historical continuity in a Christian tradition based upon the subjection of the laboring classes to their betters provided the moral and ideological rock on which the slaveholders could build a new society. Fitzhugh never did appreciate the irony: The more slaveholders he could convert to his deeply conservative, indeed proudly reactionary, vision, the more revolutionaries he would create. For the desired end, as Simpson has so well said, was not a medieval, much less an ancient, restoration, but a startlingly new world indeed.

NOTES

1. Francis Pendleton Gaines, *The Southern Plantation: A Study in the Development and the Accuracy of a Tradition* (1924; repr. Gloucester, MA: Peter Smith, 1962).

2. See e.g., *All Clever Men, Who Make Their Way* (Fayetteville, AR: University of Arkansas Press, 1982); *A Character of Hugh Legaré* (Knoxville, TN: University of Tennessee Press, 1985); and O'Brien and David Moltke-Hansen, eds., *Intellectual Life in Antebellum Charleston* (Knoxville, TN: University of Tennessee Press, 1985).

3. See e.g., J. D. B. De Bow, *Industrial Resources of the Southern and Western States* (New Orleans: The Office of De Bow's Review, 1854), I: 72–73. In general, contrast the discussions of the Middle Ages in *De Bow's Review* with the discussions in the literary journals, which tended to be much softer.

4. Daniel R. Hundley, *Social Relations in Our Southern States* (1890; repr. Baton Rouge, LA: Louisiana State University Press, 1979). T. C. De Leon, *Four Years in Rebel Capitals* (Mobile, AL: n.p., 1892), and *Belles, Beaux, and Brains of the Sixties* (1907; repr. New York: Arno Press, 1974).

5. Jaroslav Pelikan, *The Vindication of Tradition* (New Haven: Yale University Press, 1984).

6. Rev. W. G. Brownlow and Rev. A. Pryne, *Ought American Slavery to Be Perpetuated* (1858; repr. Miami, FL: Mnemosyne Publ. Co., 1969), 271.

7. De Leon, 202.

8. For an elaboration of these remarks and others on master-slave relations, see Eugene D. Genovese, *Roll, Jordan, Roll* (New York: Pantheon Books, 1974), 1: 3–6, 70–112.

9. Hundley, 174–75. In fact, many whom Hundley would have acknowledged as true Southern Gentlemen did not dress or act as he claimed. But then, his book is full of biased and even ignorant assertions.

10. Ibid., 55.

11. Perceval Reniers, *The Springs of Virginia* (Chapel Hill: University of North Carolina Press, 1941), 159–60. The South did remain the center of these tournaments, which were rare in the free states. See Esther J. Crooks and Ruth W. Csorks, *The Ring Tournament in the United States* (Richmond: Garrett and Massie, 1946).

12. Ibid., 159. The words are Reniers's paraphrase, with a few words from Dew included as sub-quotation.

13. Dew's "progressive" thought is best captured in his *Lectures on the Restrictive System, Delivered to the Senior Political Class of William and Mary College* (1829; repr. New York: Augustus M. Kelley, 1969).

14. During and after the sixteenth century Western European demand stimulated a return to large-scale enserfment ("The Second Serfdom") in Eastern Europe, which began to export agricultural commodities on a larger scale. For a theoretical introduction to the nature and consequences of the superimposition of the world market on a basically non-market society, see Elizabeth Fox-Genovese, "Antebellum Southern Households: A New Perspective on a Familiar Question," *Review* 7 (1983): 215–53.

15. These generalizations will be defended at length in a forthcoming book on "The Mind of the Master Class," by Elizabeth Fox-Genovese and Eugene D. Genovese. For the moment, let it be noted that the Know Nothings had to go to great lengths in the South to deny that they were hostile to Catholics. Religious bigotry did not play well, especially among the country people, notwithstanding their strong Protestantism. See e.g., W. Darrell Overdyke, *The Know Nothing Party in the South* (Baton Rouge: Louisiana State University Press, 1950). The border states, especially Maryland, were another matter.

16. For a splendid study of Holmes's life and work see Neal C. Gillespie, *The Collapse of Orthodoxy: The Intellectual Ordeal of George Frederick Holmes* (Charlottesville, VA: University of Virginia Press, 1972).

17. Thomas Cooper, *Lectures on the Elements of Political Economy* (New York, 1971), 8.

18. *Restrictive System*, 137–40; Dew, *A Digest of the Laws, Customs, Manners, and Institutions of the Ancient and Modern Nations* (1852; repr. New York, 1870), esp. chap. 3. For a critical approach of Dew's rich thought see Eugene D. Genovese, *Western Civilization through Slaveholding Eyes: The Social and Historical Thoughts of Thomas Roderick Dew*, "The Andrew Mellon Lectures" (New Orleans: The Graduate School of Tulane University, 1986).

19. George Fitzhugh, *Sociology for the South* (Richmond, VA, 1854; repr. New York: Burt Franklin, 1965); *Cannibals All! Or, Slaves without Masters* (1857; repr. Cambridge, MA: Harvard University Press, 1960).

20. See esp. Tate, "Remarks on Southern Religion," in Twelve Southerners, *I'll Take My Stand* (New York: Harper and Brothers Publishers, 1930), 155–75.

21. See esp. William Sumner Jenkins, *Pro-Slavery thought in the Old South* (Gloucester, MA, 1960); Drew Faust, ed., *The Ideology of Slavery: Proslavery Thought in the Antebellum South* (Baton Rouge: Louisiana State University Press, 1981).

22. Henry Hughes, *Treatise on Sociology, Theoretical and Practical* (1854; repr. New York: Negro Universities Press, 1968).

23. Among the southern biblical arguments that passed from theology and scriptural exegesis to history and sociology in defense of slavery as historically ubiquitous and divinely sanctioned, see the contributions of T. Stringfellow, Chancellor W. Harper, and Albert Bledsoe in E.N. Elliott, ed., *Cotton is King and Pro-Slavery Arguments* (1860; repr. New York: Negro Universities Press, 1969); Fred A. Ross, *Slavery Ordained of God* (1857; repr. Miami, FL: Mnemosyne, 1969); William A. Smith, *Lectures on the Philosophy and Practice of Slavery* (Nashville: Stevenson and Evans, 1856). For an elaboration see Eugene D. Genovese, *"Slavery Ordained of God": The Southern Slaveholders' View of Biblical History and Modern Politics*, "Fortenbaugh Memorial Lecture" (Gettysburg: Gettysburg College, 1985).

24. Almost all the theologians, and a great many of the secular writers, who entered the lists against the abolitionists made this point explicitly.

25. Hundley, 134.

26. Ibid., 16, 148; also George S. Sawyer, *Southern Institutes* (1858; repr. New York: Lippincott, 1967), 381. Not only did the critique of the French revolution as an opening to Socialism, Anarchism, Communism, and Abolitionism mark the work of the leading theologians and social theorists, it appeared often in the diaries of college students and ordinary farmers and planters.

27. Diary of William Hooper Haigh, May 18, 1843, in the Southern Historical Collection of the University of North Carolina at Chapel Hill; original emphasis. See, among many such in that same library, Columbus Morrison Diary, June 30, 1845.

28. *Digest*, 333.

29. George D. Armstrong, *The Christian Doctrine of Slavery* (1857; repr. New York: Negro Universities Press, 1967), 59–60 and *passim*.

30. Brownlow, 21.

31. Sawyer, 28, 134ff., 381, 255.

32. Samuel Nott, *Slavery, and the Remedy* (Boston, 1856), 36, 87–88.

33. T. R. R. Cobb, *An Inquiry into the Law of Negro Slavery in the United States* (1858; repr. New York: Negro Universities Press, 1968), cxxxi; also cix–cxx.

34. For an introduction to the yeomanry see the excellent recent study by Steven Hahn, *The Roots of Southern Populism* (New York: Oxford University Press, 1983).

35. Tate's views appear in many of his essays on southern literature and history, as well as in his fanciful yet in many ways insightful biography of Jefferson Davis.

36. Lewis P. Simpson, "The South's Reaction to Modernism: A Problem in the Study of Southern Letters," in Louis D. Rubin and C. Hugh Holman, eds., *Southern Literary Study: Problems and Possibilities* (Chapel Hill: University of North Carolina Press, 1975), 48–68.

37. Fifteen Southerners, *Why the South Will Survive* (Athens, GA: University of Georgia Press, 1981).

38. Herbert Agar and Allen Tate, eds., *Who Owns America? A New Declaration of Independence* (Boston: Little, Brown, 1936).

39. Lewis P. Simpson, *The Dispossessed Garden: Pastoral and History in Southern Literature* (Athens, GA: University of Georgia Press, 1975), 62.

40. For a good illustration see Nathaniel Beverley Tucker, *A Series of Lectures on the Science of Government* (Philadelphia: Carey and Hart, 1845).

The Interior or Hidden Life:
Medieval Mysticism in Nineteenth-Century American Evangelicalism

Theodore R. Hovet

STUDENTS OF AMERICAN CULTURE HAVE LONG BEEN AWARE OF THE INFLUENCE of mystical writers like Plotinus and Swedenborg on American Transcendentalism. What they have not yet paid much attention to is the profound influence of medieval and Renaissance mystical literature on highly influential men and women in mainline Protestant churches in America — particularly the Presbyterian, Congregational, and Methodist — during the middle decades of the nineteenth century. Such neglect is understandable since it is difficult to associate the great body of European mystical literature — a lot of it Catholic, some of it Alchemist — with a group in America usually associated with evangelical revivalism or Christocentric sentimentality.

But the body of mystical literature which flowered in the thirteenth and fourteenth centuries with the writings of Meister Eckhardt, John Tauler, John Ruysbroeck, and Thomas à Kempis and began to fade in the late seventeenth and early eighteenth centuries after works by Jacob Boehme, Teresa of Avila, Saint John of the Cross, William Law, and Madame Guyon had a profound effect on American Protestantism. This literature was seriously and sympathetically discussed in major religious publications like the *Christian Review, Christian Examiner, Methodist Review*, and New York *Evangelist*.[1] Even more importantly, several influential writers translated the medieval mystical ideal into the language and environment of nineteenth-century American life. Chief of these was Thomas C. Upham, a professor at Bowdoin College who taught Nathaniel Hawthorne and became a friend of Harriet Beecher Stowe. In two books widely reviewed in the religious press, *Principles of the Interior or Hidden Life* and *A Treatise on Divine Union*, he explained the "mystic way" to Americans who, more likely than not, had been conditioned to see the spiritual life as the by-product of an instantaneous conversion experience. Phoebe Palmer, a Methodist lay-evangelist who had inspired Upham and his wife to pursue more deeply the mystic way, was also influential in bringing mystic ideas to large numbers of American Protestants through her writings, particularly *The Way of Holiness* and through her famous Tuesday Evening in New York City. Horace Bushnell, the highly respected Congregational minister at Hartford, was another who was profoundly touched by mystical doctrines. Inspired by Upham's writings and his own mystical experience, he speculated on the symbolic nature of scripture, a speculation which is still being seriously discussed by religious and literary historians. Finally, Harriet Beecher Stowe used major images and ideas of medieval mysticism in her own novels.

Lesser known figures also left interesting monuments to the revival of medieval mysticism. Sylvester Judd, a Unitarian minister, attempted to integrate medieval mysticism with Emerson's Transcendentalism; James Barr Walker, a Presbyterian minister, wrote popular theological works which relied heavily on mystical concepts; Frederic Dan Huntington, an Episcopal bishop, vividly described the mystic "way" in a number of published sermons; and Warren Felt Evans, a former Methodist minister, searched for a grand synthesis of the teaching of medieval mystics, the ideas of Emerson, and the spiritual ideals of Upham.[2]

The mysticism these men and women imported into America from medieval and Renaissance sources left its mark on a number of aspects of American religious life. The medieval *via negativa*, for example, was reworked into Phoebe Palmer's immensely influential doctrine known as the "altar phraseology," while Madame Guyon's "Quietism" resulted in an experimentation with contemplation and meditation in the religious circle of Mr. and Mrs. Upham. But the mystical doctrine that will be explored here is that of the so-called concept of "emanation" because of the fresh perspective it brings to our understanding of an important aspect of nineteenth-century evangelicalism and its response to the modernization of American life, a response which still shapes American attitudes toward the family, society, and the economic system.

The concept of emanation had been absorbed into Christian mysticism from Dionysius the Areopagite, a sixth-century mystic who had borrowed the idea from Plotinus, the Neoplatonic philosopher of the third century, and from St. Augustine. According to the concept of emanation, the cosmos is not a hierarchical structure with God at the apex. Instead, the cosmos is, to use one of M. H. Abrams's many lucid explanations of the European mystical tradition, a *"circuitus spiritualis,"* an organic entity in which "a powerful current of 'love,' or cohesive and sustaining supernatural energy . . . flows ceaselessly from God down through the successive levels of ever remoter being and circles back to God—the force that holds the universe together and manifests itself to human awareness as the yearning to return to an undivided state."[3]

In nineteenth-century American Protestantism, the concept of emanation found expression in both poetry and prose. In a poem titled "The Sovereign Will" (1850), for example, Thomas C. Upham explained:

> 'Tis like the mystic wheel within the wheel
> The prophet saw at Chebar. Its decree
> Goes from the centre to the utmost bounds
> Of universal nature. Its embrace
> And penetrating touch pervades, surrounds
> What'er has life or form or time or place.[4]

The concept of emanation resulted in a doctrine of original sin much different from that propagated in popular theology. As interpreted by Christian mystics, the fall occurred when the soul turned away from unity with the divine center to an individual existence at the material circumference. In the words of Plotinus, "severed from the whole, the soul clings to the part; to this one sole thing, buffetted about by a whole worldful of things . . ."[5] In short, it had fallen into Selfhood, the human manifestation of division and multiplicity. In *The Principles of the Interior or Hidden Life* (1843), Upham quoted William Law in order to explain the nature of original sin to his American readers.

> Man broke off from his true CENTRE, his proper place in God, and therefore the life and operation of God was no more in him. He was fallen from a life in God into a life of SELF, into an animal life of self-love, self-esteem, and self-seeking in the poor, perishing enjoyments of this world. This was the natural state of man by the Fall. He was an apostate from God, and his natural life was all idolatry, where SELF was the great idol that was worshipped instead of God.[6]

It is this notion of the fall into Selfhood that is the hallmark of mystical literature. The object of the mystical quest is to turn back from Selfhood and its attachment to the material circumference (a step most often referred to as the "*via negativa*," "Purgation," or the "Way of the Cross") and to merge again with the divine center (the so-called "unitive life"). It is this turning back toward unity that explains why the mystical narrative line is usually a curve or "U" that recounts how an individual falls into exile and alienation in a foreign land and then finds his or her way home again. It also explains why the parable of the Prodigal Son is so frequently alluded to in mystical literature.

What gave this notion of the fall such immediacy was its marriage to the ancient concept of "correspondence" which holds, in the words of Ulrich Simon, that "nothing subsists in itself, everything is woven into a vast texture of relationships. . . . [E]vents are not other-worldly, but they fit into a design which derives from, and leads to, another world."[7] As Upham explained to his nineteenth-century contemporaries, "the original type is in the infinite; but it is reproduced and reflected with greater or less degree of distinctness in all orders of moral beings."[8] Thus the evidence of the fall from center to a disordered and divided circumference could be detected in the physical universe. For example, in *The Philosophy of the Plan of Salvation*, a work carefully critiqued before publication by the Beecher and Stowe families and one which Marie Caskey characterized as "the most widely distributed and translated book of its kind in the world,"[9] James B. Walker pointed out:

> the laws which govern physical nature are analogous to those which the Gospel introduces into the spiritual world. The earth is held to the sun by the power of attraction, and performs regularly its circuit around the central, sustaining luminary, maintaining at the same time its equal relations with its sister planets. But the moral system upon the earth is a chaos of derangement. The attraction of *affection*, which holds the soul to God, has been broken, and the soul of man, actuated by selfishness, revolving upon its own center only, jars in its course with its fellow-spirits, and crosses their orbits; and the whole system of the spiritual world upon earth revolves in disorder, the orbs wandering and rolling away from that center of moral life and power which alone could hold them in harmonious and happy motion.[10]

But even though life on earth was "a chaos of derangement," the original form of the spiritual cosmos could still be detected. In *Divine Union* (1851) – Upham's second book on the mystical tradition – the Bowdoin theologian explained that "every sphere has its *centre*. And that centre, in being constituted by a divine arrangement, and with divine approbation, may be said to harmonize with the divine and infinite centre."[11] What was the center of human society? To Upham it was self-evident.

> It is man, therefore, in his threefold nature—the father, the mother, and the child—the beautiful trinity of the family . . . which may be regarded as the earthly representation, the visible, though dim, shadowing forth of the divine personalities existing in the unity of the Godhead.[12]

One more highly significant aspect of the mystical cosmos needs to be noted here. According to a tradition given particularly forceful expression by John Scotus Erigena in the ninth century and Jacob Boehme in the late sixteenth and early seventeenth centuries, "all division in nature," to quote Abrams, "was the result of the fall of man, which occurred with very little or no lapse of time after the creation and resulted in the separation of man from God, as well as the split of primal man into male and female sexes."[13] It seems somewhat surprising to us that ministers and seminary professors associated with evangelical circles in Victorian America would repeat this idea of the fall as resulting in sexual division, but repeat it they did. Upham declared that "man, created in the divine image, is male and female and these two are one." But the fall, he argued, had split androgynous "man" into male and female and now the woman is "oppressed by man's depravity, injured in her most sacred affections—the slave of man instead of his companion."[14] Horace Bushnell, who was strongly influenced by Upham as well as the European mystics, repeated this basic argument in an essay on woman's suffrage (which, incidentally, he opposed). Male and female, he declared, were to be "one flesh," but "then follows the precipitation of the fall, in which the composite unity becomes a bond of retributive liability, even as every other blessing is touched by the pangs of disorder."[15]

As odd as it might seem to an age as secular as ours, the mystic cosmos constructed out of the concepts of the *circuitus spiritualis*, the fall, and of correspondence provided some of the more influential liberals in the Protestant churches a mythological structure of considerable power when it came to helping them to explain how the new economic forces that were transforming American life in the middle decades of the nineteenth century were affecting the traditional structure of the family. In a beautiful sermon titled "the Age of Homespun" delivered at the Litchfield County Centennial in 1851, Horace Bushnell pointed out that "domestic manufacture," as he called it, of a hundred years ago depended upon the labor of women at the spinning wheel and loom. Thus the economy of the "Puritan Arcadia," to use his term for eighteenth-

century New England, revolved around a feminine center from which ema-
nated maternal love. "In the play of the wheel," Bushnell explained, the woman
"spun fibre too within, and in the weaving wove it close and firm."[16] Hence,
she "is the centre of a happy domestic life, and becomes a mark of reverence to her children: 'Her children arise up and call her blessed.' "[17] The
domestic economy of the pre-modern rural America, therefore, reflected closely
the spiritual cosmos before the fall.

In the New England of 1851, however, the steam engine was replacing
the spinning wheel. To use Bushnell's very interesting language, "this transition from mother and daughter power to water and steam power is a great
one, greater by far than many have as yet begun to conceive—one that is
to carry with it a complete revolution of domestic life and social manners."
What caused this "transition"? It occurred when "fathers and sons" grew im-
patient of hard work out of doors, and set them at contriving some easier
and more plausible way of living through "money" and "speculation."[18]

Thus in Bushnell's symbolic world, we have a recreation of the fallen Plotin-
ian cosmos: the Puritan Arcadia or the "age of homespun" corresponded to
the pre-lapsarian cosmos, for everyone was united to the domestic center
through the power of love. But the fathers and sons turned away from that
center to seek their individual identity in the distant cities. To put it another
way, the centripetal pull of the organic, feminine domestic center—symbolized
by the spinning wheel—gave way to the centrifugal force of the mechanical
steam engine. The family disintegrated into "atoms," as Bushnell termed it.
Thus the mystic concept of the Fall, in which the individual soul turned away
from spiritual unity to the material circumference of existence, was repeated
in America, as the doctrine of correspondence held that it must be. Moreover,
the division between feminine and masculine created by the fall was repeated by the masculine and feminine spheres. Henceforth, New England existed in a fallen and divided world: the masculine sphere of money, the machine,
and the city was divided from the feminine nucleus of domesticity, handicrafts,
and love. It should be pointed out here that if one were to approach Henry
Adams's symbols of the virgin and the dynamo through Bushnell's sermon,
they would not seem as unique as literary and cultural historians have pic-
tured them.[19]

If one turns to other literature written by those touched by the mystical
vision, one finds during this period of rapid modernization and urbanization
a powerful mythological model being constructed in which the feminine, as
in Bushnell's sermon, stands in metonymic relationship to rural life, domestic labor, love, and ancient spiritual traditions. In fact, the Virgin as envi-

sioned in the art and literature of the Middle Ages is in a sense reborn in the American woman. Note, for example, how Frederic Dan Huntington, the Episcopal bishop who turned to the mystic way, in writing about his rural childhood home transforms his mother into a figure who well might be the Virgin in a Medieval stained-glass cathedral window:

> But as to the old kitchen and all that, – that is a matter that touches me in a vital point. . . . Did I not used to take sweet and holy counsel with the best and purest of mothers, by the twilight, many and many a time, in that shady old milk-room? Milton may talk about the dim religious light of Gothic cloisters; it never was half as impressive as the light that used to shine in at sundown, not exactly, to be sure, 'thro' storied windows richly dight,' but through panes stained with age as art could not do it. I say again nobody has any business to meddle with those walls.[20]

Or here is one of Harriet Beecher Stowe's masculine narrators commenting upon his gift to his bride:

> In the olden times the family linen of a bride was of her own spinning and that of her mother and kinswomen; so that every thread in it had a sacredness of family life and association. One can fancy dreams of peace would come in a bed, every thread of whose linen had been spun by loving and sainted hands. So, the gift to my wife from my mother was some of this priceless old linen, every piece of which had its story. . . . They had been through the history of family life, and came to us fragrant with rosemary and legend. We touched them with reverence, as relics of ascended saints.[21]

But what about the new world being created by industrialization and urbanization? For those looking at it with the mystic cosmos in mind, it is a masculine world constructed not by hand within the home, but by the machine in an impersonal urban complex. In *American Cottage Life* – a title which already gives the game away – Upham describes how this world forms a new kind of wheel, that of the machine, to replace the spinning wheel. This new wheel creates a centrifugal force that shatters the feminine nucleus which had existed during "American Cottage Life." To quote from one of the poems:

> The mourning daughters to the Factory went,
> that rears on high its massy stories tall,
> With noise of many looms in concert blent,

and wheels that loudly dash within its wall,
Close on the banks of darkling Salmon-Fall.[22]

A surviving fragment of Sylvester Judd's "The White Hills: An American Tragedy" (1851) is another work which illustrates how for many touched by the mystical vision the masculine identity was becoming associated with modern individualism and materialism. Not unlike Theodore Dreiser's Clyde Griffiths of the next century, Judd's hero has been seduced by Mammon dressed "in the guise of a modern gentleman." Before leaving his rural hamlet for the new world of money and power emerging in the West, he seeks a "parting interview" with his lifelong love. Standing in the dark outside her "cottage, embowered in woodbine and shrubbery," he watches her through a window "embroidering a cross." He declaims:

> I cannot enter. Nook of paradise,
> With a bright angel in it! It is no place
> For me. I'm lost, not callous or malign;
> And contrast makes me lonely, dreadfully
> Alone. Back of the cottage is the sky
> and back of this is heaven. And she's in heaven,
> Whose awful azure glories her with heart
> of maiden innocence and holy peace;
> While I retreat to what I am, to gaze
> Across a pathless gulf on what I was.[23]

Harriet Beecher Stowe provides a particularly memorable example of how the feminine and masculine became symbols for pre-modern and modern society. In *Uncle Tom's Cabin*, the runaway slave, George Harris, has found refuge in a Quaker settlement, an agrarian enclave not yet touched by modern economic forces. He watches the mother, Rachel Halliday, preside over the domestic altar. Stowe comments:

> Rachel never looked so truly and benignly happy as at the head of her table. There was so much motherliness and full-heartedness even in the way she passed a plate of cakes or poured a cup of coffee, that it seemed to put a spirit into the food and drink she offered.

George is touched by the spirit emanating from this domestic priestess administering communion to the household.

> This, indeed, was a home, — *home*, — a word that George had never yet known a meaning for; and a belief in God, and trust in his providence,

began to encircle his heart, as, with a golden cloud of protection and
confidence, dark, misanthropic, pining, atheistic doubts, and fierce
despair, melted away before the light of a living Gospel....[24]

Meanwhile the hero of Stowe's novel, Uncle Tom, has fallen into the night-
mare world of Legree's plantation, a symbol of the modern industrial capitalism
which has supplanted the "farm" which constituted his earlier life in Ken-
tucky. Legree's slaves, rather than being served by a priestess like Rachel
Halliday, struggle in disorder around the machine that grinds the corn for
their evening meal. Tom thus witnesses a microcosm of industrial capitalism:

> sullen, scowling, imbruted men, and feeble, discouraged women, or
> women that were not women, —the strong pushing away the weak,—
> the gross, unrestricted animal selfishness of human beings, of whom
> nothing good was expected and desired; and who, treated in every way
> like brutes, had sunk as nearly to their level as it was possible for hu-
> man beings to do. To a late hour in the night the sound of the grinding
> was protracted; for the mills were few in number compared with the
> grinders, and the weary and feeble ones were driven back by the strong,
> and came on last in their turn.[25]

Finally, then, the mystic cosmos drawn after Plotinus's concept of emanation
became a powerful analytical model for depicting the nature of the new
economic and social forces transforming American life. The individualism,
the materialism, the constant movement in American life—those qualities so
often noted with pride by the spokesmen of the Jacksonian era—were for
men and women familiar with the mystic quest a sign of the continuous fall
of humanity toward Selfhood at the material circumference of existence. People
were atoms spun off from the feminine nucleus of the pre-modern domestic
economy and then caught up in the accelerating force of the machine and the
new commercial complexes it was building. What was particularly frightening
to some of the men and women whom we have discussed here was the realization that the mystical vision of *circuitus spiritualis* may be forever obscured
by the fragmented materialism of modern urban culture. To quote Bushnell,

> Instead of being wrought together and penetrated, to some extent, by
> historic laws and forces common to all the members, we only seem to
> lie as seeds piled together, without any terms of connexion, save the
> accident of proximity, or the fact that we all belong to the heap. And
> thus the ... forms of organic existence, which God has appointed for
> the race, are in fact lost out of mental recognition.[26]

Thus when Judd's hero, gazing through the window at his beloved, laments that he is looking "across a pathless gulf on what I was," he is giving expression both to the mystical concept of sexual division and to the sense of loss of a social order more nurturing to the human spirit.

Social and intellectual historians continue to be puzzled why the concept of "two spheres"—that is, a masculine commercial sphere marked by materialism and competitive individualism and a feminine domestic sphere characterized by domestic affection and spiritual aspiration—emerges with such force in middle-class culture in the middle decades of the nineteenth century. In attempting to find the answer, they have paid particular attention to the individuals, with the exception of Upham, who have been discussed here. Ann Douglas has looked closely at Stowe and Bushnell, Barbara Cross at Bushnell, Anne C. Loveland at Phoebe Palmer, and Elizabeth Ammons and Jane P. Tompkins at Stowe's fiction.[27] Without exception, these twentieth-century commentators view the concept of woman's "sphere" as a futile effort to throw a veil of respectability over the role of the powerless. As Ann Douglas puts it, it was a way "to protest a power to which one has already in part capitulated."[28]

However, if we look at the two spheres from the perspective of the mystical vision of the fall, they begin to reverberate with symbolic meaning. Not only did modernization constitute a fall of the nation from an Arcadian past centered on the feminine domestic economy, but each day the man heading out from home to the marketplace reenacts the original fall when humanity turned away from its spiritual center and toward materialism and individualism at the circumference of existence. If, however, the wife and mother assumes the role of true womanhood, she recreates, in the eyes of those influenced by the mystical concept of emanation, a spiritual center in the home which has sufficient spiritual and emotional power to turn the fallen man away from the material circumference back toward his true home. The pre-modern domestic economy in which the woman at the spinning wheel, to quote Bushnell again, "spun fibre too within" and wove "it close and firm" is now replaced by the urban middle class home in which the woman creates a sacred space that replicates that at the spiritual center of existence.

Thus Phoebe Palmer, who had immense influence in middle-class evangelical circles, describes how she rose early in the morning and "bore the individual members" of her family to "the mercy seat" in order "through this medium, to crave the acceptance of their persons." After assuming this priestly function at "the family altar," she tells us, she "often had ... reason to observe throughout the day, that not only the members of her household, but also her house, which had also been specially consecrated to God, were held under a divine influence, and the Spirit, 'which, as a peaceful dove, / flies the abode of noise and strife,' was felt to be brooding over that household."[29] Similarly, Harriet Beecher Stowe, whose novels had great influence in publicizing the "cult of domesticity," explained in *The Minister's Wooing* that woman's domestic sphere was an "appointed shrine ... more holy than cloister, more saintly and pure than church or altar" in which "priestess, wife, and mother ... ministers daily in holy works of household peace, and by faith and prayer and love redeems from grossness and earthliness the common toils and wants of life."[30]

Moreover, in accordance with the mystical notion of the fall as a division of humanity into male and female, it could be argued that a well-defined feminine sphere reawakened the awareness in men that the spiritual identity was androgynous. As Bushnell put it, "the woman things of the world" have reminded Christians that Jesus had "both a manly and womanly nature, and that he became the perfect one, because in this union he was able, in so great force and authority, to bear so many things with a gentle submission and an unfaltering patience."[31] Stowe explicitly traced this quality to a feminine origin:

> The feminine element in Christ's nature was Mary's contribution to her son's greatness. It was her physical and psychological endowment as a woman that Mary, representing mankind, had given, sealing the human nature to the divine.

Hence, it is the mother who most fully reveals the nature of Christ.

> He who made me capable of such an absorbing unselfish devotion as I feel for my children so that I could willingly sacrifice my eternal salvation for theirs—He certainly did not make me capable of more love, more disinterest than he has himself. He invented mother's hearts— and he certainly has the pattern in his own. . . .[32]

Feminist religious and cultural historians have been highly critical of this kind of sanctification of woman's sphere. Rosemary Ruether, for example, argues that when "woman comes to be identified with the spiritual, pious, and altruistic impulses, whose purity can be preserved only by the strictest segregation from the public world of male materialism and power," then she is also segregated from "public influence in society or in the Church." Moreover, Ruether continues, the concept of an androgynous spiritual origin ultimately works against women:

The very concept of androgyny presupposes a psychic dualism that identifies maleness with one-half of human capacities and femaleness with the other. As long as Christ is still presumed to be, normatively, a male person, androgynous Christologies will carry an androcentric bias. Men gain their "feminine" side, but women contribute to the whole by specializing in representation of the 'feminine,' which means exclusion from the exercise of the roles of power and leadership associated with masculinity.[33]

This observation is more than born out by the example of Bushnell who argued that women must not be given the suffrage, for "still life is then no more, and the man who goes home at night from his caucus fight, or campaign speech, goes in, not to cease and rest, but to be dinned with the echo, or perhaps bold counter-echo of his own harsh speech."[34]

However, we must recognize that Ruether's argument would have been meaningless to those who embraced the mystic vision of the world. This vision reversed the traditional view of how and where freedom was obtained. It did not come from the exercise of power but from its renunciation. Palmer expressed concisely how the mystical ideal lent authenticity to the cult of domesticity when she explained:

> the female part of the church have the advantage. Retired from the turmoil and perplexities of business life, the mind is, or may be, free from the anxiety and distraction of debts, or business competitions, with a reputation and religious influence that have not been scathed and trammeled by exposure to the storms and combative elements of business or political life, they are free to throw their whole souls most effectively into the work of God.[35]

Thus the cult of domesticity for its most forceful spokespersons was not a capitulation to masculine power. Rather it imaged forth the highest spiritual ideals. In our secular age, cultural and religious historians as well as feminists will probably reject those ideals, but they should acknowledge that for a number of men and women of the nineteenth century they contained an intellectual and emotional substance which filled the woman's life with power and significance. They should also pay tribute to the continued force of one of the noblest creations of medieval society—the vision of the mystic way.

NOTES

1. Two noteworthy examples of the interest in mysticism in the religious press are "Notes on the Mystics," *Christian Review* 25 (1860): 557–76 and "The Mystical Element in Religion," *Christian Examiner* 37 (1844): 309–17.

2. Little known works of particular interest to anyone concerned with the more imaginative treatments of mysticism are Sylvester Judd's *Margaret: A Tale of the Real and the Ideal, Blight and Bloom* (1845, rev. 1851); James Barr Walker's *The Philosophy of the Plan of Salvation* (1841); and Warren Felt Evans's *The Celestial Dawn* (1862) and *The Happy Islands* (1860).

3. Meyer H. Abrams, *Natural Supernaturalism: Tradition and Revolution in Romantic Literature* (New York: W. W. Norton and Co., 1971), 152.

4. *American Cottage Life, A Series of Poems* (New Brunswick, NJ: Joseph Griffin, 1850–51), 163.

5. Elmer O'Brien, ed. and trans., *The Essential Plotinus* (Indianapolis: Hackett Publishing Company, 1964), 66.

6. *Principles of the Interior or Hidden Life* (New York: Harper and Brothers, 1843), 284–85.

7. *Story and Faith* (London: SPCK Press, 1975), 183.

8. *A Treatise on Divine Union* (Boston: George C. Rand, 1851), 297.

9. *Chariots of Fire: Religion and the Beecher Family* (New Haven: Yale University Press, 1978), 231.

10. *Philosophy of the Plan of Salvation. A Book for the Times* (Cincinnati: Jennings and Graham, n. d.), 166.

11. *Divine Union*, 291.

12. *Divine Union*, 297.

13. *Natural Supernaturalism*, 153.

14. *Divine Union*, 306.

15. *Women's Suffrage; The Reform Against Nature* (New York: Charles Scribner and Co., 1869), 74–75.

16. *The Age of Homespun. A discourse, delivered at Litchfield, Conn., on the occasion of the Centennial Celebration, 1851* (n. p., n. d.), 124. The discourse is available in slightly altered form in *Work and Play* (New York: Charles Scribner's Sons, 1903), 374–407.

17. *The Age of Homespun*, 107–08.

18. *The Age of Homespun*, 112, 123.

19. For a more detailed analysis of Busnell's *The Age of Homespun*, see Theodore R. Hovet, "Horace Bushnell's 'Age of Homespun' and Transcendental Symbolism," *ATQ* 55 (1985): 5–18.

20. Arria S. Huntington, *Memoirs and Letters of Frederic Dan Huntington* (Boston and New York: Houghton, Mifflin and Company, 1906), 28.

21. *My Wife and I* (1871; New York: AMS Press, 1967), 453.

22. *American Cottage Life,* 79.

23. Arethusa Hall, *Life and Character of the Rev. Sylvester Judd* (Boston: Crosby, Nichols and Company, 1854), 383.

24. *Uncle Tom's Cabin; or Life Among the Lowly* (1852; New York: AMS Press, 1967), I: 185.

25. *Uncle Tom's Cabin,* II: 120.

26. *Views of Christian Nurture and Subjects Adjacent Thereto* (Delmar, NY: Scholars' Facsimiles and Reprints, 1975), 26.

27. Elizabeth Ammons, "Heroines in *Uncle Tom's Cabin,*" *American Literature* 49 (1977): 161–79; Barbara Cross, *Horace Bushnell: Minister to a Changing America* (Chicago: University of Chicago Press, 1958); Ann Douglas, *The Feminization of American Culture* (New York: Alfred A. Knopf, 1977); Anne C. Loveland, "Domesticity and Religion in the Antebellum Period: The Career of Phoebe Palmer," *Historian* 39 (1977): 455–71; Jane P. Tompkins, "Sentimental Power: *Uncle Tom's Cabin* and the Politics of Literary History," *Glyph* 8 (1981): 80–104.

28. *The Feminization of American Culture,* 12.

29. *The Way of Holiness, with Notes by the Way* (New York: printed by the author, 1854), 87–88.

30. *The Minister's Wooing* (1859; New York: AMS Press, 1967), 410.

31. "Women's Suffrage," 60, 61.

32. Quoted by Caskey, 205, 187–88.

33. Rosemary Radford Ruether, *Sexism and God-Talk: Toward a Feminist Theology* (Boston: Beacon Press, 1983), 129, 130.

34. "Women's Suffrage," 62.

35. *The Promise of the Father or, a Neglected Speciality of the Last Days* (Boston: Henry V. Degen, 1859), 98–99.

A New Dimension?
North American Scholars
Contribute Their Perspective

Susan Mosher Stuard

I N NORTH AMERICA, OVER THREE GENERATIONS AND BY AN INDIRECT ROUTE, A NEW perspective on the role of women in medieval society has appeared. It now exerts some influence on general understandings of European history, and it constitutes a perspective in which the historical profession may take some pride and which feminists may value and respect. At first glance it may seem more a matter of chance than an intentional challenge to Old World interpretations that this new direction in scholarship has been advanced, but that first glance may be deceptive, masking distinctive features in the organization of higher learning in the United States and Canada, and important differences in the structure of historical studies this side of the Atlantic. But surely it would be difficult to make a case for conscious intent. The accomplishment seems to consist in roughly equal parts of the brashness of young nations encountering the high tradition of European learning, incomplete assimilation of the interests governing Positivist history (although Americans wrote Positivist history perfectly well), and a genuine impulse to rethink the medieval past and apply its lessons in the New World. If, for this century of North American scholarship it is impossible to make a claim for conscious intent, surely disclaimers are not in order either.

New world feminism began early enough in Boston to influence historical scholarship, and early in its own course recognized the importance of medieval women. Writing in *The Una* before the Civil War, Paulina Wright Davis argued that paradoxically women's journey back to the Middle Ages was a journey of progress. Then women had been physicians and notaries and held positions of authority, whereas in the nineteenth century their only job opportunities were the classroom and the factory at slave wages.[1] But this hard-headed approach to an age best known to the American reading public through the Romantic novels of Sir Walter Scott had no direct influence on the fledgling profession of medieval historical studies that began soon after the Civil War. Its influence, if it was felt at all, was indirect. In championing higher education for women feminism inspired the founding of women's colleges where young women could study the history of all ages.

In America's new colleges women pursued the same curriculum as men and studied under historians who were likely to be men trained abroad in the German methods of historical analysis proudly touted as Positivism, the "new scientific history." One such medievalist, Herbert Baxter Adams, divided his teaching year between Johns Hopkins University and Smith College after the latter was founded in the 1870s. Adams believed history was the study of documents and saw to it that his Smith women and his Johns Hopkins men pursued careful research projects. He also believed the medieval past should be made relevant through investigations into the underlying political and social institutions which the New World had inherited from the Old. Setting his students to investigate and report on these, and writing on them himself in "The German Origins of New England Villages," Herbert Baxter Adams used the curriculum to heighten interest in a European cultural heritage. Women students were made aware of the relevance of studying the Middle Ages because in the hands of this skilled teacher of history they were put in direct touch with the past. Not all historical personages women encountered in their study of history were men, nor were all the institutions presented male domains. In his four years teaching at Smith College Adams encouraged women to investigate medieval history, recommending two women to continue for the Ph.D. degree.[2]

His more famous contemporary Henry Adams was also led to medieval scholarship through the challenge of pedagogy, but the Harvard College curriculum to which he turned his efforts placed distinctly different demands upon him. Unlike Herbert Baxter Adams, who had been thoroughly trained in Rankian methods and medieval history at Leipzig University, Henry Adams had pursued only two years of advanced historical training in Germany, studying only modern history. In 1870 when President Elliot of Harvard drafted him to present a medieval bridge of lectures between Professor Gourney's classical course and Professor Torrey's modern one, Henry Adams demurred on the grounds that he knew no medieval history, but Elliot prevailed and Henry Adams began to read the documents as his brief training at Leipzig had prescribed. The result was History One, or the prototype of the American survey course.[3] By his own admission Henry Adams possessed no text and could discern no great truth with which to edify his students; yet by 1876 he had created his own interpretive framework that anticipated contemporary understanding of mentalities in uncanny ways. With all the brashness of youth he entered the field of cultural and social history and turned to the condition of women as a way of monitoring the state of health of Western society. In 1876 he was ready to challenge European authorities and, more significantly, prevailing Victorian notions on the evolution of primitive societies by reference to Europe's Barbaric Age. His Lowell lecture that year on "The Primitive Rights of Women," was presumptuous: he attacked Andrew MacLennan's respected and popular *Primitive Marriage* by implication and Henry Maine's authoritative study of *Ancient Law* directly. He offered an unsentimental review of the law, chronicles, and sagas that anticipated in important ways our contemporary formulations on gender.[4]

Adams had come to the conclusion that a "social balance" had existed between men and women in Germanic society: a parity qualified solely by a woman's subjection to guardianship. "A woman could not go to war" he asserted, that is, she risked her property and legal rights if she did so. He challenged established authority on the role of the Church: "Historians . . . have . . . assumed [that] the elevation of women from what was supposed to have been their previous condition of degradation and servitude was due to the humanitarian influence of the Church. In truth the share of the Church in the elevation of women was for the most part restricted." He goes on to be far more critical by asserting that the Church abhorred most strong women and over time actually forced a diminution of women's rights. This idea was unorthodox enough, but he asserted next that the "social balance" between the sexes, particularly in the family, explains Europe's dynamic pattern of growth, yet, paradoxically, the balance was thrown out of equilibrium by the "exigencies of a pressing immediate necessity," that is, state building. He concluded with a dire warning: we must revitalize the family by restoring the social balance between the sexes. Not to do so will carry us down the road to ruin as Rome was ruined; to do so will hasten the dawn of the bright new age.[5]

His morally uplifting conclusion might shock, but it could also appeal to a Boston audience that relished a call to reform. It twisted onto its head the

European nations' argument that their treatment of women was a proof of their superiority over decadent or primitive peoples and an imperative to enlighten and reform others. But this position also constituted an original contribution to medieval scholarship, I would argue, because Adams saw gender as a historical product, and subject to change over time, and he viewed its shifts as integral to other changes in society over the long term. Interest in the long term was, in some degree, a response to the challenge of the survey course which he presented, and in that sense his pedagogy inspired his scholarship, but his insight did not in its turn inform his teaching of history. In his attempt to echo the categories introduced by Gourney in his classical lectures and carried forward by Torrey on the modern era, Adams suppressed his own ideas about causation and presented a chronology of reigns, wars, and administrative milestones. He did not teach about women, culture and society – he taught public history, a failure by his own admission.

Adams met failure in his private life in the same years, and the weight of it led him to abandon his autobiography; he did not return to the task of examining his successes and failures for twenty years. By that time he had achieved an accommodation with the values of his age and found another formulation on the question of woman. In *Mont St. Michel and Chartres*, and later with his famous metaphor of the Virgin and the Dynamo, Henry Adams stressed medieval women's elevation in step with society's increased refinement. This conformed much more closely to the values of his Victorian audience, and consequently these were the ideas for which he became known. Adams's original interpretation, that is, that parity between the sexes had once existed in the West and that considering women's position in society had the capacity to force reinterpretation of the age, was lost to all but a few.

Instead most North American medievalists in the young discipline espoused current ideas about causality in history and accepted the lead of European authorities. For women, if they were considered at all, civilization brought progress understood as refinement, the Church served to elevate women's status in European society, and patriarchy, often synonymous in Victorian circles with advanced moral order, brought substantial benefits to women as well as to men. But if this represented the view of the majority, Henry Adams's radical early position did not disappear altogether. One scholar in particular kept his original idea alive, and thus she mounted a challenge to common assumptions about women's past and to generally held views within the historical profession. Florence Griswold Buckstaff, first woman regent of the University of Wisconsin and an organizer of social welfare services in that state, had prepared in medieval history.[6] After graduation from the

University of Wisconsin in 1883 she pursued graduate study in history in
Cambridge, Massachusetts (her obituary coyly refused to note the institution
of higher learning). She published "Married Women's Property Rights in Anglo-
Saxon and Anglo-Norman Law" in the *Annals of the American Academy* in
1886.[7] This work emphasizes early rights of women and a loss of positive
legal rights for them in England after the Norman conquest. Florence Griswold
Buckstaff left the field of Medieval Studies, but it is clear that her scholarship on early Europe informed her social activism. Her published study provided some scholarly references for Adams's innovative but less than fully
substantiated thesis on medieval women presented in the Lowell lecture of
1876.

Adams's and Buckstaff's ideas in turn played into the interests of a Stanford University historian, George E. Howard. His extensive researches during the last decade of the nineteenth century resulted in a three-volume history
of matrimonial institutions, which he was ready to publish in 1904.[8] He became the United States's leading authority on marriage as a result, and his
strong advocacy of divorce as a right for women was based upon his understanding of women's former right to divorce in the common law tradition.
His longitudinal approach associated the loss of such rights with other social
evils, and his careful scholarship was deemed sufficient authority to promote
his stand on divorce in a number of states. Reform followed, providing a
striking example of the practical application of historical scholarship to American life.[9] Howard was a major influence upon his student, Mary Roberts
Smith Coolidge, whose *Why Women Are So* helped launch modern research
into acculturation of women. Coolidge adopted a position which prevailed
among some pioneering social scientists of the day, namely that human nature is highly plastic and influenced by social conditions in different times
and places.[10] Indirectly at least, the long term of change in women's condition in the West presented in Howard's study affected her thinking.

In America, where faculties were gathered into collegial disciplines, a historical argument that carried little weight within its own established profession
might find a responsive audience elsewhere, and so the original idea suggested by Adams and researched by Buckstaff was taken up and developed
by fledgling departments of the social sciences. Within a few years it was
buttressed further by the painstaking scholarship of the British historian, Bertha
Phillpotts, whose *Kindred and Clan in the Middle Ages* (1913) thoroughly
characterized the early world in which women had played their consequential roles.[11] This work came recommended by its own air of authoritative
English scholarship, endorsed by publication at Cambridge University Press,

so it mattered not that it languished on the shelves of European libraries and was allowed to go out of print. In the quest for the legitimizing office American scholars sought from serious European scholarship the *imprimatur* was sufficient. Fortunately Bertha Phillpotts's scholarship was formidable, and her arguments could stand on their own. American scholars now had conclusive historical evidence that women had once held positive legal rights that they had long since lost.

This scholarly pursuit at the junction of the high tradition of historical writing and the new concerns of the social sciences continued through the first wave of twentieth century American feminism. In new departments at respected women's colleges like Barnard, and in major universities where women were accepted in graduate programs, scholars ventured the idea that gender roles were socially constructed and had their roots in specific historical conditions. For the most part this work was pursued in the new scholarly disciplines, not within departments of history. Elsie Clews Parsons had originally looked to history, but she found the discipline of anthropology more accommodating for the sorts of questions that she wished to raise about societies. Ruth Benedict had attempted to write the history of prominent women such as Mary Wollstonecraft, but she grew frustrated at the inability of biography to produce the answers that she sought, and, therefore, she trained in anthropology.[12] The new social sciences were pursued by thinkers who had made a conscious decision that interpretive framework was more critical to their investigations than the field of study. For this reason the case for gender as a socially constructed category was more likely to be argued in reference to remote stateless societies rather than by reference to Europe's formative age.

This highly pragmatic approach was not chosen by all aspiring scholars, however. Herbert Baxter Adams, the inspiring teacher who had recommended two of his original Smith College women for the history Ph.D., had his successors. Professors encouraged women to pursue the high tradition of historical study of the Middle Ages, and in one fashion or another convinced women that their questions would find answers in the documents of history. The essentially philological approach of history was presented to students as neutral in regard to gender and all similar cultural artifacts, and, through applying the strict rules of Rankian Positivism, capable of revealing whatever reality lay embedded in the early records of the European past. While I might argue that this was a naively idealistic view of the purposes to which Positivist history was to be directed, and that the historical profession in general had no particular desire for reappraisals of history from young and untried American scholars who had the further disadvantage of being female, this did not prevent women from entering the historical profession with all the good will in the world. Women expected to be accepted on the strength of their scholarship and of their careful reconstructions of the past. And women were, to a surprising degree, capable of finding their way as medieval historians and respected scholars in the North American university system.

Within the profession, women historians took up important posts in institutions of higher learning, and when that happened, there was a strong chance that they had been trained as medievalists. Helen Cam at Harvard University and Sylvia Thrupp at the University of Michigan were sole women in departments of history, and they were both medievalists.[13] Later Marie Borroff occupied the same sole position in Medieval Studies and comparative literature at Yale University. Catherine Boyd published her dissertation on Cistercian nuns and taught at Carleton College. Katherine Fischer Drew edited the Lombard Laws and chaired her history department at Rice University. Emily Hope Allen never completed her degree, but provided the notes for the first published edition of Margery Kempe's autobiography.[14] Mt. Holyoke provided her institutional identification regardless of an uncompleted degree. It also provided a professorship for Nelly Neilson who pioneered studies in medieval agriculture and served as the first woman president of the American Historical Association.[15] Emily Putnam produced her important study, *The Lady*, became dean, then president, of Barnard College.[16] If North America could not produce sufficient women medievalists, it could count on England to supply a few. Eleanor Shipley Duckett, a Cambridge-trained medievalist, transferred her scholarly interests to women in the Middle Ages and her home to the United States. Her own estimate of her chances of being taken seriously were not optimistic, yet she continued to study early medieval culture and to write about women who, for the variety of roles they played and the latitude permitted them, were exotic by twentieth century standards.[17]

Before World War II when women were not well represented in the American Historical Association, the Mediaeval Academy of America enrolled women at roughly 20 to 40% of membership.[18] The determined interdisciplinary stance of the Academy made this possible; women were generally better represented in the literary disciplines than in history, but women historians clustering in the medieval field became members as well. Helen Wieruszowski, a historian, served as president of the Academy for a term. Women served on the editorial and advisory boards of *Speculum*, and their works were published as contributors to the monograph series of the Academy from the very beginning.[19]

Women did not necessarily enter the historical profession with the same interests as women who brought their feminist researches to the other fields of Social Science, of course. If Helen Cam found anything interesting to investigate about women, it is not clear from her published works on the history of the law, the state, and bureaucracy, except, possibly in the title she chose for her textbook, *England before Elizabeth*. But other women in medieval history studied social and economic history, the early sagas and epics with their casts of women characters, the early law codes with their positive legal rights for women, and early European institutions like double monasteries, which were dominated by women. Their scholarly products were, for the most, securely in the mainstream of Positivist history: the thoroughly researched monograph and the well-edited text were women's contributions to medieval scholarship. It could be argued that this was a thin Positivism in some cases because it was accompanied by no effort to force a reinterpretation of the general course of medieval times based upon the cumulative evidence. But, since this scholarly literature was very respectable, and respected by the profession, neither could it be entirely ignored. Positivism's neutrality, directed toward uncovering all the documented evidence from the early European centuries, was a two-edged sword. If its concerns had been "public" history, it could just as well have suppressed information about medieval women, but in this instance it was directed in precisely the opposite direction. Without question much of the history written elsewhere, directed attention away from women. Yet the history written by some well-established historians in the field uncovered information about women's roles, their lives, and their positive legal rights, and so it tended to cut the other way. Added to the scholarship on women produced in England, this history could provide in some instances almost as substantive a cumulative Positivist history of women as the cumulative history of medieval men.

Some women scholars, then, chose this path, pursued the discipline of history, and trusted to the Positivism that in their student years had been presented to them as a scholarly weapon with the capacity to set the historical record straight. These women believed in the force of history, and perhaps, in the isolation of the New World they were free to do so. The scholarship which Americans produced pleased European historians, not because of its findings necessarily but because it confirmed Europeans' own belief in the consequence of their medieval past. But if English historians could ignore works on medieval women written by Bertha Phillpotts, Georgiana Hill, and Alice Clarke, they would have no trouble ignoring what American scholars had to say on the same subject.[20] Continental historians were less than eager to bridge the language barrier to read monographs produced by American scholars, particularly when they did not see the consequence of learning about medieval women in the first place. Americans were welcome to participate in European Medieval Studies through visiting Europe, studying, and doing research there, but Old World scholars did not necessarily believe it needed Americans to interpret the medieval past to them.

With conscious intent or less fully articulated motives, medievalists, who prided themselves on the full general picture of the Middle Ages which they presented in the classroom, continued to raise the question of medieval women for their students. Barbara Kreutz, graduate dean at Bryn Mawr College, noted of her training at University of Wisconsin with Robert Reynolds and Gaines Post that both men encouraged her to explore the lives of medieval women:

> Both of them when writing history, followed the scholarly mode of their day . . . but as teachers they were unabashedly romantic, loving anecdotes and color – and thereby delighting generations of undergraduates. Gaines Post, as I recall, always had various women or women-related topics on the list of "suggested topics for papers". . . . Of course it would be foolish to claim that either Post or Reynolds were feminist historians, yet I am firmly convinced that both of them would have been "open" to feminist history, for they were open to any ideas, any approaches, which could expand history.[21]

So women students continued to be drawn to the study of the Middle Ages, and medieval women might be subjects of scholarly papers, even though they were not a prominent part of the course lecture. For these students medieval women were authenticated and highly compelling figures, the product of an exotic age, far removed from the world of twentieth century study of history and, quite possibly, not well understood in the context of their own time, but no less interesting to inquiring students on that account.

After World War II when American historical study was enriched by the example and teaching of Europe's refugee intellectuals, and its own tradition of scholarship had achieved a higher degree of maturity, original formulations began to appear in print in greater numbers. One of the more controversial scholarly journals of the day, *The Journal of the History of Ideas*, had the presence of mind to recognize in a brief communication from a medievalist at the University of Vermont, Betty Bandel, a comment on gender roles which confirmed their editorial stance on the historical consequence of ideas. In an article entitled "The English Chronicler's Attitude Towards Women,"[22] Betty Bandel focussed upon English chroniclers' relation of well-documented political deeds in the histories of certain women rulers, particularly Saxon queens, and later, the Empress Matilda. She noted that before the Norman Conquest chroniclers expressed no wonder at women wielding political power; it was taken as a matter of course. After the Conquest such acts were singled out by the chroniclers as "manly" and remarkable. By the late Middle Ages chroniclers doubted the authenticity of the early histories, disclaiming such recorded acts on grounds that women could not have behaved in such a fashion. In the most extreme case, that of the Empress Matilda, recorded deeds were reascribed to her brother on the assumption that a woman could not have fought as actively for the right of her son to sit upon the throne as the chronicle sources insisted she had.

Bandel's contribution to the history of ideas lay in tracing the growing specificity of the concept of gender from the eleventh to the fourteenth century. What was manly or womanly had little significance in the earlier chronicles. By the time of Matthew Paris and other late medieval writers "manliness" was important and sufficiently entrenched in the mind of the chroniclers and, presumably, their audience, to number among the essential organizing ideas in their recorded histories. Bandel had seen what few scholars before her had taken the trouble to notice. By distinguishing between the perception of women and women's acts, and by charting this over a sufficient time interval so that the dynamic quality of change in perceptions could be communicated, she had turned Positivist analysis to the literary texts in such a way that it could be used to uncover gender roles. The implication of her work was that gender as an organizing idea was a relatively late accretion in the Western tradition and that women's roles would become more circumscribed as restricted gender expectations came to figure in European life. She made it clear in her brief essay that women's history did move on an upward trajectory; in fact it was evident that gender contributed to an erosion of status and opportunity for women.

This is the inheritance of medieval historiography before the great interest in economic and social history of the Middle Ages that began to flourish in the 1960s in North America. At the University of Toronto Ambrose Raftis investigated the lives of English peasants and gave a greater role to women, while Michael Sheehan began investigations of marriage, the family, and the role marriage partners' consent came to play in validating marriage.[23] In that decade Jill Kerr Conway and Natalie Zemon Davis offered the first survey course on women in European history at the University of Toronto. David Herlihy, a young medieval scholar teaching at Bryn Mawr College in those days, began to apply the insights of social and economic history to understanding women's roles. He says of his early interest that in viewing the documents of the early Middle Ages, women's importance was obvious and certainly worthy of investigation. Was their greater presence then than at later stages in Western development mysterious? It seemed to be a significant question. He is uncertain about any influence a woman's college such as Bryn Mawr may have had upon his thought, certainly his first scholarly attempt, "Land, Women and Family in Continental Europe, 700–1200" had not been written for assignment in the classroom.[24] Still Herlihy speculated that it was possible that Bryn Mawr's stated intent, that is, to prepare women to follow productive roles in society, operated to create a climate in which investigation of women's roles was an appropriate area for historical research. The result was an article that substantiated through reference to the charters that women's rights of possession had been strongest in the eleventh century and had declined thereafter. In his research Herlihy speculated on the reasons for this and continued to address the question of change in women's status because he found it a sensitive indicator of social and economic change in the medieval and Renaissance centuries.[25]

The emergence of a new interest in medieval women and a Positivist method for analyzing literary texts to reveal assumptions about gender or sex roles corresponded with other important changes in the American world of letters. By the 1960s Europeans had ceased to view American contributions to medieval scholarship as unnecessary offerings. In the train of that American scholarship came ideas about medieval women and their roles, which, if they had earlier aroused the interest of German historians (the celebrated *Frauenfrage*), and had always been a peripheral interest in English historiography, had nonetheless remained largely outside the interests of the national schools of historical writing.[26] Since so much of the American contribution to scholarship ignored the boundaries laid down by the national traditions, this was hardly surprising. Medieval women as a proper subject for historical research received some encouragement from the fact that some American scholars used women's condition as a means to measure other changes in society. In emphasizing the social and economic structures which had promoted Europe's development, and in casting the question over a long term, Americans offered women's roles as a bellwether of substantive change. Their work even suggested a new chronology: the emergence of institutions in the centuries after the break-up of the Carolingian empire when women played consequential roles, and a later stage, beginning in the late eleventh and twelfth centuries when women were separated from the institutions and positions that had permitted them to play forceful roles. Finally in the thirteenth century increasingly powerful institutions deprived women of positive legal rights, relegating them more and more to the domestic household. Perspectives that disturbed the old categories and chronologies were in vogue in the intellectual world by the late sixties and seventies, and ideas about medieval women received a hearing on that account—a hearing that would have been unlikely at any earlier date.

This spate of scholarship on women corresponded with the second wave of American feminism of the 1960s as well. If late twentieth century feminism was less tied to scholarship and institutions of learning than early feminism, there were still numerous questions that feminists wished to ask of history, their own history as women viewed over the long term. Medieval history, as it had developed, could offer two specific and complementary perspectives to feminists. First, it could, in the tradition of Positivist history, point to accomplishments in the era before the constraints of a division of the private from the public sphere inhibited women from playing effective roles. There was proof available from the medieval record that women were capable of assuming authoritative roles: they could write learned treatises, administer institutions, yes, serve as physicians—what the early nineteenth century feminist, Paulina Wright Davis, had noted long before. The findings of Positivism suggested that women's history was written on a separate trajectory from men's. History became a subject worth investigating for those feminists who wanted an explanation for this divergence in the course of men's and women's distinct histories.

Along with this uncovered past feminists could also find an additional tradition of scholarship that had begun to look at the notion of gender itself as a socially constructed product. Women's behavior and perceptions of women's behavior could be compared as Bandel had done in 1955. While investigations of sex roles were frequently undertaken in the disciplines of cultural anthropology and sociology, medieval history could provide comparable opportunities for investigation because of the wealth of documentation and the tradition of scholarship that had uncovered essential evidence. Since European history, particularly the history of the Enlightenment, the Renaissance, and the Middle Ages was understood to be our heritage, and a proud tradition to own, investigating gender in this context might hold more consequence for contemporary women than raising the same question about more geographically remote societies.

The sum of the two strains in the hands of gifted historians could produce innovative history which had the capacity to affect general understandings of the European past. In *Doctrine of the Lady in the Renaissance* Ruth Kelso questioned whether women were full participants in an era commonly understood to mark a major transition for men in Western society. Joan Kelly asked directly whether women had a Renaissance at all?[27] The implication of both was to place back in the medieval past a major transition for women which preceded the transitions and watersheds claimed for men. David Herlihy noted of the Mediaeval Academy of America: "In 1982 the sex ratio of entering members, 92, dropped to its historic low. There are no indications that this fall in sex ratios is abating."[28] With the conviction that critical answers lay in the medieval past women have flocked to the field of medieval history. Within the medieval past many of them hope to uncover the roots of the condition of women before and during the onset of modern times.

Since the Second World War contemporary scholarship on medieval women has some impressive accomplishments to its name. Three at least deserve mention. First, the contribution of medieval women, particularly women in monastic orders, to the creation of European society and culture, has been uncovered. The extent and variety of the influence exerted by monastic women began to be investigated in England in the nineteenth century with Lina Eckenstein's still valuable study, and it was later joined by Eileen Power's important work on monastic houses and women in Orders.[29] A major literature on the religious institutions which women created and staffed now exists. American women have added to it, revealing not only how critical women were to the development of institutions in the West but also how long they remained important in the power equation of medieval society. Second, scholars now recognize that charting dynamic change within the family provides some of the earliest indications of Europe's transition to the modern age. It now appears evident that, within the family, roles women played underwent earlier change than men's in reaction to the increase in complexity and the shift to a cash economy, which marked the earliest phases of modern development. Third and last, a careful monitoring of medieval women's history allows the investigator to identify by region and locale those moments when the public and the private spheres grew separate and distinct from each other. With the divergence came those gender expectations that clearly circumscribed future expectations and roles for women and for men in modern Western societies. Women's history from the Middle Ages to the present is no longer construed as progress, and its separate course stands as a caution against constructing any general interpretive framework in the progressive idiom. Adams's dire warning that a society's treatment of women determines its ultimate fate may have gone the way of most other Victorian moral dictums, but his early formulation on women led to observations of a critical nature on how societies define gender and how mentalities change and new gender associations emerge. If Adams's early ideas about medieval women were unthinkable in America's Gilded Age of institution building, they are not unthinkable in our age with its re-evaluation of our Western heritage.

In the present generation scholars in the tradition of those women noted in this essay continue to investigate medieval society, but today the edited text and the narrowly defined monograph composed in the Positivist tradition are only two of the means available for investigating the past. History has borrowed from sociology, economics, and cultural anthropology. Quantitative studies have confirmed what could only be suggested before: the extent of medieval women's landholding, the number of convents in Europe, the growth of women's dowries. Sensibilities and the mental equipment of the age are standard subjects for research, and gender formulations figure among those topics. The validity of the transitions associated with the Renaissance and the Reformation have been questioned by reference to women's experience. In such instances woman's experience takes on the same consequence as men's for interpreting important change.

Today, scholarship on medieval women is frequently conducted in collaborative efforts where a wealth of documentation produced by numerous scholars drawing upon different bodies of evidence confirms a shared interpretive approach and purpose. James Bruce Ross and Mary Martin McLaughlin began their collaboration with *The Portable Medieval Reader* in 1949, giving "The Body Social" and some commentary on women first place in their collection. They have continued their collaboration in paired articles. Jo-Ann McNamara and Suzanne Wemple collaborated on path- breaking studies of the early Middle Ages.[30] Anthologies often carry the burden of the interpretation of medieval women in contemporary scholarship.[31] These collaborative studies, produced largely but by no means exclusively by women, bear the particular stamp of American scholarship, and the work is no longer overlooked on that account, but rather known and considered for this dimension afforded our general understanding of the past. The peculiar American combination of brashness, an idiosyncratic reading of the purposes which Positivist history might serve, and a genuine impulse to understand the Old World and apply its lessons in the New, have brought Medieval Studies to this unexpected pass. Entering into an era of historiography that transcends the limits of national schools of history, scholarship in medieval women constitutes a genuine contribution to the investigations that lie ahead.

NOTES

1. Paulina Wright Davis, "Remarks at the Conventions," *The Una* (September, 1853): 136–37. See Susan Conrad, *Perish the Thought* (Metuchan, NJ: Citadel, 1978), 157–59, for comment on these Boston feminists. I am grateful to Ann Koblitz for pointing out this early American feminist reference to medieval women.

2. Herbert Baxter Adams, "Special Methods of Historical Study as Pursued at the Johns Hopkins University and at Smith College," *Johns Hopkins University Studies in Historical and Political Science* 2 (1884): 5–23; see also his "German Origins of New England Towns," ibid., Ser. 1, pt. 2. A New Englander, Adams spent his spring semesters at Smith looking into the origins of his native region, eastern New England; see John Higham, "Herbert Baxter Adams and the Study of Local History," *American Historical Review* 89 (1984): 1125–1239. On Herbert Baxter Adams's impact on his Smith College students see Natalie Zemon Davis, *Women's History as Women's Education*, (Northampton: Smith College, 1985). On the "scientific" history of Herbert Baxter Adams and Henry Adams see Dorothy Ross, "Historical Consciousness in Nineteenth Century America," *American Historical Review* 89 (1984): 909–28.

3. *The Education of Henry Adams* (Boston: Houghton Mifflin, 1918). William Courtenay, "The Virgin and the Dynamo," in Francis G. Gentry and Christopher Kleinhenz, eds., *Medieval Studies in North America, Past, Present and Future* (Kalamazoo: Medieval Institute Publications, 1982), 1–16.

4. Henry Maine, *Ancient Law*, 1st ed. (London: J. Murray, 1861); by 1876, and Adams's Lowell lecture, this work had undergone six editions. John F. MacLennan, *Primitive Marriage* (Edinburgh: Black, 1886). MacLennan's works were also very popular, but his posthumous *Patriarchal Theory* (London: Macmillan, 1885) published under the editorship of Donald MacLennan was an even more influential work, marking the ascendancy of Maine's and MacLennan's views on primitive phases of European development.

5. Henry Adams, "The Primitive Rights of Women," in *Historical Essays* (New York: Scribners, 1891), 36–41. Adams's biographers have not emphasized this early interpretation of medieval women and the change in his opinion over the decades. On this topic T.J. Jackson Lears, *No Place of Grace* (New York: Pantheon Books, 1981), 261–96 is interesting.

6. Obituary of Florence Griswold Buckstaff, Oshkosh, Wisconsin *Daily Northwestern*, 11 February, 1948, p. 4.

7. Florence Griswold Buckstaff, "Married Women's Property Rights in Anglo-Saxon and Anglo-Norman Law," *Annals of the American Academy* (1886): 233–64.

8. George E. Howard, *A History of Matrimonial Institutions*, 3 vols. (Chicago: University of Chicago Press, 1904).

9. William L. O'Neill, *Divorce in the Progressive Era* (New Haven: Yale University Press, 1967).

10. Mary Roberts Smith (Coolidge), *Why Women Are So* (New York: Holt, 1912). Her earlier study in sociology, which established her reputation, was *Chinese Immigration* (New York: Holt, 1909). She had studied with George E. Howard in the 1890s. Later with Clelia Mosher she launched modern sex research. See Rosalind Rosenberg, *Beyond Separate Spheres* (New Haven: Yale University Press, 1982).

11. Bertha Phillpotts, *Kindred and Clan in the Middle Ages* (Cambridge: Cambridge University Press, 1913). On this seminal work going out of print see Sylvia Thrupp, *Early Medieval Society* (New York: Appleton Crofts, 1967), ix.

12. After graduating from Vassar College in 1909 Ruth Benedict tried writing about important women in history but found it difficult to work in complete isolation. She returned to school in 1919 at the New School for Social Research and soon began her productive years under the influence of the anthropologist, Franz Boas. See Rosalind Rosenberg, *Beyond Separate Spheres* (New Haven: Yale University Press, 1982), 223.

13. Helen Cam, *The Hundred and the Hundred Roles* (London: 1930) marked her entry into the field of scholarship on administrative, legal, and state history. She served a term as chair of the Department of History at Harvard University; she also produced a textbook for college students, *England before Elizabeth* (London and New York: Hutchinson's University Library, 1950). Sylvia Thrupp, *A Short History of the Worshipful Company of Bakers of London* (Croydon, England: Galleon, 1933) wrote social history. See also her *Merchant Class of Medieval London* (Chicago: University of Chicago Press, 1948) and numerous articles.

14. Marie Borroff, *Sir Gawain and the Green Knight, A Stylistic and Metrical Study* (New Haven: Yale University Press, 1962), among other works. She has been on the Yale faculty since 1971. Hope Emily Allen, *The Book of Margery Kempe* (Oxford: Oxford University Press, 1940); idem, ed., *The English Writings of Richard Rolle* (Oxford: Oxford University Press, 1931); idem, *The Manuel des Pechiez and the Scholastic Prologue* (New York: Columbia University Press, 1918). Katherine Fischer Drew, *The Burgundian Code* (Philadelphia: University of Pennsylvania Press, 1949; rev. ed. 1972); idem, "Note on Lombard Institutions," *Rice University Institute* 48 (1956). Catherine Boyd, *A Cistercian Nunnery in Italy in the Thirteenth Century* (Cambridge, MA: Harvard University Press, 1943); idem, *Tithes and Parishes in Medieval Italy* (Ithaca: Cornell University Press, 1952). This list is far from exhaustive but provides a sample of women in the medieval field and their scholarly contributions.

15. Nellie Neilson, "Economic Conditions on the Manors of Ramsey Abbey," Thesis, Bryn Mawr College, 1898; idem, *Customary Rents* (Oxford: Oxford University Press, 1910); idem, *Fleet* (Oxford: Oxford University Press, 1920); idem, *Medieval Agrarian Economy* (New York: Holt, 1936). See also Emil Pocock, "Presidents of the American Historical Association," *American Historical Review* 89 (1984): 1240–58.

16. Emily Putnam, *The Lady* (New York: 1910; repr. Chicago: University of

Chicago Press, 1975). Mary Beard, *Women as a Force in History* (New York: Macmillan, 1945) also featured prominent medieval women in her longitudinal study, although the framework she employed did not direct her to the question of gender and changes in roles and status for women.

17. Eleanor Shipley Duckett, *Women and their Letters in the Early Middle Ages* (Northampton: Smith College, 1964); idem, *Anglo-Saxon Saints and Scholars* (New York: Macmillan, 1947); idem, *Gateway to the Middle Ages* (New York: Macmillan, 1938). Duckett produced works for a scholarly audience and a popular audience as well. See the article on historiography of women by Elizabeth Fox-Genovese in *Signs: Journal of Women in Culture and Society* 11 (1986). See also Bonnie Smith, "The Contribution of Women to Modern Historiography," *American Historical Review* 89 (1983): 709–32. Helen Cam was also English.

18. David Herlihy, "The American Medievalist," *Speculum* 58 (1983): 881–88. Natalie Zemon Davis estimated women at 1% of the membership of the American Historical Association in 1885, and 4 1/2% in 1984. "Discovery and Renewal in the History of Women," American Historical Association Centennial Session, Chicago, Illinois, 30 December, 1984.

19. Cornelia Catlin Coulter served on the first Advisory Board of *Speculum* in the 1930s, Margaret Schlauch served on its editorial board, while Nellie Neilson served on the Advisory Board. Women returned to this responsibility in the 1970s with Margaret Hastings and Joan Ferrante both serving on the Advisory board. Alice Beardwood, *Alien Merchants in England* (Cambridge, MA: Mediaeval Academy of America, 1931) was the eighth publication in the monographic series of the Mediaeval Academy of America. Florence Edler (de Roover) *Glossary of Mediaeval Terms of Business* (Cambridge, MA: Mediaeval Academy of America, 1934) was the eighteenth. Pearl Kibre's *Scholarly Privileges in the Middle Ages* (Cambridge, MA: Mediaeval Academy of America, 1962) was one of two monographs composed by Kibre which the Academy published.

20. On English historiography see Barbara Hanawalt, "Golden Ages for Medieval Women in English Historiography" in Susan M. Stuard, ed., *Women in Medieval History and Historiography* (Philadelphia: University of Pennsylvania Press, 1987), 1–24.

21. Personal correspondence with Barbara Kreutz, Dean of the Graduate School Bryn Mawr College, 5 July, 1982.

22. Betty Bandel, "The English Chronicler's Attitude Toward Women," *Journal of the History of Ideas* 16 (1955): 113–18.

23. J. Ambrose Raftis, *The Estates of Ramsey Abbey* (Toronto: Pontifical Institute of Mediaeval Studies, 1957); idem, *Tenure and Mobility: Studies in the Social History of the Mediaeval English Village* (Toronto: Pontifical Institute of Mediaeval Studies, 1964); idem, ed., *Pathways to Medieval Peasants* (Toronto: Pontifical Institute of Mediaeval Studies, 1981). Michael Sheehan, "Marriage and Family in English Conciliar and Synodal Legislation," in J.R. O'Donnell, ed., *Essays in Honor of Anton*

Charles Pegis (Toronto: Pontifical Institute of Mediaeval Studies, 1974), 205–14; idem, "The Formation and Stability of Marriage in Fourteenth-Century England: Evidence of an Ely Register," *Mediaeval Studies* 33 (1971): 228–63. More recently see Paolo Brezzi and Egmont Lee, eds., *Sources of Social History: Private Acts of the Late Middle Ages* (Toronto: Pontifical Institute of Mediaeval Studies, 1984).

24. David Herlihy, "Land, Family and Women in Continental Europe, 700–1200," first published in the 1962 volume of *Journal of Social History*, reprinted in Susan Mosher Stuard, ed., *Women in Medieval Society* (Philadelphia: University of Pennsylvania Press, 1976), 13–47. For a list of Herlihy's studies which feature women's condition as an indicator of change, see the bibliography in David Herlihy and Christiane Klapische-Zuber, *Les Toscans et leurs familles* (Paris: S.E.V.P.E.N., 1978).

25. Personal interview with David Herlihy, San Francisco, California, 29 December, 1982.

26. See essays on German historiography by Suzanne Wemple and Martha Howell, and on English historiography by Barbara Hanawalt in *Women in Medieval History and Historiography* (Philadelphia: University of Pennsylvania Press, 1987), 101–31.

27. Joan Kelly-Gadol, "The Social Relation of the Sexes," *Signs: Journal of Women in Culture and Society* 1 (1976): 809–23. Ruth Kelso, *Doctrine for the Lady of the Renaissance* (Urbana, IL: University of Illinois Press, 1956).

28. "The American Medievalist," 886–88.

29. Eileen Power, *Medieval English Nunneries* (Cambridge: Cambridge University Press, 1922); Lina Eckenstein, *Women under Monasticism* (Cambridge: Cambridge University Press, 1896).

30. *The Portable Medieval Reader* (New York: Viking, 1949) went through fourteen printings in its first dozen years; idem, paired articles in Lloyd DeMause, ed., *The History of Childhood* (New York: Psychohistory Press, 1977). James Bruce Ross is a woman. See articles by Jo-Ann McNamara and Suzanne Wemple in Berenice Carroll, ed., *Liberating Women's History* (Urbana, IL: University of Illinois Press, 1979) and *Becoming Visible* (Boston: Houghton Mifflin, 1976).

31. See, for example, the ten contributors in *Women in Medieval Society* and recently, Barbara Hanawalt, *Women and Work in Pre-industrial Europe* (Bloomington, IN: Indiana University Press, 1985).

Personification and the
Idealization of the Feminine

Marina Warner

I
N HENRY JAMES'S SHORT STORY OF 1879, "THE MADONNA OF THE FUTURE,"
the narrator, who is an artistically minded American abroad in Florence,
meets a compatriot who has lived in the city a long time:

> He confessed with a melancholy but all-respectful head-shake to his
> American origin. "We are the disinherited of Art!" he cried. "We are
> condemned to be superficial! We are excluded from the magic circle.
> The soil of American perception is a poor little barren, artificial deposit.
> Yes! we are wedded to imperfection. An American, to excel, has just
> ten times as much to learn as a European."[1]

The narrator discovers that his engaging, cultured companion is a painter,
who had at first been courted by the wealthy expatriate community of Florence, but was now shunned and living in Bohemian indigence. He is dedicated to art, or more specifically to the creation of a single masterpiece, a
new Madonna, in the tradition by which he is surrounded in Florence, from
Giotto and Fra Angelico to Raphael. Though their conversation devolves principally on Raphael's Madonna of the Chair, the exchange which follows between them can illuminate for us one of the aspects of an older Europe that
made an enduring impact on the imagination and work of nineteenth century and early twentieth century American writers and painters.

"Don't you imagine [asks the narrator] that he had a model, and that some pretty woman— "[2]

The artist of the Madonna of the Future interrupts sharply:

"As pretty a young woman as you please! It doesn't diminish the miracle! He took his hint, of course, and the young woman sat smiling before his canvas. But meanwhile, the painter's idea had taken wings. No lovely human outline could charm it to vulgar fact. He saw the fair form made perfect; he rose to the vision without tremor, without effort of wing; he communed with it face to face, and resolved into finer and lovelier truth the purity which completes it as the perfume completes the rose. That's what they call idealism; the word's vastly abused, but the thing is good. It's my own creed at any rate. Lovely Madonna, model at once and Muse, I call you to witness that I too am an idealist!"[3]

To this the narrator, who is more worldly-wise than this ardent artist, responds:

"An idealist then," I said, half-jocosely, wishing to provoke him to further utterance, "Is a gentleman who says to Nature in the person of a beautiful girl, 'Go to, you're all wrong! Your fine is coarse, your bright is dim, your grace is *gaucherie*. This is the way you should have done it!' "

The irony of James's story turns on the delusion of the painter, who has chosen for his model a woman of easy virtue, Serafina, but remains fixed in his splendid vision of her, unable to see the truth of her life and character. Indeed he is so entranced by his vision of her that he proves incapable of painting her picture at all. The narrator finds that when he meets her, she has grown old, and when he visits the artist's studio, the canvas is blank. The power of idealism can, it transpires, so charm "vulgar fact," as to make the form so perfect that reality vanishes. The narrator inadvertently opens his new friend's eyes, and the loss of his illusion kills him.[4]

For this essay, I want to develop two questions that arise from the story: first, how the legacy of medieval Neoplatonist personification, representing ideal concepts in the female form, translates into public consciousness through the imagery of certain official buildings in the United States; and secondly, how this convention of depicting allegorically virtues and principles in the female form relates to the portrayal and interpretation of a real person, Joan of Arc, the fifteenth-century French heroine who was taken into the hearts of Americans from the War of Independence to the Second World War through a variety of media, from children's books to film.

The theme that Henry James's story, "The Madonna of the Future," explores, as it dramatizes the constant interplay between reality and idealism and between female and a notion of the feminine, infuses the tradition of female personification. If one can generalize about such a vast topic, it can be said that the Greeks and the Romans, who, following the dictates of linguistic grammar, also represented abstract concepts in the female form, did not however speculate on the association between women and divine daimons who happened to be feminine in linguistic gender. By contrast, nineteenth century romanticism was preoccupied with developing that very notion of congruity into perceiving something essentially feminine about allegorical Justice or Peace or Wisdom or Mercy. In this concern, artists, thinkers and writers were carrying much further an idea that does surface intermittently in early and medieval philosophy. Philo Judaeus, in the first century, rationalized in this way:

> Indeed all the virtues have women's titles, but powers and activities of consummate men. For that which comes after God, even though it may be the highest of all other things, occupies a second place, and therefore was termed feminine to express its contrast with the Maker of the universe, who is masculine. . . . For preeminence always pertains to the masculine, and the feminine always comes short and is lesser than it. . . .[5]

In the twelfth century Guillaume de Conches, writing about Boethius's figure of Philosophy in the *Consolation of Philosophy*, argued from female characteristics rather than status, saying that Philosophia appeared to Boethius in a vision under the guise of a woman because

> a woman softens the ferocities of the soul, nourishes children with her milk, and is better accustomed to taking care of the sick than men.[6]

But in general, the Fathers were careful to separate feminine allegory from femaleness through a series of fine discriminations. By erecting a structure delimiting the world of forms from the fallen created universe below, the thinkers of the early Church and the Middle Ages took care to distinguish real women from the ideals which the female form represented. Methodius of Olympus (second century), for instance, made it clear in his Symposium of Ten Virgins that while his ten speakers on the various benefits of Chastity were all women, and were led by the greatest among them, Arete, whose name in Greek means "virtue," they were in spirit honorary males, since "the enlightened spiritually receive the features and image and manliness of

Christ."[7] Bernard of Clairvaux was characteristic of his time too when he
warned that the Bride in the Song of Songs, the beloved and amorous Shula-
mite who, in his rapturous sermons, he interpreted as the spouse of Christ,
the Church, the Virgin Mary and even each faithful soul, should never be
confused with women themselves, even though the bride is called "beautiful
among women" because "women signify carnal and secular souls, which have
nothing virile in them, which show nothing strong or constant in their acts,
which are completely languid, soft and feminine."[8]

But confuse real women with allegories of the virtues is exactly what the
green and idealizing visitors to Europe from the United States were apt to
do, like Henry James's Florentine expatriate. They perceived in the icons
and statues of the French cathedrals, the frescoes and sculptures of Italy,
a type of woman who they desired often enough to live in their own time
and their own class too. Henry Adams, for instance, rhapsodizes about the
Madonna whom he conjured from the perfection of Chartres Cathedral's architecture and decorations, glass and sculpture programs. His praises, taken
out of context, could describe a society hostess from the pages of an Edith
Wharton novel except that Wharton would have shown a sense of irony and
waste. *Mont St. Michel and Chartres* was an inspiration when I first read it,
and I still feel very strongly that the development of positive female symbolism can nourish a society. But such passages as this make me wonder,
above all, if it is ever possible to write history that escapes the stamp of its
own time, and makes the imaginative leap necessary to remember another.
Here is Henry Adams's Madonna, demonstrating all the supposedly female
characteristics of caprice, temperament, taste, lovableness, indulgence, idleness, charm, service: a child in expensive grown up clothes, playing at houses
in Boston's most salubrious districts at the turn of the century. In this case,
she is the hostess of Chartres cathedral:

> Whatever Chartres may be now, when young it was a smile. . . . To us,
> it is a child's fancy; a toy house to please the Queen of Heaven, to please
> her so much that she would be happy in it, — to charm her till she
> smiled.
>
> The Queen Mother was as majestic as you like; she was absolute;
> she could be stern; she was not above being angry; but she was still
> a woman, who loved grace, beauty, ornament — her toilette, her robes,
> jewels; who considered the arrangements of her palace with attention,
> and liked both light and color; who kept a keen eye on her Court, and
> exacted prompt and willing obedience from king and archbishops as
> well as from beggars and drunken priests. She protected her friends

and punished her enemies. She required space, beyond what was known
in the courts of Kings, because she was liable at all times to have ten
thousand people begging her for favors mostly inconsistent with law —
and deaf to refusal. She was extremely sensitive to neglect, to disagree-
able impressions, to want of intelligence in her surroundings. . . . Her
taste was infallible, her sentence eternally final. This church was built
for her in this spirit of simple-minded practical utilitarian faith — in this
singleness of thought, exactly as a little girl sets up a doll house for
her favorite blonde doll. Unless you can go back to your dolls, you are
out of place here. . . .[9]

Mont St. Michel and Chartres (1905) contains many more accurate evoca-
tions of the cathedral's enchantment and beauty and genius, and it is a bit
unfair to quote only this glutinously belittling vision of a paragon of turn-of-
the-century womanhood. The passage does, however, reveal that Henry Adams
accepted the *prima facie* female aspects of the profuse allegorical imagery,
in French and Italian medieval art, inspired not only by the figure of the
Virgin Mary, a historical woman become a type of the highest Christian ideals,
but by other medieval schema.

The three theological virtues (Faith, Hope, and Charity), the four Cardi-
nal Virtues (Prudence, Justice, Fortitude, and Temperance), the Seven Liberal
Arts (composed of the trivium, or threefold path to Eloquence — Dialectic,
Rhetoric, and Grammar — and the quadrivium or fourfold path to Learning —
Philosophy, Astronomy, Music, and Geometry) were all personified in feminine form. There were other divine guilds of allegorical female figures: the
Nine Beatitudes classified from the blessings of the Sermon on the Mount,
whom the twelfth-century visionary Hildegard of Bingen saw helping to raise
the edifice of the church,[10] and whom the anonymous master of the mosaics
in St. Mark's placed on the dome of one of the chapels, where they dance
in a ring around the figure of the Christ Pantocrator in the apex, on either
side of Mary *orans* in the center. Humility, a thin girl with scarecrow hair,
is dancing like a maenad crossed with an angel. The repertory of Wisdom's
representations, both as a type of the Church, *Ecclesia*, and as an allegory
of Learning, or *Sapientia*, inspired Herrad of Landsberg (or Hohenburg),
another great twelfth-century abbess, in her work the *Garden of Delights*. She
included an illumination of a seated Wisdom, nourishing the seven Liberal
Arts from streams issuing from her breasts.[11] The Sapiential texts of the
Bible — the Book of Proverbs, Wisdom, Ecclesiasticus, the Song of Songs —
informed much of the iconography which celebrated the Virgin Mary as Mother
of the Virtues, or the Seat of Wisdom, the ground where the Logos found

his being. Allegorical poems like Alain de Lille's *Anti-Claudianus*, and Dante's *Divine Comedy* developed in different ways the theme of redemptive love and creativity through female figures; the symbolism of women was rich, radiant, and deserves more attention from contemporary readers than it is receiving. But the writers and artists who explored its possibilities were not making social comments or feminist pleas about the nature of the female sex. They were elaborating a complex and multilayered metaphor. Hildegard of Bingen, for instance, could exclaim in a letter to a fellow abbess:

> The form of woman flashed and radiated in the primordial root. How so?.... Both by being an artifact of the finger of God and by her own sublime beauty. O how wondrous a being you are, you who laid your foundations in the sun and who have overcome the earth![12]

She developed in her visions a magnificent body of self-affirming female allegories from this pre-eminent symbol of unblemished woman. Yet at the same time, Hildegard constantly deplored the secondary status of women on the earthly plane, without openly challenging it: "I am wretched and more than wretched in the name of woman," she wrote for instance to Saint Bernard.[13] She frequently avoids this lamentable "name," and refers to herself in the generic, as *homo*, human creature.[14]

The potency of this early medieval body of imagery arises out of some clear misogynist roots, and these remain in evidence in the later American manifestations of tradition. Aside from the well-aired problem of Mary's uniqueness, which sets up an insidious contrast with other, less perfect women, there is the status of women in allegory as *subject matter*, with both terms of the phrase taken at full force. They are containers of meaning, ascribed to them from without, not enunciated by them from within. The figure of woman comes to mean Justice, or Rhetoric, or the Beatitudes, or Humility, according to the idealizing mind of the creator; woman is the stuff from which the artist or writer's concept is made, just as, according to ancient, Aristotelian biology (which was known in the twelfth century), woman provided the matter of creation, while man provided the insubstantial form which pulled the amorphous, incoherent natural substance together.[15] She was *meter* or *mater*, "mother," as well as *materia*, "matter," while he provided *eidos*, "form" and *nous*, "mind." The analogy holds for the creation of a work of art: and woman is the raw material of creation, protean in her possibilities because she does not control her individual identity. Furthermore, the allegorical cycles of the French and Italian cathedrals established the difference between the real world and ideal: Take virtues like the beautiful, majestic *Pax* or Peace

who presides beside her sister Justice and other civic Virtues like Temperance, Magnanimity, and Prudence in the *Allegory of Good Government* by
Ambrogio Lorenzetti in the Palazzo Pubblico in Siena, painted at the beginning of the fourteenth century. They are twice as large again as the real citizens
of Siena, all male, who process at their feet; here scale makes the distinction.
In cycles of the Liberal Arts, the exponents or the protagonists who bring
these skills onto our earthly plane are luminaries and sages of the past, either
from the Bible, like Tubal-Cain, who was credited with the invention of Music
(as at Chartres), or from classical antiquity, like Euclid, Cicero, Pythagoras
and other great men, as in a fifteenth-century illumination of the Hill of
Knowledge (the school of Botticelli). The only woman who sometimes appears as an active practitioner, not as a muse, is Naamah, or Noemi, Tubal-
Cain's sister, who was sometimes thought to have invented weaving and wool
working. As this was work performed by women, Noemi illustrates the craft
in cycles of the *artes mechanicae* established by Hugh of St. Victor, and appears, with a spinning wheel, for instance, in an early fifteenth-century roll,
now in the Bodleian Library in Oxford, illustrating the descendants of Noah.
But other skills practiced by women in the Middle Ages are almost always
ignored: their painting, their building, their clerical and manuscript work,
their medicine, their learning. In the moving, beautiful, undoubtedly powerful iconography of medieval religious art, however inspiringly woman is in
evidence as type, model, ideal, she rarely closes the rift between fantasy and
reality: and in the connection lies the power of images, written and visual,
to structure our world for the better.

The disjunction seems to correspond to an aspect of gender in language
itself, since in Latin, Greek and the languages which derive from them, it
is common for agent nouns to be masculine, like *judge* (*iudex*), and for nouns
of action, for the thing done, to be feminine, like *justice* (*iustitia*), and almost
all other words for virtue in both Latin and Greek. Linguistic gender, no more
than the mythology of Homer and Hesiod, does not conceptualize a distinction between abstract and concrete, but between the doer and the deed. When
Hesiod writes that Justice is the daughter of Zeus, we can puzzle, as people
have done for centuries, whether he means that she is a personification or
a person.[16] What is germane to our theme is that Greek classical polytheism allowed numbers of gods and goddesses and godlings so that Homeric
and Hesiodic forces, like *Eris* (Strife), *Ate* (Ruin or Folly), *Dike* (Justice), *Themis*
(Order or Law) or *Metis* (Cunning Intelligence) could be divine beings, theologically, without censure; Roman personified principles, like *Pax*, *Fortuna*,
or *Victoria* could receive religious worship. But under Christianity, the unique-

ness of the Godhead made it imperative for the orthodox to see similar divine principles, like the Christian Virtues, as personifications not persons. Justice or Prudence, which were developed, in the work of medieval philosophers, from the classical masters' writings on ethics, could not be prayed to as saints, could no longer be revered as anthropomorphic valencies, and could no longer be personal goddesses, the daughters of Zeus, except in a manner of speaking. Under Christianity, feminine gender words for virtue were disinfected of individual personality, and in this sense, attenuated as figures of speech, they ceased to be real.

This may seem a departure from the theme of the medieval impact on the United States. These principles, however—women as subject matter, the conflict between real and ideal, and men as active agents of skill and art—are present in a good deal of public imagery, mainly erected at the turn of the twentieth century. Meanings are inscribed upon the female form while at the same time the imagery conveys a careful sense of these forms' difference from real women, *unless*, and this unless is crucial, the concept they convey is properly restricted to a prevailing notion of exemplary femininity: Henry James's Madonna of the Future—Serafina—must be an angel of purity, and the painter is shattered when he discovers that this is not so; Henry Adams's Madonna of Chartres is girlish, hostessy, charming.

The art historian Norman Bryson, in a thought-provoking work, *Word and Image*, suggested that accounts of the development of art should no longer concern themselves with analyzing and defining a succession of styles and their characteristics, but concentrate instead on developing a history of changing discourses.[17] My argument here is that the premises of some of the allegorical iconography of the Middle Ages are present in American public statuary and ornament, even though they do not bear much resemblance visually to medieval art. A classicizing monument, like Robert Aitken's statue of *The Past*, which was completed c. 1935, outside the National Archives Building in Washington DC, shows a majestically enthroned seated figure, carved in the heavy, pseudo-Roman folds of the Thirties (Fig. 1).[18] But she is a closer cousin of the *Sedes Sapientiae* images of the eleventh or twelfth centuries, emblematic of knowledge, than the seated Tyches or classical goddesses of the city whom she more superficially resembles.[19] Personification, separate from worship and cult, from observance and prayer, characterizes the allegorical thought of the early Middle Ages, the age of belief that retrieved a classical past's philosophy by interpreting its mythological deities and plethora of divine beings as so many abstractions.

Nineteenth-century American sculpture often carries medieval attributes.

1. Robert Aitken, *The Past*, National Archives, Washington (Author's photo).

William Rush's carving of *Justice* was made between 1812–24 for one of the triumphal arches erected to welcome Lafayette to Philadelphia in 1824 (Fig. 2).[20] Though she is draped in a classical toga, she carries here the sword which characterizes the virtue in medieval paintings like Lorenzetti's; another contemporary figure of *Justice*, sculpted by John Dixey for City Hall, New York, in 1811, carries the scales of justice that the Archangel Michael traditionally wields in images of The Last Judgment (Fig. 3). In the Loren-

2. William Rush, *Justice*, Pennsylvania Academy of Fine Arts, Philadelphia (Photo: John Dewe Mathews).

zetti, for instance, the same scales fall under Justice's authority as they balance on the finger of Sapientia above. The sword of Justice again appears in the avenging hand of America, personified by Constantino Brumidi on the fresco on the Dome of the Capitol in Washington, the *Apotheosis of Washington*, painted in 1865; America here has been conflated with the figure of Free-

3. John Dixey, *Justice*, City Hall, New York (Photo: John Dewe Mathews).

4. *Labor*, Woolworth Building, New York (Author's photo).

dom, and again, wears classical mantle and tunic, and a starry diadem like a latter-day Diana. But she resembles, in her pose, and her righteous on-rush, the figure of avenging Justice, who appears in allegorical tapestries about the Virtues and Vices and the struggle of Everyman, as here in a sixteenth-century work from Flanders, in Hampton Court Palace, London.[21] The woven narrative drama illustrates one of the popular medieval morality plays that warn against the perils of a sinful life.[22]

In other major works of American sculpture, the tradition of medieval thought was mediated through Paris where many of the American sculptors studied, and its influence can be seen more clearly. Henry Adams commissioned the funerary monument to the memory of his wife, Marion Hooper, who had committed suicide, from the great Irish-born sculptor of French descent, Augustus Saint-Gaudens, after he had seen his designs for another tomb, for Edwin Morgan, published in *American Figures* by Mariana Van Rensselaer in 1886. The Morgan figures were angels, and stood, on either side of the entrance to the Mausoleum. Saint-Gaudens had also designed the Farragut monument with figures of Loyalty and Courage carved in bas relief. But the Adams tomb, one of the most impressively dignified architectural ambiences in Washington, contains only one figure, Grief, a shrouded, brooding presence keeping a silent and awesomely motionless vigil at the sepulchre (Fig. 8). The sculpture was intended to recall Michelangelo's Sistine ceiling, and in particular, the Sibyls and the figure of the prophet Jesse.[23] But there is no doubt as to the sculpture's sex, and the characteristic medievalizing shift, from person (Jesse or Sibyl) anchored in space and time of this world, to the personification, the type of Grief, has informed the sculptor's vision. In this case too, she resembles stylistically the mourning bearers of catafalques who, hooded and mantled, seem to step slowly to an unheard dirge as in the sculptures of Claus Sluter (d.1404) at Dijon, on Philip The Bold's tomb.

Cass Gilbert's justly famous Woolworth building in downtown New York was dubbed "the cathedral of commerce" because it was inspired by the pinnacles and tracery of Gothic cathedrals.[24] Its jewelled lobby emulates the mosaic glints and Byzantine splendors of St. Mark's and Ravenna's basilicas. In the lunettes on either side of the entrance hall are painted two frescoes, on the mezzanine floor: of Commerce on one side, personified as a queenly maiden, a Madonna of Trade, receiving goods from children who kneel to her, and facing her, a figure of Labor, spinning thread on a distaff, like Naamah all those hundreds of years before in cycles of the technical arts (Fig. 4).

Another example of the medieval vision and its influence can be found in the sculpture of the New York Public Library. Paul Bartlett's successful,

5. Paul W. Bartlett, *Philosophy*, *Romance*, *Religion*, New York Public Library (Author's photo).

6. Bartlett, *Poetry*, *Drama*, *History*, New York Public Library (Author's photo).

free-standing, exuberant figures surmount the entablature above the entrance; again the curving contrapposto of their pose, the swirling robe and classical attributes, like the mask Drama holds in her hand, mark them out as eclectic amalgams of baroque and classical elements of style; but again they are also scions of the Liberal Arts, the youthful maidens who draw our eyes upwards and contemplate higher things. But the men, unlike them, seem to practice the arts they represent. History on the right holds his chin to express his active thought processes, while Poetry and Drama, its female form next to him (Fig. 6), only body forth the art rather than perform it, even though they were sculpted at a date when women were writing and acting with comparative freedom; they stand over the doors as muses, as objects of desire, conduits to channel our aspirations, rather than examples to follow. Similarly on the building's right flank, Philosophy is a venerable magus, literally plucking his beard as he stands deep in thought, while Romance and Religion, both areas of expertise for women—one should think—are embodied, not narrated, by the Flora-like maiden and the ecstatic Madonna beside her (Fig. 5).[25]

The use of the female form, its status as subject matter deprived of a speaking voice, was noticed by the painter Mary Cassatt, and she attempted to reclaim the tradition of personification to reflect women's capacities and gifts and contributions to the movements of the real world. In her murals for the south tympanum of the Women's Building of the World's Columbian Exhibition in Chicago in 1893, Mary Cassatt took the theme "Young Women Plucking the Fruits of Knowledge and Science," and thereby neatly replaced the subject back into the image: the Seven Liberal Arts, as it were, no longer stood for the arts but were learning to be artists themselves. She situated her young women in a realistic French orchard, their feet either planted on the ground or supported by a stepladder, engaging in daily tasks that at a literal level are performed by women in agriculture, and at a metaphorical level, express the inversion of Eve's sin when she took the apple of knowledge and precipitated the Fall (Fig. 7).

The Women's Building at the Exhibition was designed by a woman architect, Sophia B. Hayden, and entirely decorated by women artists, all commissioned by a rich patron, Mrs. Potter Palmer, to proclaim the extent of women's abilities. Mary Cassatt was aware of the allegorical cycles which adorned French buildings of the time; she noted that the *pompier* Paul Baudry (whom she admired) represented virtues in the form of "The Modern Woman as glorified by Worth! [the couturier]." She said that she was attempting something very different:

7. Mary Cassatt, detail from *Modern Woman*.

That would hardly describe my idea of course. I have tried to express
the modern woman in the fashions of our day and have tried to represent
those fashions as accurately and as much in detail as possible. . . . [The
subject] enabled me to place my figures out of doors and allowed of
brilliancy of colour. My figures are rather under life size although they
seem as large as life. I could not manage women in modern dress eight

8. Saint-Gaudens, *Grief.*

or nine feet high. An American friend asked me in rather a huffy tone
the other day, "Then this is woman apart from her relations to man?"
I told him it was. Men I have no doubt are painted in all their vigor
on the walls of the other buildings; to us [what counts is] the sweetness
of childhood, the charm of womanhood, if I have not conveyed some
sense of that charm, in one word, if I have not been absolutely feminine, I have failed.[26]

This passage occurs in a letter to the patron, Mrs. Potter Palmer, and it
is most revealing. Mary Cassatt states that she has explored conventional personification for its possible bearing on the real; she has turned the Otherness
of women on its head, and placed them in the center of her theme, not in

an ideal stratosphere, not over life-size like Lorenzetti's magnificent virtues, but instead portrayed them in contemporary dress. But she is stung by her friend's accusation of misanthropy, and defensively, reasserts that this reclamation of woman as thinking, acting, speaking subject, not the vehicle of another's idea or template of a man's potential, is still a feminine being, with all the charm and sweetness of conventional and approved femininity at the turn of the century. She subverts her own challenge to the rubric of Woman in her day, in a similar way to Henry Adams, who goes out of his way to lavish adoration on Mary and her cathedral, but then belittles both for readers today by using metaphors that restrict her range of meaning sentimentally and condescendingly; by portraying her as light, charming; in short, "feminine":

> The rudest ruffian of the Middle Ages, when he looked at this Last Judgment, laughed; for what was the Last Judgment to her! An ornament, a plaything, a pleasure! A jewelled decoration which she wore on her breast! Her chief joy was to pardon; her eternal instinct was to love; her deepest passion was pity![27]

If personifications were to touch upon the real, if fantasy were to feed back into the empirical world and shape its structure, then the symbolic woman must abide by the prevalent trivializing and acceptable definitions of what womanliness meant.

In the case of Joan of Arc, and her cult in the United States, this principle can be demonstrated very clearly. Joan of Arc stood for many heroic qualities, she epitomized courage, the love of freedom, the undaunted defense of right and victory over evil; she was even in her own day perceived by such contemporaries as Christine de Pisan as a personification come true. But in the main, her American apologists include the palinode that in the midst of her derring-do and daring, she was nothing but a charming little thing, whom God had called to display incongruously virile virtues.

A stirring and interesting drama, *Female Patriotism, or the Death of Joan of Arc*, was written in 1798 by John Daly Burk, an Irish-born American revolutionary, and it is the earliest American interpretation of the heroine's life that I have come across.[28] Burk paid little attention to the historic Middle Ages, for he was chiefly concerned with evoking a national liberator of her people who rose against the common enemy—of fifteenth century France, of eighteenth century Ireland and of America—Britain. His play, written in lyrical and often powerful blank verse, breathes the gusty air of romanticism and manages to create in Joan of Arc a forerunner of staunch republicanism, notwithstanding that she established a Valois king on his anointed throne. Joan is the messenger of Liberty, the agent of Justice, and the spirit of democracy well before her time:

> 'Tis not to crown the Dauphin prince alone
> That hath impell'd my spirit to the wars.
> For that were petty circumstance indeed;
> But on the head of every man in France
> To place a crown, and thus at once create
> A new and mighty order of nobility,
> To make all free and equal, all men kings,
> Subject to justice and the laws alone:
> For this great purpose have I come amongst you.
>   (Shout: Liberty and Equality).[29]

Even Burk's rousing sense of a world turned upside down, prefigured by the Hundred Years War in France, cannot however encompass equality for women, and his Joan makes the reservation that will become customary in American portraits of her, and avows her deep-seated femininity. She says later in the play:

> For tho' the love of liberty sublimes my soul
> And makes me do such things to compass it,
> As my soft sex would shrink at; yet I feel
> Those timid, soft and virgin sentiments
> Play on the silken fibres of my heart
> Which speaks me all the women: let me heaven
> Sooner resign my laurels in an hour
> Than loose one single thought that's feminine. . . .[30]

Another aspect of Burk's play illuminates medievalism in America. Burk sees Joan's time as a beginning, the start of a new order in France, and he conjures her as an innocent simple instrument of high principles; in this he presages other later treatments of her life, which similarly see her youth and innocence as representative of the youth and childlikeness of the Middle Ages themselves. Henry Adams often returns, without self-consciousness, to the simplicity of medieval people. "The mediaeval pilgrim," he writes "was more ignorant than we, and much simpler in mind. . . ."[31] By casting Joan as a child, out of a Rousseauesque admiration for untouched and uncorrupted savage nobility, Burk inaugurates in American literature a long tradition that sees the Middle Ages as an enviable age of belief and sincerity, itself like children before cynicism and sophistication have adulterated their pure motives and responses.

Sarah M. Grimké, the great campaigner for emancipation, produced in 1867 an English version of Lamartine's biography of Joan of Arc. She added a preface, where she developed connections between femininity and childlikeness. She wrote:

> Enthusiasm is a sacred flame. We do not analyse it; we are dazzled, rapt, and silent before it. When this passion takes possession of a nation, women feel it in a higher degree than men. As they are by their nature more sensitive, more impressible, more loving, they identify themselves more fully through their imagination and their affections with their country. . . .[32]

Here the idealization of women dovetails into a reverence for the Middle Ages as a time of "enthusiasm," of a capacity for sacrifice and selflessness, which women are more capable of than men:

> Her [the country's] image is incorporated with that of their mothers, their husbands, their children, their homes, their sepulchres, their temples and their gods.[33]

Burk's tragedy and Grimké's biography are both comparatively isolated instances in the early American cult of Joan Arc, though they adumbrate many of the themes that continue. The climax of adulation came after the turn of the century and during the first World War, when the struggle in France against another, different invader was interpreted by the French and the British and their American allies as a recapitulation of the events of the early fifteenth century, when Joan of Arc's exploits had turned the tide of defeat and helped drive the English off her soil. It was in 1915, for instance, that the equestrian bronze by Anna Hyatt Huntingdon was installed over the Hudson River in New York City, as a defiant, rallying cry to the soldiers fighting in Europe (Fig. 10).[34]

The cult of Joan in France itself had burgeoned after the defeat of France by Prussia and the loss of the province of Alsace-Lorraine, her birthplace in 1870. Joan became the figurehead of the French attempt to rally themselves again in the midst of humiliation; one of the offshoots of the fervor was the resplendent children's picture book, Maurice Boutet de Monvel's *Jeanne d'Arc* of 1896. His frontispiece showed the heroine leading her troops into battle; but in this instance they are dressed in the uniforms of the contemporary French army, ready to face the Prussians, overcome and defeat

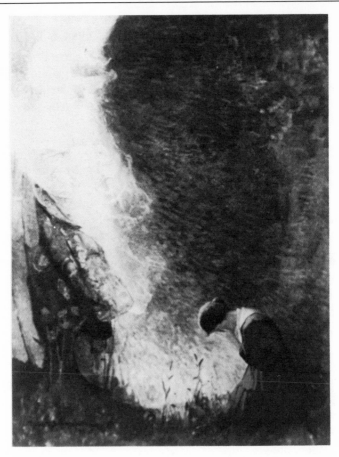

9. Frank Schoonover, *Joan of Arc*, from Lucy Foster Madison, *Joan of Arc*.

them. Boutet de Monvel's interpretation was otherwise medievalizing in the thoroughgoing spirit of the Gothic revival, and his account of Joan's life stressed her virtuousness as a little girl, her exemplary modesty, submissiveness and obedience to her vocation as a female, and explained her unique mission, her unusual cross-dressing and her life of soldiering as imposed upon her by God from without, not from within. In the view of Burk the revolutionary and Deist, Joan had embarked upon her exploits only by controlling her inner feminine softness; in the view of Grimké, Joan had brought to her military adventures a woman's heart and capacity for self-sacrifice; in Boutet de Monvel's story, she was *called*: all the irregularities of her heroic life were explained by recourse to God summoning her and her dutiful obedience, against her deeply feminine nature.[35]

10. Anna Hyatt-Huntingdon, *Joan of Arc.*

In Boutet de Monvel she is much smaller than the angels who appear to her. She is a child in the hand of God. He wrote about his conception of Joan:

[She] had such a tender breast, so much pity—I find in her so much of womanly grace in contrast with her decision in the hour of action—that I can see her only blonde. . . . Side by side with the brutal soldier she appeared feeble and delicate. Her force, then, was entirely moral, and art must preserve for her this character. . . . No; she was not what is ordinarily termed beautiful, but she became so at certain moments—beautiful with the beauty of a soul which was noble and true.[36]

Boutet de Monvel's work had an enormous influence on American medi-aevalism; Senator William Andrews Clark visited the artist in Paris and found in his studio the unfinished sequence of large panels, in watercolor and gold-leaf, which had been commissioned for the new basilica to Joan of Arc, who had been declared Venerable, then Blessed, but was not yet a saint. That was to come in 1920. Boutet de Monvel was ill and had not been able to complete the commission, which consisted of variations on the children's book; Senator Clark bought the existing six large panels, and brought them to New York, where he hung them in his Gothic room in 1911. He gave them to the Corcoran Gallery of Art in Washington in 1925.[37] In structure they resemble the panels of the children's book, in their emphasis on pageantry, costume, military splendors and colorful chivalry, in the direct communion of Joan, as a representative child of the age, with the angels and saints. But Boutet de Monvel's effect on American mediaevalism is by no means limited to Senator Clark's gorgeous picture book series.

Lucy Foster Madison's biography of Joan of Arc for children, published in 1918, "the story of the most marvellous girl the world has ever known" was illustrated by Frank E. Schoonover (Fig. 9).[38] The cover illustration bor-rowed the pose of Anna Hyatt's statue, sword raised up to cry the cavalry charge and at the same time point up to heaven in the sign of the cross. But inside, Boutet de Monvel's slender, small child is as awed by the mission Divinity springs upon her, and submits humbly, or appears frail and little as she pleads before the hard men whom she managed to persuade so miraculously to support her. The embattled rebel who would not put on a woman's dress in prison even when she was offered the right to hear Mass and have communion, who felt that virility and manliness were God's modes, and that she had been directed to live in the fashion of a man by angels, always appears childishly feminine: even in her most heroic and exalted mo-ments on the battlefield.

The vision of Boutet de Monvel influenced media far beyond the audience of picture books. The film Cecil B. De Mille made in 1916, *Joan the Wom-an*, shows traces of its influence. De Mille undertook the film in retaliation. D. W. Griffith's *Intolerance* had been the most ambitious movie so far in the young film industry, and De Mille was determined to outdo him. He filmed it during the War, but it was only released to fanfares of publicity in July 1920. It included passages of color—the film had been tinted—and it deployed most of the 2000 cowboys available in Hollywood, in armor carefully recon-structed to evoke the period. The film only exists in fragments today, but the startling realism of the scenes of assault and siege is noteworthy; it is not surprising to read that after it was shown, audiences were upset that men and horses might have been truly injured. De Mille intercut and superimposed scenes of fighting over scenes of idleness at court, and later scenes of debauchery while Joan suffered in prison. This sophisticated editing was called by the critic of *Kiné Weekly* "a most effective dramatic device."[39] De Mille's screenwriter Jeanie McPherson took liberties with the historical story, even if the costume department was eager for veracity. She adapted Schiller's drama of 1801, *Die Jungfrau von Orleans*. Schiller's Joan falls in love with an English soldier, and thus weakens her enchanted virginity; her death comes to her on the battlefield, not at the stake.[40] In *Joan the Woman* – the title is significant – Joan also exhibits womanly virtues of compassion and gentleness of heart and susceptibility and falls for an English general whom she attempts to deflect from his warrior path; he is then wounded by a deserter whom her co-villagers in Domremy are sheltering, but is freed at her request. Later, after many rousing battles, Joan encounters him once again, and he captures her and, failing to return her generosity, hands her over to her enemies; she dies, in this version, at the stake. De Mille's scriptwriter gave the story a further, modern twist: the whole film is framed by scenes of the trenches of the First World War, and the same actor plays the general and a modern soldier. He digs up a medieval sword and then dreams of Joan of Arc; for his betrayal of her, in his earlier life, he receives his penalty, a shell burst that kills him.

De Mille's *Joan the Woman* starred Geraldine Farrar, one of the most famous opera singers of the day. The association with opera is revealing; De Mille's Joan of Arc, both as a loving woman in the fifteenth century, undone and yet confirmed in virtue by her capacity to love against her own interest, and as a redemptive vision for the soldier of the first World War, recalls the eternal feminine celebrated in the operas which only precede the film by a few decades: Wagner's *Tannhäuser* for instance. Geraldine Farrar was praised: she was "modesty, strength and spirituality personified" wrote one critic.[41] Farrar does not resemble the Joan we have grown to expect, the urchins and androgynous children whom Boutet de Monvel helped to crystallize in the collective imagination. But the visualization of the film resembles his picture book closely: the scene in the market place at Rouen, where Joan was burned to death, seems modelled on Boutet's illustration, while De Mille's battle scenes were inspired by the superimposed, busy, interlacing of weapons, horses and men, spread across a wide double page, which were themselves harking back to Uccello's fantastic studies. Boutet's images have a decidedly cinematic feel about them, not because they imitate the movement and mêlées of the cinema, but because the cinema imitates them.

It continued to be unacceptable to portray Joan as a rebel, an individual who rose up against a country girl's ordinary lot, refused the marriage which had been arranged, and ran away from home, rather than as someone who submitted, obediently, to an unlikely calling. The personification of justice had her resonance muffled by restricting justice's meaning to a womanly compassion. In *Joan of Arc*, the 1948 movie made by Victor Fleming from Maxwell Anderson's stage play, *Joan of Lorraine*, the film makers returned to another theme central to Boutet de Monvel's tender view of the Middle Ages, and cast Ingrid Bergman, then fifteen years old, as Joan of Arc, in order to stress her innocence and unworldliness, her girlishness. Much is made at the start of Joan's reluctance to leave home. She conveys modesty, shyness, feminine effacement, in direct contradiction to the assertiveness, courage, and other supposedly masculine virtues she represents by her actions in the story. She gives voice to a diffidence nowhere visible in her historical story, viz., that it is not her proper place to go to the wars; she repeats, "It is nothing in me, but in my Lord"; she tells her mother, "I never wanted to hurt you, mother," and when she has her hair cut in a boy's style in order to accomplish her great deeds, the tears fall down both their cheeks. The interesting thing about this image of her haircut is that it is a publicity still. The scene does not occur in the version of the film I have seen. There, Joan's transformation from dutiful orthodox young girl, at her pastoral and domestic tasks, to a tomboy in armor happens seamlessly, without a break, without drawing attention to itself, as if it were perilous to notice at all Joan of Arc's unusual departure from traditional girlhood, and her subversive usurpation of men's qualities and roles. And so an apology for her feminine attractions is made, not only by the personableness of the young Bergman herself, but by the sexual attention of her jailers. In Boutet de Monvel, they assault her physically with drawn dagger; in the 1948 movie, their intentions are carnal, and the jailer wants to kiss her.

Through these American interpretations of Joan of Arc, we see ideas about universal human virtue and ideas about female propriety in tension; Joan of Arc was a pre-eminent heroine, exhibiting courage, fortitude, justice, the personification in history of many of the qualities habitually represented in the female form in rhetoric and iconography. But the disjunction between that tradition and nineteenth and twentieth century concepts of femininity was deep, and accommodations were continually made to adjust Joan of Arc's personality and life to conform to a more acceptable womanly model. This womanly model was provided by a vision of the French Middle Ages channelled through American male gallantry, at a time when women were reverenced for their gentleness, *courtoisie*, lovingness, indulgence, and simple, unlettered inspiration, when madonna, model, and muse called men to a higher ideal than "vulgar fact." In the process vulgar fact was indeed forgotten, or perhaps could not quite be faced, and the historical splendors and possibilities of women's participation in the Middle Ages were neglected in favor of contemporary romancing.

NOTES

1. Henry James, "The Madonna of the Future," in *The Complete Tales of Henry James*, ed. Leon Edel (London: J. B. Lippincott Company, 1962–64), III, 14–15.

2. Ibid., 20–21.

3. Ibid., 20–22.

4. Ibid., 20–21.

5. Philo Judaeus, "On Flight and Finding," 51, quoted by Marvin W. Meyer, "Making Mary Male: The Categories 'Male' and 'Female' in *The Gospel of Thomas*," paper kindly lent by author, forthcoming in *Journal of Theological Studies*; see also, Richard A. Baer, *Philo's Use of the Categories Male and Female* (Leiden: E. J. Brill, 1970).

6. Guillaume de Conches, MS. Paris BN Lat. 14380, trans. and quoted in Joan M. Ferrante, *Woman as Image in Medieval Literature* (New York: Columbia University Press, 1975), 43.

7. Methodius of Olympus, *The Symposium, A Treatise on Chastity*, trans., annot., Herbert A. Musurillo, S. J. (Westminster, MD and London: Newman Press, 1958), 113.

8. Bernard of Clairvaux, *Sermo in Cantica Canticarum* XXXVIII, iii.4, quoted by Ferrante, 28.

9. Henry Adams, *Mont St. Michel and Chartres* (New York: Houghton Mifflin, 1905; repr. Princeton, 1981), 90–91.

10. Hildegarde, *Scivias* in *PL* 197.424; also, ed. Adelgundis Führkötter and Angela Carlevaris, *Corpus Christianorum Series Latina* 43–43A, (Turnhout, 1978).

11. Herrad of Hohenburg, *Hortus Deliciarum*, ed., Rosalie Green, et al., 2 vols. (London: Warburg Institute, 1979), fol. 32r. (p. 104), and Pl. 18, Vol. 2.

12. Hildegarde, *Letter to Tengswindis*, trans., Peter Dronke, *Women Writers of the Middle Ages* (Cambridge: Cambridge University Press, 1984), 165–66.

13. Hildegarde, *PL* 197.189–90.

14. See the opening invocation of *Scivias*, *PL* 197.

15. Michael Evans, "Allegorical Women and Practical Men: The Iconography of the Artes Reconsidered," in Derek Baker, ed., *Medieval Women* (Oxford: Basil Blackwell, 1978), 305–28.

16. Hesiod, *Theogony*, ed., M. L. West (Oxford: Oxford University Press, 1966).

17. Norman Bryson, *Word and Image* (Cambridge: Cambridge University Press, 1981), XVI, 6–7.

18. *The WPA Guide to Washington DC: The Federal Writers' Project Guide*, intro., Roger G. Kennedy (George Washington University, 1942; repr. New York: Pantheon Books, 1983), 186.

19. Ilene H. Forsyth, *The Throne of Wisdom* (Princeton: Princeton University Press, 1972).

20. William H. Gerdts, "William Rush: Sculptural Genius or Inspired Artisan?" in *William Rush, American Sculptor*. Exhibition of Pennsylvania Academy of Arts. Philadelphia, 1982, 66.

21. H. C. Morillier, *The Tapestries at Hampton Court Palace* (London: Her Majesty's Stationery Office, 1962), 11.

22. See Alan E. Knight, *Aspects of Genre in Late Medieval French Drama* (Manchester: Manchester University Press, 1983), 8–11, 32–34.

23. John Dryfhout, *The Work of Augustus Saint-Gaudens* (Hanover: University Press of New England, 1982); Larado Taft, *The History of American Sculpture* (New York: Macmillian, 1930), 297–98, fig. 44.

24. *The WPA Guide to New York City: The Federal Writers' Project Guide*, intro., William H. Whyte (The Guilds Committee for Federal Writers' Publications, 1939; repr. New York: Pantheon Books, 1982), 326; Phyllis Dain, *The New York Public Library* (New York: The New York Public Library with Astor, Lenox and Tilden Foundations, 1972), 24.

25. Ibid., 325.

26. Frederick A. Sweet, *Miss Mary Cassatt, Impressionist from Pennsylvania* (Norman: University of Oklahoma, 1966), 125, 130.

27. Adams, 145.

28. Joseph Shulin, "John Daly Burk: Irish Revolutionist and American Patriot," *Transactions of the American Philosophical Society* New Series, 54, Part 6, (October, 1964). I am also deeply indebted to the unpublished thesis of Marcelline Brun-Reyniers, "Jeanne d'Arc aux Etâts-Unis. De l'Histoire au Mythe" (Tours, 1981), which was made available to me through the efficient help of Marie-Veronique Clin, at the Centre Jeanne d'Arc, Orléans.

29. Brun-Reyniers, 188; Burk, Act IV, Sc. 1.

30. Brun-Reyniers, 195; Burk, Act IV, Sc. 2.

31. Adams, 142.

32. Sarah Moore Grimké, trans., cond., Alphonse Lamartine, *Joan of Arc* (Boston: Adams & Co., 1867), 5.

33. Ibid., 5.

34. Taft, ibid., 572–55, fig. 114.

35. Maurice Boutet de Monvel, *Jeanne d'Arc* (repr. Paris: Gautier Languereau, 1973); see 4–7.

36. Maurice Boutet de Monvel, "The National Hero of France," *The Country Magazine*, vol. 53, no. 17, 119–30. I am indebted to Katherine Kovacs, Archivist at the Corcoran Gallery of Art, Washington, for this and other materials on the Boutet de Monvel paintings in the museum's collection.

37. Agnes Kendrick Gray, "Jeanne d'Arc after Five Hundred Years," *The American Magazine of Art* (May 1931): 369–74; Michael Patrick Hearn, "Maurice Boutet de Monvel, Master of the French Picture book," *The Horn Book Magazine* Vol. 55, no. 2 (April 1979): 170–80.

38. Lucy Foster Madison, *Joan of Arc The Warrior Maid*, with illustrations and decorations by Frank E. Schoonover (London: Skeffington & Son, 1918).

39. *Kiné Weekly*, 22 January 1920.

40. Kevin Brownlow, author of *The Parade's Gone By* (London: Secker and Warburg, 1968), showed me fragments of Cecil B. De Mille's *Joan the Woman*; the Centre Jeanne d'Arc in Orleans has some other fragments. Otherwise information on the film comes from the British Film Institute clippings library.

41. *Kiné Weekly*, 22 January 1920; *Bioscope*, January 1920.

Part Two: Literature

"By Chaucer's Boots":
Some Medieval Strains in
Colonial American Literature

Harrison T. Meserole

O N THE VERY SURFACE OF IT, THE IDEA THAT A MEDIEVAL STRAIN PERSISTED
in colonial American writing strongly enough to be perceived and
evaluated is an unpromising one. To begin with, the era of the seventeenth century is so fraught with rapid change, in virtually every aspect of
inquiry, whether social, political, geographical, economic, or belletristic, to
say nothing of theological, philosophical, or aesthetic, that it would be reasonable to assume the submergence and gradual disappearance of even the most
central themes or currents of emphasis inherited from the Middle Ages.
Moreover, between the Middle Ages and the seventeenth century stood the
dramatic event of the Reformation, the determined frontal attack on the Roman Catholic church, the institution whose power and influence had been
so predominant in the medieval world. On this side of the Atlantic, particularly in the northeastern colonies in which much of our early literature origi-
nated, the Reformation manifested itself in perhaps its severest form in the
antipathy of New England Puritans toward all things Roman.

This antipathy, well known to students of early America, can be quickly
demonstrated. Richard Steere, who may best be known to specialists in English literature for his rejoinder to Dryden's *Absalom and Achitophel*, which
had mounted the most satiric attack on Shaftesbury shortly before the Earl
was arrested on a charge of treason following the dissolution of the Oxford

Parliament in July 1681, voiced his response in the 36-page *History of the Babylonish Cabal; or the Intrigues, Progression, Opposition, Defeat, and Destruction of the Daniel Catchers. In a Poem* (London, 1682).[1] Seeking to contravene Dryden's mockery in *Absalom*, Steere begins his poem in majestic tones and stately measures, but soon his outrage at what he saw as Roman Catholic attempts to subvert the Whig cause explodes into invective, with focus on the perjured oath. More effective in its assault on Rome is Steere's broadside verse, "Romes Thunder-Bolt, or, Antichrist Displaid," with its title continuing in typical seventeenth-century fashion, "Being a brief Character of the Sorded Ignorance of the Church of *Rome*, called in Scripture *MISTRY BABYLON* THE Great: With the certainty of her Totall Fall, Finall Destruction, and Desolation; the Assurance of which produceth Comfort and Consolation to the afflicted, Persecuted, Despised, and Dejected Protestant Churches, Published for the Necessary Use of all Protestant Families in the Three Kingdomes" (1682). In rhymed iambic pentameter couplets, the verse is better than in the *Babylonish Cabal* because it is more controlled, and Steere sharpens his attack at key points in his polemic by using a rhymed triplet for percussive emphasis. For example, after indicting the Catholic Church for its cheats and lying wonders meant to deceive the *mobile vulgus* into believing in miracles, so that by blind

> *Implisset* faith the people grope
> After the blind Directions of the *Pope*,
> And his black tribe of *Locust[s]*, which devour
> And eat the Labour of the Labourer,

Steere concludes:

> Thus *Rome* defiles her lawful marriage bed,
> And by successive *Popes* to lewdness led,
> Controuling all the dictates of her Head.

And Steere illuminates his broadside with a well-conceived woodcut accompanied by eight couplets keyed by letters to details in the emblem. The first, appropriately "A," stands for Christ,

> The worlds Redeemer in the Clouds above,
> Amids't the Angels doth in Glory move,

while the other seven, "B" through "H," excoriate, in order, the Pope, the Whore of Babylon, the Seven-Headed Beast, the Popish Army, the Strumpet, the Beast again, and of course Rome.

Another example of this anti-Papist mood was John Wilson, first teacher of the Church at Charlestown, Massachusetts, who developed among his Puritan colleagues in New England the reputation of being the most skillful anagrammatist since Adam—at least, so remarked Cotton Mather, adducing the patristic interest in Pilate's famous *Quid est veritas?* and its response, *Est vir qui adest.*

In 1657 Claudius Gilbert, pastor of Limerick, Ireland, and implacable defender of the old religion, published *The Libertine School'd*, in which he mounted a vigorous attack on Quakerism, and he sent Wilson a copy. Delighted, Wilson anagrammatized Gilbert's name into " 'Tis Braul I Cudgel" and wrote on the title-page verso of Gilbert's tract a fourteen-line diatribe in which he found yet another reason for laying the ills of the world at Rome's feet:

Claudius Gilbert

Anagram. Tis Braul I Cudgel

[Tis Braul I Cudgel,] Ranters, Quakers Braul,
Divels, and Jesuites, Founders of them all.
Their Brauling Questions whosoever reades
May soone perceive, These are their proper heades.
What Better Cudgels, then Gods holy word,
(For Brauls so cursed,) and the Civil sword?
By God Ordained to suppresse such evils,
Which God Abhorreth, as he doth the Devils.
Oh! Lett these blessed Cudgels knocke them downe.
Lett Sathan fall, that Christ may weare the
     Crowne.
Let Baal pleade for Baal; who are Christs,
Abhorr, oppose, Confound these Antichrists.
Yea Lett the Lord confound them, who with spight
Against his Truth maliciously Fight.

J W.[2]

Yet we know that elements, interests, and predilections of a culture or an age persist in a later era despite that era's antipathy to the principal tenets of the earlier time. Such is the case with American Puritanism itself, which as a predominant force found its last great spokesman in Jonathan Edwards, who died in 1758, but today after three and a half centuries still exerts measurable influence on identifiable aspects of our culture—Pennsylvania's continuing resistance, for example, to Sunday shopping, particularly in rural districts. And so it was with a considerable number of ideas, points of view, and currents of emphasis from the Middle Ages, which made themselves felt in our earliest American writings.

Evidence for this assertion appears in its most obvious and most elementary form in the number of allusions to medieval writers and books that echo in the lines of verse and passages of prose composed by our colonial forebears. In just the first two books of his *Magnalia Christi Americana*, for example, Cotton Mather refers to, among others, Richard I of England, Phillippe de Commines the historian, Chrysostom, Bernard of Clairvaux, Eusebius of Caesarea, Johannes Cassianus, and, expectedly frequently, to the four great church fathers Ambrose, Augustine, Gregory, and Jerome. To introduce Book II of his history, moreover, devoted to the lives of governors and magistrates who have been "SHIELDS unto the CHURCHES of *NEW-ENGLAND*," Mather adjures his readers:

> Prudentius *calls* Judges, The Great Lights of the Sphere; Symmachus *calls* Judges, The better part of Mankind. *Reader, Thou art now to be entertained with the* Lives *of* Judges *which have deserved that Character. And the* Lives *of those who have been called,* Speaking Laws, *will excuse our History coming under the Observation made about the Works of* Homer, *That the Word, LAW, is never so much as once occurring in them. They are not written like the* Cyrus *of* Xenophon, *like the* Alexander *of* Curtius, *like* Virgil's AEneas, *and like* Pliny's Trajan: *But the Reader hath in every one of them a Real and a Faithful History. And I please my self with hopes, that there will yet be found among the Sons of* New-England, *those Young Gentlemen by whom the Copies given in this History will be written after; and that saying of Old* Chaucer *be remembered,* To do the Genteel Deeds, that makes the Gentleman.[3]

Always erudite, Mather chose his references appropriately. Aurelius Clemens Prudentius (d. ca. 410) was perhaps the chief Christian poet of the early church, who had also been a lawyer and had had a successful career in civil administration. Quintus Aurelius Symmachus (d. 410) was the orator, statesman, and letterwriter who pleaded with the emperor Valentinian II to restore to the Roman senate the statue and altar of the pagan Victory and who thus provoked Prudentius' verse refutation "Contra Symmachus." And of course there is "*Old* Chaucer." It would be satisfying to report that Mather had read in the original "The Wife of Bath's Tale," from which he quotes, as it can be established that he had so read both Prudentius and Symmachus. He apparently had not, for as Kenneth Murdock demonstrated in his admirable edition of Books I and II of the *Magnalia*, Mather took the quotation he uses not from the *Canterbury Tales* but from Josiah Dare's etiquette book, *Counsellor Manners His Last Legacy to His Son* (London, 1673), compiled "out of the dying advice of 'an ancient Gentleman.' " In his notebook, Mather copied down ten quotations from Manners, of which this is the first, and later used his notes in preparing the manuscript of the *Magnalia* for publication in 1702.

Yet Mather's use of Francis Manners' apothegmatic rendering of lines 1115–16 and 1170 from "The Wife of Bath's Tale,"

> To do the gentil dedes that he kan;
> Taak him for the grettest gentil man

and

> he is gentil that dooth gentil dedes,

is somehow appropriate, for elsewhere Mather voices clear approval of the accomplishments and attitudes of the Sixth Earl of Rutland, who was made Privy Councillor in 1617. And though we can be sure that Mather would have looked with favor on Chaucer's irreverent characterizations of Roman churchmen in various of the *Canterbury Tales*, we can be just as sure in visualizing with what tight-lipped disapproval the renowned religious and political leader of Puritan Massachusetts would have viewed Chaucer's earthy account in, say, "The Miller's Tale" or indeed, his lusty portrait of the five-times-wed Wife.

Such was not the case with another seventeenth-century American reader of Chaucer, the sharp-tongued Nathaniel Ward, minister of the church at Aggawam (now Ipswich, Massachusetts), who died eleven years before Cotton Mather was born. Principal author of the Massachusetts "Body of Liberties" (1641), a fundamental document in American constitutional history, Ward is better known for his *Simple Cobler of Aggawam* (1647), in which he assumed the persona of Theodore de la Guard, an eccentric frontier shoemaker whose conscience forces him to speak out against the sad state of affairs in England and whatever else annoyed him. No less than Mather a staunch defender of the true Protestant religion as a shield against Papists from without and heretics from within, Ward nevertheless possessed an irrepressible wit which rings as amusingly from his pages for the modern reader as does, say, Franklin's or Swift's. It is to Ward's verse apart from his *Simple Cobler* that we turn.

A short time before Ward's death, some members of Anne Bradstreet's family, without her knowledge, took her manuscript of original poetry to London, and in 1650 was published *The Tenth Muse Lately Sprung Up in America*, prefaced by a collection of commendatory verses by friends and acquaintances. Among these was Ward's tribute:

> Mercury shew'd *Apollo, Bartas Book*,
> *Minerva* this, and wisht him well to look,
> And tell uprightly, which did which excell,
> He view'd and view'd, and vow'd he could not tel.
> They did him Hemisphear his mouldy nose,
> With's crackt leering-glasses, for it would pose
> The best brains he had in's old pudding-pan,
> Sex weigh'd, which best, the Woman, or the Man?
> He peer'd, and por'd, and glar'd, and said for
>   wore
> I'me even as wise now, as I was before:
> They both 'gan laugh, and said, it was no mar'l
> The Auth'ress was a right *Du Bartas* Girle.
> Good sooth quoth the old *Don*, tel ye me so,
> I muse whither at length these Girls will go;
> It half revives my chil frost-bitten blood,
> To see a woman once do, ought, that's good;
> And chode by *Chaucers* Boots, and *Homers* Furrs,
> Let Men look to't, least Women wear the Spurrs.[4]

The allusion is explicit, but it is more than mere reference. Like most Puritan intellectuals Ward was convinced that names reflected personality, clues to character as well as to occupation, and he doted, as did many early American poets, on word- and letter-games. Thus, to sign his *Simple Cobler* he adopted his pen-name Theodore de la Guard, which, as P. M. Zall has recorded in his useful edition of that text,[5] is a linguistic transformation: *Theodore* = the Greek equivalent of *Nathaniel*; *de la Guard* = the French for *Ward*. In that context, then, Ward's "Chaucer's boots" plays on French *chausser*, and slyly extends the game with the concluding image of Anne Bradstreet's delicate slippers replete with spurs.

This is typical Wardian wit. The *Cobler* is full of comparable examples. Moreover, when the opportunity arose, Ward could be as earthy in his humor as ever his master Chaucer was. In recognizing, for example, that his ministerial colleague John Wilson had been enthroned as the prince of New England anagram makers, Ward characterized Wilson's process of composition in a wicked and windy image:

> We poor Agawams
> are so stiff in the hams
> that we cannot make Anagrams,
> But Mr John Wilson
> the great Epigrammatist
> Can let out an Anagram
> even as he list.[6]

It must not be thought that these are isolated instances of allusion to medieval texts. Indeed, it is hardly possible to read through the canon of any writer of the era for whom a substantial body of writing has survived without marking such references in measurable numbers, and occasionally even in clusters. In his Preparatory Meditation 56, Second Series, for example, Edward Taylor catalogued a representative list of mechanical wonders to emphasize the theme that, admirable though they may be, works of art are subordinate to those of nature, and both art and nature subordinate to works of God. Taylor writes:

> Art, natures Ape, hath many brave things done:
>   As th' Pyramids, the Lake of Meris vast,
> The Pensile Orchards built in Babylon,
>   Psammitich's Labyrinth, (arts Cramping task)
>   Archimedes his Engins made for war,
>   Romes Golden House, Titus his Theater.
>
> The Clock of Strasburgh, Dresdens Table-sight,
>   Regiamonts Fly of Steele about that flew,
> Turrian's Wooden Sparrows in a flight,
>   And th' Artificiall man Aquinas slew,
>   Mark Scaliota's Lock and Key and Chain
>   Drawn by a Flea, in our Queen Betties reign.[7]

Clearly there is a purpose to the catalogue beyond mere enumeration. By mixing references to the wonders of the ancient world with those of phenomena of the Middle Ages and to marvels of the Renaissance, Taylor adds the sweep of history to the range of geography, peoples, and kingdoms to underscore the fact that despite his ingenuity, inventiveness, and craftsmanship, man has created only "Wits Wantonings and Fancies frollicks" when these achievements are measured against God's "Doings rare."

Taylor's reference to "Regiamont" is interesting, in passing, because of its subject. Johann Müller, the great fifteenth-century mathematician and astronomer born in Königsberg (hence his pseudonym "Regiomontanus" in Latin), was well known in Colonial America for his treatise on trigonometry, the study of which he pioneered in his home country, and for his observations on the great comet of January 1472—later to become known as Halley's Comet. Typical is John Josselyn's citation in his *Account of Two Voyages to New-England* (1674) of Regiomont as authority in a detailed discussion of the natural causes and preternatural effects of comets (pp. 51–52). Taylor, too, was keenly interested in astronomy, as may be demonstrated by the considerable number of astronomical images in his *Preparatory Meditations* and the presence in Taylor's personal library of such volumes as Peter Heylyn's *Cosmographie* (1652) and Increase Mather's *Kometographia* (1683). Yet Taylor's allusion here is not to Regiomont's learned treatises but to that mathematician's avocation, that of the construction of automata, and in this case specifically to the mechanical eagle that as a youth Regiomont built to greet Maximilian I upon his entry into Nürnberg.

As such, the allusion coheres with the one Taylor makes two lines later to the "Artificial man Aquinas slew," which, as Robert Hodges has demonstrated,[8] is to the talking head constructed by Albertus Magnus, which Albert's famous pupil, Thomas Aquinas, later destroyed.

More than an exercise in trivial pursuit—the process of ferreting out of sources with which every textual editor perforce becomes familiar—the evidence provided by such congeries of references to well- and less well-known figures of the Middle Ages suggests to what degree the learning and culture of that era engaged the imaginations of our seventeenth-century American forebears. When the references are explicit, like the ones to Chaucer, Regiomontanus, Aquinas, and the others I have discussed so far, the directional signals are clear. Not quite so clear, but perhaps more significant, are those we find fully woven into the fabric of our earliest writings.

Some important scholarship points the way here. More than a century ago, John Harvard Ellis compared one of Anne Bradstreet's quaternions, "The Foure Elements," with the early morality play "The Interlude of the Four Elements," and in one of the earliest essays to be published after Edward Taylor's verse was made accessible in Thomas Johnson's edition, Nathalia Wright convincingly linked Taylor's *Gods Determinations* to morality play conventions. In a number of essays, Ronald Sterne Wilkinson has provided background material for the study of John Winthrop, Jr., the first scientist of note in the New England colonies who was dubbed by Cotton Mather our "Hermes Christianus." And most recently, in a thoroughly entertaining and perceptive article, Jennifer Goodman has persuasively argued the case for Captain John

Smith as chivalric biographer, focusing particularly on the essential role of a chivalric ideal in Smith's image of himself, especially in his *The True Travels, Adventures, and Observations of Captaine John Smith in Europe, Asia, Africa, and America from ... 1593 to 1629 ...* (1630).[9]

Goodman's argument derives a part of its strength from Louis B. Wright's demonstration in his *Middle Class Culture in Elizabethan England* (1935) that the romances generally associated with the Middle Ages were eagerly read through the late sixteenth and seventeenth centuries, and we know, of course, that elements of those romances—the quest, the maturation and triumph of the hero after facing stern trials, the accounts of strange or far-off lands, the encounters with fabulous beasts or larger-than-life persons, for example—derived, in part, from an earlier tradition, found their way into narratives, chronicles, and even histories of later eras. Some, indeed, became mythic, as Philip Young has shown in his exploration of one incident from Captain John Smith's narrative, the famous account of Smith's deliverance from death by Pocahontas.[10]

That these elements appear in our earliest American writing is thus not surprising. The quest, to begin with, is pervasive. It appears in virtually every travel account that has come down to us from the period, including those of the Cabots, Henry Hudson, Jacques Cartier, Cabeza de Vaca, and many others. The grail of the romance has become the treasure of the New World, of course, or the golden dream of colonizers, or the fabled city of Norumbega in New England, a legend which David Ingram, an English sailor, sought to confirm in his sensational 1568 tale of brooks containing fist-sized gold nuggets and the city of crystal domes and gold pillars occupied by citizens bedecked with pearls and silver. Even Daniel Denton, in his quite circumspect *Brief Description of New-York: Formerly Called New Netherlands* (1670), entices the reader in a brief foreword:

> The Bowels of the earth [are] not yet opened,
> though the Natives tell us of Glittering Stones
> ... and the *Dutch* hath boasted of Gold and
> Silver ... yet I shall not feed your
> expectation with any thing of that nature....
>
> (Fol. A3ᵛ)

The journey beset by describable and indescribable dangers is there too. Another captain, of somewhat lower degree than John Smith but perhaps even more dauntless, was memorialized in an epic graphically describing the tragic ambush and almost total annihilation by Indians of Michael Pierce and his whole company at Rehoboth on the 26th of March 1676 during King Philip's War. Using what in sum is the most uninhibited orthography to be met with in seventeenth-century documents, and verse that reminds us of the poorest of the Bay Psalm Book renderings, Deacon Philip Walker nevertheless captures much of the ominous atmosphere that the colonial soldiers experienced as they trudged through dark woods that hid

> Thes murthros Rooges like wild Arabians thay
> Lurk heare & there of every thing make pr[ey]
>
> all Lives Estats in Cruill wise thay take
> throuout the Cuntry dredfull havok make[.]

"Captain Perse and his coragios Company" are slaughtered, and Walker then proclaims:

> ffor thers no sister of the musis nine
> with Ovids pen nether Tertulas witt
> No Homer in hes Trogan warr define
> a Cruel actt so as thes Rooges actt it.[11]

Less well-known than it should be to scholars outside the field of Colonial American studies is William Wood's *New Englands Prospect* (1634). Too frequently categorized as merely another of the considerable number of promotional tracts of the time designed to whet the economic appetites of prospective colonizers and investors in New World plantations, it is far more than that, as Moses Coit Tyler suggested more than a century ago in his *History of American Literature 1607–1775*. Tyler was a severe and frequently acerbic critic who showed no mercy when the text he was assessing did not measure up. In the light of Tyler's severe criticism of most seventeenth-century American verse and prose, then, it is refreshing and not a little startling when the reader of Tyler's *History* comes upon passages of unreserved praise for a particular book: "very sprightly and masterful specimen of descriptive literature, embodying the results of precise observation. . . . Besides the extraordinary raciness and vivacity of his manner, [the author] has an elegance of touch by no means common in the prose of his contemporaries. His style, indeed, is that of a man of genuine literary culture, and has the tone and flavor of the best Elizabethan prose-writers . . ." (p. 166). The book, continues Tyler, "has a wide range of topics and a multitude of details; but it moves easily through them all, with an alert and thorough treatment, not once blundering out of the straight path or lapsing into dulness" (p. 167).

And Tyler was right on the mark. Wood promises in his subtitle "A true, lively, and experimentall description of . . . NEVV ENGLAND . . . Laying downe that which may both enrich the knowledge of the mind-travelling reader, or benefit the future Voyager," and we are not disappointed, particularly as we move through the twenty short chapters of the second part of the book, which focus on the Indian tribes, their food, customs, personal characteristics, politics, superstitions, and other matters. And it is in this section that Wood's prose provides further testimony for the accuracy of Louis Wright's assertion about the wide-spread popularity of the medieval romance in the seventeenth century.

In describing marriages among the Indians, Wood writes that the

> Kings or great *Powwowes, alias* Conjurers, may have two or three Wives, but seldome use it. Men of ordinary Ranke, having but one; which disproves the report, that they had eight or tenne Wives apeece. When a man hath a desire to Marry, he first gets the good-will of the Maide or Widdow, after, the consent of her friends for her part; and for himselfe, if he be at his owne disposing, if the King will, the match is made, her Dowry of *Wampompeage* payd, the King joynes their hands with their hearts, never to part till death, unlesse shee prove a Whore; for which they may, and some have put away their Wives, as may appeare by a story. There was one *Abamoch* married a Wife, whom a long time he intirely loved above her deservings, for that shee often in his absence entertained strangers, of which hee was oftentimes informed by his neighbours; but hee harbouring no sparke of jealousie, beleeved not their false informations (as he deemed them) being in a manner angry they should slander his Wife, of whose constancy hee was so strongly conceited: A long time did her whorish gloazing and Syren-like tongue, with her subtle carriage, establish her in her Husbands favour, till fresh complaints caused him to cast about, how to finde out the truth, and to prove his friends lyars, and his Wife honest, or her a Whore, and his friends true: whereupon hee pretended a long journey to visite his friends, providing all accoutraments for a fortnights journey; telling his Wife it would be so long before she could expect his returne, who outwardly sorrowed for his departure, but inwardly rejoyced, that she should enjoy the society of her old *Lemman*; whom she sent for with expedition, not suspecting her Husbands plot, who lay not many miles off in the Woods; who after their dishonest revelings, when they were in their midnight sleepe, approaches the Wigg-

wamme, enters the doore, which was neither barred nor lockt; makes
a light to discover what hee little suspected; but finding his friends words
to bee true, hee takes a good bastinado in his hand brought for the
same purpose, dragging him by the haire from his usurped bed, so
lamentably beating him, that his battered bones and bruised flesh made
him a fitter object for some skilfull Surgeon, than the lovely object of
a lustfull strumpet; which done, hee put away his wife, exposing her
to the curtesie of strangers for her maintenance, that so curtesan-like
had entertained a stranger into her bosome. (pp. 81–82)

The elements of the tale are familiar ones: the love-struck husband unwill-
ing to suspect his wife of infidelity, the faithless wife who takes advantage
of her husband's absence, the inquisitive friend who informs on the wife,
and the denouement in which the wife's adultery is discovered and punished.
Wood changes only one or two surface features, such as the husband's name
and the substitution of wigwam for castle, in adapting the story from the Arthurian romance cycle and similar medieval narratives to entertain his mind-
travelling reader at just the point when his interest might have flagged during
descriptions, however informative, of fire-building, tribal government, and
the Indian language. And it is clear, I think, that Wood tells the tale with
such obvious gusto that even the most staid of readers would be attracted
by its fabliau character.

There are other areas, too, in which the medieval influence is perceiva-
ble. In the curriculum at Harvard in the mid-seventeenth century, for example, which as Samuel Eliot Morison has shown,[12] owes much to the trivium
and quadrivium of the Schoolmen; in the meditative process followed by Edward Taylor, which as Louis Martz has argued, derives from Ignatius of Loyola
(despite John Wilson's attack on the Jesuits) as transmitted by Richard Baxter;[13] in the alchemy and astrology which dominate much of the imagery of
seventeenth-century American poetry and provide subject matter for a substantial body of prose; in the iconography of Puritan gravestones and its sources
in the medieval *memento mori*.[14]

As a generalization we may accept the assertion that the Marianism of the
Middle Ages was conspicuously absent in seventeenth-century New England,
just as we may also accept the argument that the prohibition against celebration of the feast of Christmas explains the paucity of reference to that subject
in our early poetry. Yet as early as 1650 Anne Bradstreet included in the
"Winter" portion of her Quaternion on *The Four Seasons* the couplet

> Through *Christendome* with great Feastivity
> Now's hold, (but ghest) for blest Nativity.[15]

And the redoubtable Richard Steere from whom we heard earlier composed, a few years later, his "Upon the Caelestial Embassy Perform'd by Angels, to the Shepherds on the Plains of Bethlehem, at the Birth of our Redeemer,"[16] in whose 92 lines every member of the traditional *dramatis personae* associated with the event is mentioned except the Virgin Mary. Until recently, moreover, Steere's poem was thought to be the first, and only, seventeenth-century American poem on the Nativity.

However, we now know that David Dunster, eldest son of Henry Dunster, second president of Harvard College, antedated Steere with not one but four Christmas poems and also composed the only poem that has so far come to light from early America in praise of Mary. Dunster's "The songe of the Blessed Virgin," written in 1683, is quite ordinary verse in which Mary speaks:

> The songe of the Blessed Virgin
>
> My Soule doth Magnifie the LORD
>
> My Spirit doth doe the same,
> And all the powers that are in mee
> Ioy in my SAVIOURS Name.
> . . . .
> To Him, therfore, and to his sonne
> with the blest Spir't of grace
> Be glory, honour, power, ascribed
> by each succeeding race.[17]

But it is in Dunster's "On christmas day" that we find the mother, the babe, and the manger in the scene so familiar today but elsewhere unrecorded in Puritan New England.

> On christmas day
>
> Looke Sheapherds! Why? Where?
> See yee not yonder! yonder! There!
> LORD! what a glorious Light
> streames through the aire!
> Never was Sunne so bright
> nor Morne so faire.
> Methinkes it doth appeare
> Like glory comeinge neare.
>
> Listen Sheapherds, Listen round!
> Harke! heare yee not a sound?

LORD what a heavenly noise
   beats through the aire!
Never was sweeter Voice,
   nor Noate so cleare!
     Heavenly Musick! Heavenly Musick!
     Glorious Light! Glorious Light!
Yet more fearfull, fearfull, fearfull, then the Night.

Feare not, Sheapherds; For behold!
   Better Tydings, ne're were told,
     News wee bringe you this same tide
     This blessed MORNE
   That to you, & all mankinde beside
   a Saviour is Borne.

Post to Bethlehem, post to Bethlehem, post about,
   Post and finde the Infant out;
     With these Signes, you shall begin,
     In a Stable att an Inne,
     You shall finde his Mother Maide
     poorly Friended
     And the BABE in a manger laid
     worse attended.
When you finde Him Loudly Crie
   Glory be to GOD on high.
     Glory be to GOD above
     Peace on Earth; & to Men, Love.
   Death, and Hell, are now beguilded
   GOD, and Men, are reconciled.
     Hallelujah! Hallelujah!
     Hallelujah! Hallelujah!

The generalizations hold, of course. Half a dozen poems on the Nativity among the 2,200 we have record of, so far, from seventeenth-century America do not invalidate the positions we know the Puritans maintained toward Christmas, and certainly the two references to Mary do not establish Marianism as a strain in the literature. Yet it is important to document their presence as one additional piece of evidence in my argument: that there is a medieval influence in Colonial America, that this influence may be perceived in a variety of manuscript and published writings of the era in a variety of contexts, and that continuing study of this presence can add a significant dimension to our understanding of the earliest American literature.

NOTES

1. Donald P. Wharton, *Richard Steere: Colonial Merchant Poet* (University Park, PA: Pennsylvania State University Press, 1979), 16. I have also drawn on Wharton's excellent discussion of Steere's "Romes Thunder-Bolt."

2. Unless otherwise noted, citations of early verse in this essay are from my *American Poetry of the Seventeenth Century* (1968; repr. University Park, PA: Pennsylvania State University Press, 1985). For Wilson's poem, see 385–86.

3. Cotton Mather, *Magnalia Christi America*, Books I and II, ed. Kenneth B. Murdock with the assistance of Elizabeth W. Miller (Cambridge, MA: Belknap Press of Harvard University Press, 1977), 200.

4. Meserole, 367.

5. P. M. Zall, ed., *The Simple Cobler of Aggawam in America* (Lincoln, NB: University of Nebraska Press, 1969).

6. Meserole, 368.

7. Meserole, 135–36.

8. Robert R. Hodges, "Edward Taylor's 'Artificiall Man.' " *American Literature* 31 (1959): 76–77.

9. John Harvard Ellis, *The Works of Anne Bradstreet in Prose and Verse* (Charlestown, MA: Cutter, 1867), xli; Nathalia Wright, "The Morality Tradition in the Poetry of Edward Taylor," *American Literature* 18 (1946): 1–18; Ronald Sterne Wilkinson, " 'Hermes Christianus': John Winthrop, Jr. and Chemical Medicine in Seventeenth Century New England," in Allen G. Debus, ed., *Science, Medicine and Society in the Renaissance: Essays to Honor Walter Pagel*, 2 vols. (London: Heinemann, 1972) I, 221–29; Jennifer Goodman, "The Captain's Self-Portrait: John Smith as Chivalric Biographer," *Virginia Magazine of History and Biography* 89 (1981): 27–38.

10. Philip Young, "The Mother of Us All: Pocahontas Reconsidered," *Kenyon Review* 24 (1962): 391–415, reprinted in Young's *Three Bags Full: Essays in American Fiction* (New York: Harcourt Brace Jovanovich, 1973), 175–203.

11. Richard Le Baron Bowen, ed., *Early Rehoboth* (Rehoboth, MA: Privately Printed, 1948) 3: 37–38.

12. Samuel Eliot Morison, *Harvard College in the Seventeenth Century*, 2 vols. (Cambridge, MA: Harvard University Press, 1936). See esp. Vol. I, Chapters VII–XII on the curriculum.

13. Louis L. Martz, "Foreword," *The Poems of Edward Taylor*, ed. Donald E. Stanford (New Haven: Yale University Press, 1960), xiii–xxxvii, esp. xxiv–xxviii.

14. These and other subjects I shall explore more thoroughly in chapters of the book I am doing on the medieval influence in early America.

15. Meserole, 29.

16. Meserole, 266–68.

17. For this and the next Dunster poem, see my "New Voices from Seventeenth-Century America," 24–45 in Calvin Israel, ed., *Discoveries & Considerations: Essays on Early American Literature & Aesthetics Presented to Harold Jantz* (Albany, NY: State University of New York Press, 1976), 24–25. I am presently completing an edition of the manuscript "Gospelmanna" (1683), in which Dunster's poetry appears. The MS is held in the rare book collection of the Pattee Library of the Pennsylvania State University.

Medievalism and the Mind of Emerson

Kathleen Verduin

RALPH WALDO EMERSON (1803–82) WAS NOT ONE TO BUILD THE SEPULCHRES of the fathers or disavow his own generation. All forms of antiquarianism were antithetical to his values: as Stephen Whicher has written, "the whole trend of [Emerson's] thought, once he set about building his personal philosophy, was to cut loose from the past as the past in order to emphasize the timeless present" (Introd., *EL*, II, 1). And Emerson himself established his position in an early lecture:

> In ordinary nothing is so disesteemed as the present moment. Men's eyes seem bewitched. . . . They forget, that the finest moments of fame were once the unguarded beat of the household clock; that the dull sunshine of the present moment is the torch of glory to the great; that time, nature and the mind hold out the same courteous invitation at this hour to the race of man, as in the Augustan or the Italian or the elder English periods. . . . (*EL*, II, 157)

Similarly, he could defy popular taste by dismissing Scott's fascination with "the ringing of old ballads and the shape and glitter and rust of old armor" as "tricks of fancy" (*EL*, I, 376); and though he dutifully visited Ruskin at Oxford in 1870, in the privacy of his journal he mocked the man's "doleful opinions of modern society" (*JMN*, XVI, 288).[1]

Nevertheless, as has frequently been argued, Emerson's independence from the past was by no means a repudiation of its creative uses.[2] More particularly, an examination of Emerson's public and private writings over the course of his long career reveals the deep influence of the Medieval Revival that flourished so prodigiously in the nineteenth century and of which both Scott and Ruskin were prominent examples. An active reader whose Unitarian background encouraged self-culture, Emerson was exposed throughout his life to works whose titles read like a catalogue of nineteenth-century Medievalism. He was acquainted not only with contemporary abridgements of the *Morte d'Arthur* but with the scholarship of Joseph Ritson, Thomas Warton, Sharon Turner, and George Ellis—whose *Specimens of Early English Metrical Romances* (1805) he read in the inexpensive edition issued by Bohn's Library, a series Emerson praised and which introduced him to many medieval texts (*JMN*, XI, 137). He knew, and admired, the work of William Morris and the Arthurian poems of Tennyson (*JMN*, XIV, 288; XVI, 115–16); and his medieval interests were further stimulated by new translations of Dante (a translation of whose *Vita Nuova* Emerson himself attempted in the early 1840s), and of Icelandic sagas, which he apparently encountered first in Bishop Percy's version of the *Northern Antiquities* of Paul-Henri Mallet (1770).[3]

Emerson's Medievalism, in short, was part of the complex fabric of art, scholarship, and nostalgia that also produced, in his own country, such poetical works as Lowell's *Vision of Sir Launfal* (1848) and Longfellow's *Golden Legend* (1850) and translation of Dante's *Commedia* (1867), in addition to the Gothic architecture of Andrew Jackson Downing and a multitude of other manifestations.[4] His lifelong interest in medieval history and literature helps document the pervasiveness and vitality of Medievalism in America and sheds particular light on the directions taken by the movement in New England. It is equally evident, however, that Emerson's contemplation of the medieval world was uniquely fitted to his own imagination, and that it shaped and stimulated to a considerable degree his resounding affirmation of his own era.

I

"You have always the earliest antiquity in your nursery today," Emerson reminded an audience in 1869, and the foundation for his own response to the Middle Ages was laid, as is often the case, already in childhood.[5] Some of his earliest letters (1816) mention Southey's *Joan of Arc* and "a French novel by Madame de Genlis called 'Chevaliers de Cygne' " (*L*, I, 21, 23), and by the age of ten he was applying his literary talents to writing "The History of Fortus." This was a long poem in rhymed couplets set down in a fair copy a few years later and, as the title page has it, "Embellished with elegant Engravings" by his friend William Henry Furness. That chivalric conventions were already well known in American popular culture is evident in the poem's opening lines:

> In days of chivalry of old
> When knights perform'd atchievements [sic] bold
> Fortus the great the strong the brave
> Who oft had stretch'd his hand to save
> A helpless damsel from the foe
> And laid full many a ruffian low
> Travers'd the earth an errant knight. . . .[6]

These interests persisted into Emerson's adolescence. Samuel Eliot Morison, in his history of Harvard University, has observed that in the first decades of the nineteenth century "curricular requirements were not exacting, so that boys like Emerson and Thoreau had ample time to browse and dream," and the journals of Emerson's student years bear this out in good measure.[7] The earliest entries reveal his eager absorption of Arthurian legend, and evidently he planned an Arthurian composition of his own:

I would plunge into the classic lore of chivalrous story and of the fairy-land bards and unclosing the ponderous volumes of the firmest believers in magic and in the potency of consecrated crosier or elfin ring I would let my soul sail away delighted in to their wildest phantasies. Pendragon is rising before my fancy and has given me permission to wander in his walks of Fairy-land and to present myself at the bower of Gloriana. (*JMN*, I, 10–11)

To compound the Arthurian emphasis, Emerson belonged in these days to a student literary club who called themselves the Knights of the Square Table.[8]

Significantly, however, he soon placed himself on guard against the meretricious spell of medieval romance and its contemporary imitations. "Romance grows out of ignorance and so is the curse of its own age, and the ornament of those that follow," he wrote in 1823. "It is things cruel and abominable in act that become romantic in memory. Unprincipled bandits are Red Cross Knights, and Templars and Martyrs even in the Song of this Century" (*JMN*,

II, 193). Though in 1826 he confided to his journal that he loved "the flourish of the silver trumpet of Chivalry," he immediately countered,

> Let the fictions of Chivalry alone. Fictions whether of the theorist or poet have their value as ornaments but when they intrude into the place of facts they do infinite injury inasmuch as it is only by the perception and comparison of Truth that we can percieve [sic] and enjoy the harmonies of the system of human destinies which the Deity is accomplishing from age to age. (*JMN*, III, 19)

To his credit, Emerson was obviously uncomfortable with what he perceived as a romantic distortion of historical reality, and his aversion to violence is evident in his assessment of chivalry as stylized bloodshed. His reading of medieval history had shown him a different medieval world, one shockingly divested of gentility. Interestingly enough, his first publication was an article, still uncollected, entitled "Thoughts on the Religion of the Middle Ages," which appeared anonymously in *The Christian Disciple* (later *The Christian Examiner*) in 1823.[9] But as this essay makes clear, the young Emerson did not view medieval history in the rosy colors of Arthurian romance: if anything, his tone conveys suppressed horror. "Whatever may have been the causes," he writes, "we are sufficiently sure of the fact, that, for a period of eight or ten centuries, in the best part of the world, the human mind endured a melancholy captivity, and blindly pursued certain miserable ends, while the whole mass of society languished under barbarous ignorance, and barbarous institutions" (402). Not surprisingly, Emerson considered the medieval mind to have suffered absolute bondage to the Church, and he decries the superstitious rites imposed by Rome. Finally, and in words startling in their distance from his later and more characteristic view of human nature, he defines the entire period as a mysterious "departure of the divine presence, like Jehovah's abandonment of his temple at Jerusalem," whose example "admonishes man of his miserable errors when left to himself" (407). The moral is unmistakable: Emerson presents the medieval world as one well outgrown, its darkness superseded first by a Protestant emphasis on inward piety, then by a Unitarian adherence to virtue and enlightenment.

The essay is essentially what one would expect from a young man about to enter the liberal Protestant pulpit; in a later sermon Emerson would refer again to "those ignorant Middle Ages, so emphatically known as the night of the world."[10] It is easy to smile at such antiquated notions, and easier still to consign this diffident and faulty essay — as scholarship indeed has done — to the relative oblivion of Emerson's juvenilia. Yet its subject, one suspects, was not randomly chosen, nor is it an accident that Emerson's contemplation of the medieval world marked the inception of his career. For a young man of Emerson's training and background, the very fact of the Middle Ages posed a challenge to Unitarian optimism and more specifically to the view that God, even in his more abstracted form as Providence, was good and benevolent and directing human affairs. Could such conditions recur? The past was most useful, in a principle Emerson was to apply repeatedly, as a perspective from which to view the present, and Emerson's idea of medieval religion, to him a dismal and authoritarian system, eventually suggested a parallel to the petrified forms he discovered in his own day: indeed, it may have been the impetus for his later rejection of the Lord's Supper in the controversy over which he left the ministry in 1832. A note from Emerson's journal for 1822 implies that while drafting the *Christian Disciple* article, he was also outlining for himself methods for evaluating all religion (*JMN*, II, 18), and some years later, in 1826, he noted that medieval errors bore an uncomfortable resemblance to dogmas and traditions more contemporary:

> It cannot be denied, the avowal is on every page of ecclesiastical history, that the most absurd and frivolous superstitions have been defended as the most precious doctrines which Jesus Christ came into the world to teach.... And now it may be another set of opinions is taught in the Councils and illustrated in pulpits; but what security is there that these are more genuine than those that went before or that another age may not treat them with the same irreverence.... (*JMN*, III, 48–49)

Accordingly, the sermon setting forth his views on the sacrament surveys the progressive enlightenment of the Christian church since the ninth century.[11] "Not knowing what to do, we ape our ancestors," he wrote later in *The Conduct of Life*; "the churches stagger backward to the mummeries of the Dark Ages" (*W*, VI, 209).

In general, then, Emerson's early writings indicate a powerful ambivalence toward the Middle Ages, a simultaneous attraction and revulsion springing respectively from his idealistic imagination and his insistence on hard reality. If he retreated from medieval superstition and violence—and he seems to have been especially skeptical about the Crusades (*JMN*, III, 18; *L*, I, 246)—he remained strongly drawn to other aspects of the period. Much as he doubted the historical authenticity of knighthood as popularly understood, for example, he continued to look to the chivalric pattern for emblems of manhood and purposeful activity. The chivalric tradition engaged his attention throughout his life: his personal view of women, even after the death of his idealized first wife Ellen Louisa Tucker, retained courtly associations, and even the uncouth John Brown, to Emerson's imagination, reflected "the oath of gentle blood and knighthood . . . to protect the weak and lowly against the oppressor" (*W*, XI, 281).[12] "What makes the true knight?" he asked in a late lecture. "Loyalty to his thought. That makes the beautiful scorn, the elegant simplicity, the directness, the commanding port which all men admire and which men not noble affect" (*W*, X, 55). Between 1869 and 1872, near the termination of his career, he delivered at least three versions of a lecture on chivalry.

But the figure of the knight was clearly of greatest importance to Emerson as a young minister, exactly the years when he was most resistant to the violence of medieval history. In a journal entry for 1827, bemoaning his own indolence and expressing impatience for the great deeds he intends, Emerson quotes the famous line from Milton's sonnet, "They also serve who only stand and wait," and adds,

> Aye but they must wait in a certain temper in a certain equipment. They must wait as the knight on the van of the embattled line standing in his stirrups, his spear in rest, his steed foaming, ready for the career with the speed of a whirlwind. Am I the accomplished cavalier? (*JMN*, III, 78–79)

Shortly after, drafting a sermon, he makes reference to "The Chivalry of Virtue" (*JMN*, III, 82).[13] If Emerson's fancy consoled him in these years with visions of himself as a sort of Fortus of the moral life, the reasons were no doubt rooted in his immediate psychic condition. Like other biographers, B.L. Packer in her recent study *Emerson's Fall* points to the "[r]ecurrent laments over want of stamina and of animal spirits, over feelings of exhaustion and despair" that pervade the early journals, and Emerson seems to have been aware for most of his life of what he took to be a limited vigor (see *L*, II, 376; IV, 101).[14] Significantly enough, perhaps, Emerson confessed in 1868 that "in Morte d'Arthur I remember nothing so well as Merlin's cry from his invisible inaccessible prison" (*JMN*, XVI, 138): an arresting image of isolation, protest, and frustrated ambition.

Despite his earlier rejection of medieval violence, then, Emerson by the 1830s was coming to behold in the period an energy exciting in its contrast to his own self-acknowledged lack of vitality, and we find him drawn increasingly to the Saxon and Teutonic past, perhaps in a conscious attempt to offset what he later termed, rather ambiguously, "the tender and delicious mythology of Arthur" (*W*, V, 55). Since his boyhood at the Boston Latin School when he first cited the Saxon king's achievements, Emerson had revered Alfred the Great, whom he later saw as a Representative Man in his own right: "Not the fabulous St. George, but this great man is the very Genius of the English nation already embodied" (*EL*, I, 252).[15] Unlike the knights of Camelot, Alfred possessed the hardy substance of reality: "His praise rests not upon monkish eulogy or vague tradition, but upon *facts*" (*JMN*, II, 77). But Alfred was ultimately less important to Emerson's imagination than was a far more primitive image from the Nordic world. In 1835 Emerson discovered Sharon Turner's *The History of the Anglo-Saxons* (1799–1805), and though Turner's long section on Alfred must have confirmed Emerson's admiration, it was Turner's image of the Berserkir that had a greater impact.[16] From this point on, Emerson's response to the Middle Ages takes on a significantly new and positive direction, an increasingly strong approval of medieval crudity and violence. Walking the woods with his brother Charles the same year he was reading Turner, Emerson invoked the Nordic vigor in contrast to his own lethargy, adding that in Charles's view "it is only by an effort like a Berserkir a man can work himself up to any interest in any exertion" (*JMN*, V, 109; see also 153). "Curse, if thou wilt, thy sires," he would write later, drafting a never-to-be-finished poem:

> Who, when they gave thee breath,
> Failed to bequeath
> The needful sinew stark as once,
> The Baresark marrow to thy bone.... (*PN*, 226)

The private interest soon invaded Emerson's professional activities, stimulating new speculations about history and culture. In a lecture delivered in 1835, Emerson notes that "the chivalry of Arthur" was powerless against the stronger Saxons—presumably because it had been refined away into decadence (*EL*, I, 241). Though on the same occasion he terms the Berserkir "a class of fiends" (242), Emerson also asserts the need for a periodic revitalization of culture, though such a revitalization might seem at first like anarchy. "But this"—the rude Anglo-Saxons—"was the rugged soil in which the splendid flowers of English wit and humanity should bloom. Out of the strong came forth sweetness" (242; cf. Judges 14:14). "What of these atrocious ancestors of Englishmen the Briton, Saxon, Northman, Berserkir?" he demanded in his journal. "Is it not needful to make a strong nation that there must be strong wild will? If man degenerates in gardens he must be grafted again from the wild stock" (*JMN*, V, 100). And it is the figure of the Berserkir, again, that empowers in 1837 the mature and confident challenge of "The American Scholar":

Not out of those on whom systems of education have exhausted their culture, comes the helpful giant to destroy the old or to build the new, but out of unhandselled savage nature, out of terrible Druids and Berserkirs, come at last Alfred and Shakespeare (*CW*, I, 61; see also *JMN*, V, 217).

II

By the time he was writing the major essays, then, Emerson's picture of the Middle Ages had undergone radical revision. No longer a welter of sinister Gothic darkness fraught with crime and ecclesiastical repression, the medieval world now represented to his mind an exhilarating source of color and primitive energy, perhaps reflecting his own desire for similar qualities. The Berserkir continued to fascinate him—both he and Carlyle agreed, for example, that Daniel Webster's oratorical force recalled a "*silent Berserkir rage*" (*JMN*, VIII, 327).[17] He loved George Borrow's translation of the Danish ballad "Svend Vonved," often reciting it to his children; according to Emerson's son Edward, the ballad described "the Berserker madness of the hero from whom it takes its name."[18] And the Anglo-Saxon interest stimulated by Turner was replicated to some degree in 1847 when Carlyle introduced Emerson to the *Heimskringla* and the Eddas of Snorri Sturluson, both available in recent translations by Samuel Laing and G.W. Dasent (*JMN*, X, xii et passim).

It should be recognized, however, that Emerson's affirmation of Nordic culture, like his earlier attraction to the Arthurian matter, was hardly idiosyncratic. From the mid–1830s on, Emerson's participation in the various assumptions of nineteenth-century Medievalism, particularly with regard to race, reflected emphatically the attitudes of his generation. Vaguely imitating contemporary nationalistic movements in Europe, Americans were seeking their origins in the medieval past. In 1843, to cite one example, the American merchant and philanthropist George Perkins Marsh addressed the Philomathesian Society of Middlebury College on "The Goths in New England," arguing that "The Goths, the common ancestors of the inhabitants of North Western Europe, are the noblest branch of the Caucasian race. We are their children. It was the spirit of the Goth, that guided the May-Flower across the trackless ocean; the blood of the Goth, that flowed at Bunker Hill." The founders of New England, Marsh asserted confidently, "belonged to the class most deeply tinctured with the moral and intellectual traits of their Northern ancestry."[19]

The extent to which Emerson held similar views of Saxon supremacy is evident, as Philip L. Nicoloff has admirably demonstrated, in *English Traits* (1856). During his second visit to England in 1847, Emerson had been pleased by the robust vitality of the British, imagining in them "[t]he Berserkir in all his hairy might here still" (*JMN*, X, 184).[20] But he was more immediately concerned with his own countrymen, whose putative crudity might also be dignified by their vigorous origins. "The blood of the Berserkir runs red in our veins," Emerson declared in the final lecture of a series on "New England" (1843): "his restlessness and energy, his love of intoxication and abandonment to his object have found new game[s] to play, new enemies to conquer[,] in physical nature but may still be discerned." If Emerson prudently struck out "victims" to replace the word with "enemies" in this passage, his embrace of the primitive spirit is nevertheless wholehearted. He was much taken by the description of Germanic tribes in Tacitus, quoting it in the same series ("and they were blue eyed men[,] lovers of liberty, yielding more to authority than to command, and respecting the female sex") and citing the passage again in 1853: "The English have always read with fondness the chapters of Tacitus on the Germans, as if they found themselves in the picture of their ancestors. At still another remove, it has new interest on the American prairie."[21]

Reborn in America, the Goths were surging westward. All cultures, Emerson had come to believe, rose from primitive beginnings, achieved a period of perfect fruition—the refinement of the primitive energy, marked by the appearance of a great man—and then inevitably began to decay. In his generation, the British were dominant, but Emerson could make out the handwriting on the wall:

> Indeed it is easy to see that soon the balance of power/center of gravity which long ago began its travels and which now is still on the eastern shore will shortly hover midway over the Atlantic main and then as certainly fall within the American sphere so that the writers of the English tongue will write to the American and not to the island public and then will the great Yankee be born.[22]

As Nicoloff puts it, "All of America's rawness and youthful innocence, even her penchant for preposterous boasting, could thus be interpreted in her favor. America was young, Europe was old, and historical necessity would take care of the rest" (p. 236). Emerson apparently thought, as Nicoloff suggests (p. 131), that the Saxon race was in for a longer run that other nations had enjoyed, and a fragment from Emerson's journals verifies this: "And I think it specially characteristic of the Saxon Race that it is tough, manyheaded, and does not so readily admit of absorption, of being picked and vampyrized by a representative man as feebler races."[23] It would be unfair, however, to brand this aspect of Emerson's Medievalism as little more than Anglo-Saxon self-aggrandizement. In an age of largely unexamined racism, Emerson welcomed immigrants who in their turn might stir America from inertia:

> The world is as rich as it ever was, but it cannot live on old corn, or old men, or books, or in short on its memory, but must have new men, new instincts, new will, new insights and spontaneities every day. The first boat-load of Norse pirates took many generations to trim and comb and perfume into royal highnesses and most noble Knights of the Garter and cabinet counsellors; but every sparkle of ornament dates back to the Norse boat. And a new boat-load of ragamuffins is arriving every hour who are the sure successors to their pomp and fortune, and will stamp the twentieth century as these fatigue the nineteenth (*JMN*, XIII, 166).[24]

III

Strikingly blue-eyed himself and described in boyhood as "a Saxon blonde," Emerson took an innocent pleasure in imagining elemental savage forefathers.[25] Of greater importance, however, are the implications of these medieval interests for his developing theory of literature. On the whole, he displays a complacent acceptance of the contemporary equation between the art of the Middle Ages and a rude but forceful primitivism. A. O. Lovejoy, in the seminal essay on the Gothic revival he published in 1932, documents the eighteenth-century idea of "the Gothic" as an imitation of nature in all its wildness and irregularity: the vaulted arches of the Gothic cathedral were widely held, as Lovejoy points out, to have been inspired by the over-arching branches and awesome darks of the northern forests.[26] Emerson reiterates this belief on several occasions:

> The Gothic church plainly originated in a rude adaptation of forest trees, with their boughs on, to a festal or solemn edifice. . . . Nor, I think, can any lover of nature enter the old piles of Oxford and the English cathedrals, without feeling that the forest overpowered the mind of the builder, with its ferns, its spikes of flowers, its locust, its oak, its pine, its fir, its spruce.[27]

Medieval architecture, in other words, drew strength from its immediate source

in nature, and similar views on the primitive naturalism of medieval literature are stated explicitly in works Emerson is known to have read. The preface
to the Bohn edition of Ellis's *Specimens*, for instance, praises "our early writers"
for "the truth and vitality of their pictures, the ingenuous frankness of their
sentiment, the force and simplicity of their language, and the buoyancy and
joyfulness of their general character."[28] However unsophisticated—indeed,
perhaps through their very simplicity—the ballads and romances had the breath
of life. George Borrow, on rather the same principle, writes in the preface
to his *Romantic Ballads*,

> The old Danish poets were, for the most part, extremely rude in their
> versification. . . . But, however defective their poetry may be in harmo-
> ny of numbers, it describes, in vivid and barbaric language, scenes of
> barbaric grandeur, which in these days are never witnessed; and which,
> though the modern muse may imagine, she generally fails at attempt-
> ing to pourtray, from the violent desire to be smooth and tuneful, for-
> getting that smoothness and tunefulness are nearly synonymous with
> tameness and unmeaningness. (pp. vii–viii)

And Walter Scott, whose *Minstrelsy of the Scottish Border* Emerson borrowed
from the Boston Athenaeum in 1834, notes in his introduction to the 1830
edition that "early poets almost uniformly display a bold, rude, original cast
of genius and expression. They have walked at free-will, and with uncon-
strained steps, along the wilds of Parnassus, while their followers move with
constrained gestures and forced attitudes, in order to avoid placing their feet
where their predecessors have stepped before them."[29]

Emerson's absorption of these attitudes, from the period of his early lectures to the close of his career, is unmistakable. Consistently impervious to
signs of sophistication in medieval civilization, he firmly denies, for example, any allegorical level of meaning in medieval romance—"Nothing was farther from the minstrel's intentions than the discovery of a hidden sense" (*EL*,
I, 259)—and only belatedly admits the potential symbolism in Norse mythology (*JMN*, X, 131–32; see also *W*, VI, 320–21 and *W*, VIII, 64). What he
appreciated most was what he called the "metallic force" of primitive literature:

> It cost the early bard little talent to chant more impressively than the
> later, more cultivated poets. His advantage is that his words are things,
> each the lucky sound which describes the fact, and we listen to him
> as we do to the Indian or the hunter, or the miner, each of whom
> represents the facts as accurately as the cry of the wolf or the eagle

tells us of the forest or the air they inhabit. The original force, the direct smell of the earth or the sea, is in these ancient poems, the Sagas of the North, the Nibelungen Lied, the songs and ballads of the English and Scotch. (*W*, VIII, 57)

Like the Saxon invasions, medieval literature had functioned as a jarring but ultimately salutary intrusion on mannered over-refinement. Emerson notes in "The Age of Fable" that "[t]he Latin literature had become formal and merely imitative. Nothing vigorous or useful any longer issued out of it" (*EL*, I, 261–62). Similarly, he approved the earthy vitality of Chaucer, remarking that the downfall of Latin poetry forced a return to "the primitive and permanent sources from which the human mind draws excitement and delight" (*EL*, I, 273).

Again, as with his study of early English history, Emerson's approval of medieval poetry reverberates with implications for the American nation— also, according to its European detractors, a new, raw, and unformed civilization. James Macpherson, in his "Dissertation on the Poems of Ossian," had argued that the "irregular manner of life, and those manly pursuits, from which barbarity takes its name are highly favorable to a strength of mind unknown in polished times"; times of "regular government, and polished manners, are therefore to be wished for by the feeble and weak in mind," a view clearly shared by Emerson.[30] It was the older poetry, then, that might best inspire the American writer: not in slavish or inauthentic imitation, but in a similar presentation of objective experience, piercing rotten diction, fastening words once more to things (*CW*, I, 20), and bringing poetry "back to Nature,—to the marrying of Nature and mind, undoing the old divorce in which poetry had been famished and false, and Nature had been suspected and pagan" (*W*, VIII, 66). "Our poetry is an affectation," Emerson complained, "but read Chaucer, and the old lays in which Merlin and Arthur are celebrated, and you will find it as simple as the speech of children" (*JMN*, XI, 42). To Emerson, Merlin provided a model for "the orator or singer who can control all minds" (*JMN*, XIV, 288); and as Nelson F. Adkins proved a generation ago, a scattered knowledge of the Welsh bardic tradition inspired Emerson's own Merlin poems—poems now recognized as among his best. And if, as Hyatt H. Waggoner has more recently shown, the Merlin poems reveal a purposeful irregularity "echoing nature's own ways," Emerson may indeed have been attempting to recreate the natural irregularity attributed to Gothic style.[31] Hence, no doubt, Emerson's approval of the poetical activity of his friends William Ellery Channing and Caroline Sturgis: rude though it was, it was "the right poetry of hope, no French correctness but Hans Sachs and Chaucer rather" (*JMN*, VII, 372).

This same fidelity to nature, and not romantic medieval distance, was what Emerson rejoiced to find in Dante. Though his early attraction to the Florentine was by way of the *Vita Nuova*, which he called "the Bible of Love" (*JMN*, VIII, 430), Emerson did not see Dante as an ethereal, daydreaming lover. In 1849, Emerson in fact considered that if he were a "professor of Rhetoric" he would use Dante as his textbook.

> Come hither, youth, and learn how the brook that flows at the bottom of your garden, or the farmer who ploughs the adjacent field, — your father and mother, your debts and credits, and your web of habits are the very best basis of poetry, and the material which you must work up. Dante knew how to throw the weight of his body into each act. . . . [H]e knows "God damn," and can be rowdy if he please, and he does please. (*JMN*, XI, 133–34)

Dante's imagination, Emerson adds, is "the nearest to hands and feet that we have seen" (*W*, XII, 49; *JMN*, XI, 152). In light of Dante's immense erudition, Emerson's idea of the poet of the *Commedia* is decidedly simplistic. Again, however, he reflects his era: English critics who rediscovered Dante near the end of the eighteenth century and in the early years of the nineteenth spoke of him habitually as a rude, uncultivated artist whose appeal stemmed chiefly from his primitive medieval vigor. William Hayley, whose *Essay on Epic Poetry* (1782) included a translation of the first three cantos of *The Inferno*, was obliged to acknowledge Dante's lapses of taste:

> Thy failings sprang from thy disastrous Time;
> Thy stronger Beauties from a soul sublime,
> Whose vigour burst, like the volcano's flame,
> From central darkness to the sphere of fame.

And Henry Hallam, from whose history Emerson derived material for several early lectures, is similarly ambivalent toward Dante: "The most forced and unnatural turns, the most barbarous licenses of idiom, are found in this poet, whose power of expression is, at other times, so peculiarly happy." This roughness, however, Hallam acknowledges, is only to be expected, since Dante was "writing almost in the infancy of a language, which he contributed to create."[32]

Like the ballads and romances, Dante's poetry as Emerson was led to understand it belonged to one of the world's mornings. Like Chaucer,

Shakespeare, and Homer, other great originals, Dante was "a new and pro-
digious person" (*JMN*, VIII, 97), and his merit lay in forsaking books and
traditions (*JMN*, V, 105) to write of the world he knew. When Emerson invoked Dante in "The Poet" (1842?), it was thus as a model for the American
genius to come:

> Dante's praise is, that he dared to write his autobiography in colossal
> cipher, or into universality. We have yet had no genius in America,
> with tyrannous eyes, which knew the value of our incomparable materials,
> and saw, in the barbarism and materialism of the times, another car-
> nival of the same gods, whose picture he so much admires in Homer;
> then in the middle age; then in Calvinism. (*CW*, III, 21)

In the unpublished lecture "Anglo-American Notes," quoted earlier, Emerson identifies Dante as another representative man "who knots up into himself the genius or idea of his nation"—and Dante looms a forerunner to the
consummately American poet that Emerson envisioned. "That the Event and
the Person meet, we must believe, and that Dante is Italian because, that
moment he could most live as an Italian. At this moment he would be born
American" (*JMN*, XI, 399).

IV

For many of Emerson's English contemporaries, as Alice Chandler has
shown, Medievalism involved a rejection of the distasteful modern world; it
might take the form of nostalgia, in Carlyle and Ruskin, for the patriarchal
security of feudalism or, in Tennyson and the Pre-Raphaelites, of romantic
withdrawal into a chivalric and in some ways feminized dreamworld.[33]
Emerson's Medievalism, by contrast, was unremittingly democratic, a call
to action and an affirmation of the cultural promise of America. It would not
do to recreate the Middle Ages, as Walter Scott had attempted: this for a
time might "take the attention like truths and things," but "the design was
not natural and true" (*EL*, I, 376). Instead, the example of the medieval world
was in its very unselfconsciousness: the simplicity of romance, the elemental
Nordic force, Dante's authentic response to Nature.[34] We may protest that
Emerson's picture of the Middle Ages was a fragmented and distorted image; he was not a rigorous scholar, and it may be, as one of his friends observed, that he "sipped from books" instead of reading them.[35] But by the
end of his life, Emerson's Medievalism—stimulated by his early interest in

chivalry, compounded by his attraction to Nordic and Saxon civilization, and refined by his knowledge of the ballad tradition and of Dante—had become integrated with nearly every facet of his thought. Underlying even the major essays, Medievalism is inextricable from Emerson's most characteristic themes and paradoxically informs his unshakable faith in his own nation and the present moment. The medieval world showed him, as in Merlin's mirror, a model of the potential greatness of America and an iconography of the vigorous personal life: and though he found much of what he admired in other primitive literature—Homer, primarily, and the Vedas—his debt to the currents of Medievalism that extended to America in his century was demonstrably of greater importance. Indeed, Emerson reveals awareness of the Medieval Revival as a phenomenon in a late essay, "The Progress of Culture":

> In modern Europe, the Middle Ages were called the Dark Ages. Who dares to call them so now? They are seen to be the feet on which we walk, the eyes with which we see. It is one of our triumphs to have reinstated them. Their Dante and Alfred and Wickliffe and Abelard and Bacon; their Magna Charta, decimal numbers, mariner's compass, gunpowder, glass, paper and clocks; chemistry, algebra, astronomy; their Gothic architecture, their painting, are the delight and tuition of ours. (*W*, VIII, 214)

Part, as he recognized, of a movement that absorbed much of Europe and America, Emerson's Medievalism also ministered to his immediate circumstances. As his professedly low physical vitality may account for his attraction to the prowess of knight and Berserkir, he seems to have been similarly disturbed by contemporary myths of decline, the pervasive notion that New Englanders were lesser men than their fathers. Echoes of Emerson's medieval views occur from time to time when he invokes the Puritan forebears, and his description of Concord's old men recalls, though in subdued form, the robust Berserkers: "We shall never see Cyrus Hubbard or Ephraim Wheeler or Grass-and-oats or Oats-and-grass, old Barrett or Hosmer in the next generation. These old Saxons have the look of pine-trees and apple-trees, and might be the sons got between the two; conscientious laborers with a science born in them from out the sap-vessels of these savage sires."[36] From the local perspective, too, Medievalism may well have accommodated other, more inward needs. Octavius Brooks Frothingham, in his book *Transcendentalism in New England* (1876), observed that "The Unitarian was disquieted by mysticism, enthusiasm and rapture," being distinguished instead by "practical wisdom, sober judgment, and balanced thoughtfulness"; Emerson once remarked, in the same vein, "The Unitarian church forgets that men are poets" (*L*, III, 118), and Perry Miller goes so far as to define Transcendental literature as "a protest of the human spirit against emotional starvation." If these statements are valid, Emerson and others of his generation may have turned to the Middle Ages—as did many of their descendants—for the color and imaginative richness absent in good part from the liberal Protestantism of nineteenth-century New England.[37]

Closer to the core, however, Emerson's ultimate affirmation of the Middle Ages represents a personal, even existential triumph over the cosmic anxieties of his youth. Nearly all of Emerson's observations on medieval culture hark back in some way to his first essay, the long-forgotten "Thoughts on the Religion of the Middle Ages," which had opened with a disquieting thesis: "That there is a decline in nations, and a period of semi-barbarous repose following the decline, is a fact of awful interest, whose causes are not fully explained" (401). The young writer professed bafflement at this pattern, ending the essay rather lamely with promises of an eternal security in heaven (408). In a demonstration of the remarkable consistency of his thought, Emerson's very late lecture on chivalry (1871) both recapitulates earlier themes and puts forever to rest the doubts of a younger self:

> What we call Chivalry, was a strange mixture of hunger, barbarism, and violence, with aspirations, of religion and thought. . . . Here was misrule, war, ambition, but also intellect and conscience. But the laws of the universe are absolute. . . . The Divine Providence never sleeps. Out of this blind confusion, a better civilization has grown. The nations of Europe and America today are slowly sifting the poison and the bran,—slowly erecting new institutions far more humane than any which history has recorded.

Rightly understood, the Dark Ages had been the necessary "period of incubation for the new birth of Europe."[38] From an initial horror, Emerson's idea of the Middle Ages had become a benign acceptance of the rhythms of the universe, a conclusive recognition of the "harmonies of the system of human destinies," as he had expressed it many years earlier, "which the Deity is accomplishing from age to age" (*JMN*, III, 19).

In old age, then, Emerson looked back with gratitude on his early reading, acknowledging its lasting influence. "The ballad and romance work on the hearts of boys," he wrote, "who recite the rhymes to their hoops or their skates if alone, and these heroic songs or lines are remembered and determine many practical choices which they make later" (*W*, VIII, 67). Planning his lecture on chivalry in 1870, he discovered a similar pattern. "Every reading boy has marched to school and on his errands, to fragments of this music, and swinging a cut stick for his broadsword, brandishing it, and plunging it into the swarm of airy enemies whom his fancy arrayed on his right and left." The next line, from the journal of a man become a sage, may stand as a final comment on Emerson's Medievalism. "The life of the topic," he adds cannily, "would be the impatience in every man of his limits; the inextinguishableness of the imagination" (*JMN*, XVI, 198).

NOTES

1. References to Emerson's published writings, indicated parenthetically in the text, are from the following editions: *The Collected Works of Ralph Waldo Emerson*, introd. and notes by Robert Spiller et al., text established by Alfred R. Ferguson et al. (Cambridge, MA: Harvard University Press, 1971–), abbr. *CW*; *The Complete Works of Ralph Waldo Emerson*, Concord Edition ed. Edward Waldo Emerson (Boston: Houghton Mifflin, 1903–4), abbr. *W*; *The Early Lectures of Ralph Waldo Emerson*, ed. Stephen E. Whicher, Robert E. Spiller, and Wallace E. Williams (Cambridge, MA: Harvard University Press, 1959–72), abbr. *EL*; *The Poetry Notebooks of Ralph Waldo Emerson*, ed. Ralph H. Orth et. al. (Columbia, MO: University of Missouri Press, 1986), abbr. *PN*; *The Letters of Ralph Waldo Emerson*, ed. Ralph L. Rusk (New York: Columbia University Press, 1939), abbr. *L*; *The Journals and Miscellaneous Notebooks of Ralph Waldo Emerson*, ed. William Gilman et al. (Cambridge, MA: Harvard University Press, 1960–82), abbr. *JMN*. This edition of the Journals has been painstakingly edited, retaining all the orthographic idiosyncrasies of Emerson's manuscript; for the sake of a more readable text, however, I use "and" where Emerson has "&," obvious insertions are silently incorporated, and words struck out have similarly been deleted.

2. See Jeffrey Steinbrink, "The Past as 'Cheerful Apologue': Emerson on the Proper Uses of History," *ESQ* 27, 4th Quarter (1981): 207–21; Gustaaf Van Cromphout, "Emerson and the Dialectics of History," *PMLA* 91 (1976): 54–65; David G. Hoch, " 'History' as Art; 'Art' as History," *ESQ* 18, 4th Quarter (1972): 288–93; Jonathan Bishop, *Emerson on the Soul* (Cambridge, MA: Harvard University Press, 1964), 60–66.

3. On the self-culture movement in New England, see David Robinson, *Apostle of Culture: Emerson as Preacher and Lecturer* (Philadelphia: University of Pennsylvania Press, 1982), 7–29. Emerson's immersion in the texts of the medievalist movement is evident from Kenneth Walter Cameron's bibliographical study *Ralph Waldo Emerson's Reading* (Raleigh, NC: Thistle Press, 1941). Cameron's list of books Emerson withdrew from the library of Harvard and the Boston Athenaeum includes (in

the apparent order of Emerson's reading) Walter Scott, *Minstrelsy of the Scottish Border*, 4th ed. (Edinburgh, 1810); Thomas Warton, *The History of English Poetry* (London, 1824); Sharon Turner, *History of the Anglo-Saxons*, 2nd ed. (London, 1807); Dante, *A Vision of Hell*, trans. Cary (London, 1819); Henry Hallam, *View of the State of Europe during the Middle Ages* (Philadelphia, 1824); Thomas Percy, *Reliques of Ancient English Poetry*, 4th ed. (London, 1812); *Ancient Scottish Poems* (London, 1815); *Lays of the Minnesingers*, ed. Edgar Taylor (London, 1825); A. F. Ozanam, *Dante et la Philosophie Catholique* (Paris, 1839–45); Paul-Henri Mallet, *Northern Antiquities* (London, 1847); John Ruskin, *Stones of Venice* (London, 1851–53); Edward Davies, *The Mythology and Rites of the British Druids* (London, 1809); Thomas Fuller, *History of the Worthies of England* (London, 1811); John Mitchell Kemble, *The Saxons in England (until the Norman Conquest)* (London, 1849); William Camden, *Britain* (London, 1637); John Allen Giles, *History of the Ancient Britons* (London, 1847); Augustin Thierry, *History of the Conquest of England by the Normans* (London, 1841); J. A. Froude, *History of the Worthies of England*, new ed. (London, 1811); John Allen Giles, *The Life and Times of Alfred the Great* (Oxford, 1854); *The Mabinogion*, ed. Lady Charlotte E. Guest (London, 1849); Thomas Malory, *The Byrth, Lyfe, and Actes of King Arthur*, ed. Robert Southey (London, 1817); Snorri Sturluson, *The Heimskringla*, trans. Samuel Laing (London, 1844); *Njal's Saga*, trans. George Webster Dasent (Edinburgh, 1861); Alban Butler, *The Lives of the Fathers, Martyrs, and Other Principal Saints* (New York, 1846); Thomas Carlyle, *Specimens of German Romance* (Edinburgh, 1827); William Forbes Skene, *The Four Ancient Books of Wales* (Edinburgh, 1868); *La Chanson de Roland* (Paris, 1850); F. G. Bergmann, *The San Grëal: An Inquiry* (Edinburgh, 1870); Dante, *Opere* (Florence, 1830–41; Karl Witte, *Dante Forschungen* (Berlin, 1869). Walter Harding, *Emerson's Library* (Charlottesville: University Press of Virginia, 1967), lists some of these titles also, in addition to Jacob Abbott, *History of King Alfred of England* (1849); Boccaccio, *Vita di Dante Alighieri* (Milan, 1823); *Chanson de Roland* (London, 1880); *Chronicles of the Crusades* (London: Bohn, 1848); G. W. Dasent, *Story of Gisli the Outlaw* (Edinburgh, 1866); Claude Fauriel, *History of Provençal Poetry* (1860); John Gilchrist, *A Collection of Ancient and Modern Scottish Ballads, Tales and Songs* (1815); James Macpherson, *Ossian* (1857); Erwin Nasse, *On the Agricultural Community of the Middle Ages* (1871); Benjamin Thorpe, *Northern Mythology* (London: 1851–52); and various translations of Dante, including those of Parsons and J.A. Carlyle.

The journals make reference to George Ellis, *Specimens of Early English Metrical Romances* (London, 1848); Robert Jamieson, *Popular Ballads and Songs* (London, 1806); Joseph Ritson, *Ancient Songs and Ballads* (London, 1829); and D.W. Nash, *Taliesin, or the Bards and Druids of Britain* (London, 1858). In 1850 Emerson jotted in his journal a list of books for Caroline Sturgis Tappan which includes Ellis, Mallet, Bede, *The Heimskringla* and *Eddas*, *Six Old English Chronicles*, and Simon Ockley, *The History of the Saracens* (London, 1848), many of them in the

Bohn editions (*JMN*, XI, 224–25); finally, see Emerson's late essay "Books," where he comments on his own sources (*W*, VII, 205–6).

4. See Alice P. Kenney and Leslie J. Workman, "Ruins, Romance, and Reality: Medievalism in Anglo-American Imagination and Taste, 1750–1840," *Winterthur Portfolio* 10 (1975): 131–63; also *Studies in Medievalism* 1, no. 2 (Spring, 1979), issue on Medievalism in America.

5. "Chivalry" (1869), bMS Am 1280.211 (1). Unless otherwise noted, quotations from Emerson's sermons and unpublished lectures are taken from manuscripts in the Houghton Library and quoted by permission of the Houghton Library and the Ralph Waldo Emerson Memorial Association.

6. *Records of a Lifelong Friendship 1807–1882: Ralph Waldo Emerson and William Henry Furness*, ed. H[orace] H. F[urness] (Boston: Houghton Mifflin, 1910), 177–85.

7. Morison, *Three Centuries of Harvard 1636–1936* (Cambridge, MA: Harvard University Press, 1946), 201.

8. Ralph L. Rusk, *The Life of Ralph Waldo Emerson* (New York: Charles Scribner's Sons, 1949), 72; see also Beverly Taylor and Elisabeth Brewer, *The Return of King Arthur: British and American Arthurian Literature since 1900* [sic] (Cambridge: D. S. Brewer/Totowa, NJ: Barnes and Noble, 1983), 165–67. A context for Emerson's Arthurian interests may be found in James Douglas Merriman, *The Flower of Kings: A Study of the Arthurian Legend in England Between 1485 and 1835* (Lawrence: The University Press of Kansas, 1973), esp. 83–136.

9. "H. O. N." [Ralph Waldo Emerson], "Thoughts on the Religion of the Middle Ages," *The Christian Disciple* n.s. 4, no. 24 (Nov.–Dec. 1822, [actual date 1823]): 401–8. Emerson derived much of this essay from his reading of Froissart and from J. C. L. de Sismondi, *A History of the Italian Republics* (London, 1832[?]).

10. Sermon no. 8, "God to be loved not feared" (1827), bMS Am 1280.215. Emerson did not title his sermons; titles assigned follow the list in William B. Barton, *A Calendar to the Complete Edition of Emerson's Sermons* (Memphis: Bee Books, 1977).

11. Sermon No. 162 (1832), "The Lord's Supper," bMS Am 1280.215.

12. After a conversation with Margaret Fuller in 1843, Emerson wrote, "For me today, Woman is not a degraded person with duties forgotten, but a docile daughter of God with her face heavenward and endeavoring to hear the divine word and convey it to me" (*JMN*, VIII, 372). For a discussion of chivalry in America during a later period, see John Fraser, *America and the Patterns of Chivalry* (Cambridge: Cambridge University Press, 1982).

13. The following passage appeared in Emerson's sermon "The freedom of inquiry is the most precious right we possess" (No. 175, n.d.): "Patriots turn pale when some paper priviledge [sic] some national punctilio is withheld or disputed to their country and Christians should not sit still and ignorant when the honour of their Order no transient institution of one age or one realm but the Chivalry of the Universe is trampled in the dust" (bMS Am 1280.215). Moncure Conway, in his reverential

memoir *Emerson at Home and Abroad* (Boston: James R. Osgood, 1882), calls Emerson "our virginal Sir Galahad in America" who "refused any longer to touch the chalice of his Boston Church" (175). In spite of Conway's rather careless inversion of the Grail story, this remark and the imagery infusing the chapter (entitled "Sangreal") from which it is taken testify to the presence of Arthurian paraphernalia in nineteenth-century New England. Emerson, perhaps in anticipation of Conway's medieval compliment, thought Conway resembled Dante. See Gay Wilson Allen, *Waldo Emerson: A Biography* (New York: Viking, 1981), 573.

14. Packer, *Emerson's Fall: A New Interpretation of the Major Essays* (New York: Continuum, 1982), 152. See also Allen, 62 and Richard Lebeaux, "Emerson's Young Adulthood: From Patienthood to Patiencehood," *ESQ* 25, 4th Quarter (1979): 203–10.

15. "Themes showed by Mr. Gould to the Latin School Committee" (1816), bMS Am 1280.214 (200).

16. Turner's description of the Berserkir is as follows: "These men, when a conflict impended, or a great undertaking was to be commenced, abandoned all rationality upon system; they studied to resemble wolves or maddening dogs; they bit their shields; they howled like tremendous beasts; they threw off covering; they excited themselves to a strength which has been compared to that of bears, and then rushed to every crime and horror which the most frantic enthusiasm could perpetrate. This fury was an artifice of battle like the Indian war-whoop. Its object was to intimidate the enemy. It is attested that the unnatural excitation was, as might be expected, always followed by a complete debility. It was originally practised by Odin. They who used it, often joined companies. The furor Berserkicus, as mind and morals improved, was at length felt to be horrible. It changed from a distinction to a reproach, and was prohibited by penal laws. The name at last became execrable." I quote from the 4th ed. (London, 1823), I: 442–43. See also *JMN*, XI, 69, and Mallet's description in *Northern Antiquities*, trans. Thomas Percy (1770; repr. New York: Garland, 1979), 71.

17. See also *The Correspondence of Emerson and Carlyle*, ed. Joseph Slater (New York: Columbia University Press, 1964), 240. Carlyle, interestingly enough, called Cromwell a "Baresark" (280), suggesting a provocative parallel with the forcefulness both he and Emerson attributed to Calvinism.

18. Edward Waldo Emerson, *Emerson in Concord: A Memoir* (Boston: Houghton Mifflin, 1889), 172–73; see also *W*, VII, 437n; *JMN*, VII, 481; IX, 14. For the ballad itself, see Borrow, *Romantic Ballads* (London: Wightman and Cramp, 1826), 61–81.

19. Marsh, "The Goths in New-England" (Philomathesian Society of Middlebury College, 1843), pp. 14, 19; Emerson addressed the same society in 1845. I am indebted to Professor Buford Jones of Duke University for drawing this document to my attention.

20. Nicoloff, *Emerson on Race and History: An Examination of English Traits* (New York: Columbia University Press, 1961).

21. "New England V: Results," bMS Am 1280.199 (5); "New England I: Origin," bMS Am 1280.199 (1); "Anglo-American Notes," bMS Am 1280.202 (2).

22. "New England IV: Literature," bMS Am 1280.199 (4).

23. See David M. Stevens, "Emerson on the Saxon Race: A Manuscript Fragment," *ESQ* 47, 2nd Quarter (1967): 103–5; see also *JMN*, XIII, 120.

24. Emerson's sanguine comments on the Irish immigrants in New England may be found in "New England II: Traits," bMS Am 1280.199 (2).

25. The description comes from Samuel Kirkland Lothrop, to whom Emerson was tutor at Harvard. See Rusk, 66; also John McAleer, *Ralph Waldo Emerson: Days of Encounter* (Boston: Little, Brown, 1984), 53.

26. Lovejoy, "The First Gothic Revival and the Return to Nature," *Modern Language Notes* 47, no. 7 (Nov. 1932): 419–46, esp. 435–38.

27. "Thoughts on Art" (written for the *Dial* in 1841), in Ralph Waldo Emerson, *Uncollected Writings* (New York: Lamb, 1912), 48. Emerson used similar passages elsewhere (*EL*, II, 52; *CW*, II, 11–12; *JMN*, V, 109, 403).

28. J. C. Halliwell, Preface to *Specimens of Early English Metrical Romances* by George Ellis (London: Henry G. Bohn, 1848), iii.

29. Scott, "Introductory Remarks on Popular Poetry," in *The Minstrelsy of the Scottish Border* (Edinburgh: Robert Cadell, 1850), I: 7.

30. "Dissertation concerning the Poems of Ossian," in *The Poems of Ossian*, trans. James Macpherson (New York: Edward Kearney, n.d.), 58.

31. Adkins, "Emerson and the Bardic Tradition," *PMLA* 63 (1948): 662–77; Waggoner, *Emerson as Poet* (Princeton: Princeton University Press, 1974), 138. For discussions of the Merlin poems ("Merlin I," "Merlin II," "Merlin's Song," and "The Harp"), see Carl Dennis, "Emerson's Poetics of Inspiration," in *Characteristics of Emerson Transcendental Poet*, ed. Carl Ferdinand Strauch (Hartford: Transcendental Books, 1975), 22–28; John Q. Anderson, *The Liberating Gods: Emerson on Poets and Poetry* (Coral Gables: University of Miami, 1971), 20–39; R. A. Yoder, *Emerson and the Orphic Poet in America* (Berkeley: University of California Press, 1978),144–53; David Porter, *Emerson and Literary Change* (Cambridge, MA: Harvard University Press, 1978), 88–90; Carl F. Strauch, "The Mind's Voice: Emerson's Poetic Styles," *ESQ* 60, 1st Quarter (1970): 43–59.

32. Hayley, *An Essay on Epic Poetry (1782): A Facsimile Reproduction*, ed. Sister M. Celeste Williamson, S.S.J. (Gainesville, FL: Scholars' Facsimiles and Reprints, 1968), 120; Hallam, *View of the State of Europe during the Middle Ages* (Philadelphia, 1824), II, 369. On Emerson's interest in Dante, see Angelina La Piana, *Dante's American Pilgrimage: A Historical Survey of Dante Studies in the United States 1800–1944* (New Haven: Yale University Press, 1948), 89–93; J. Chesley Mathews, Introd. to *Dante's Vita Nuova*, trans. Ralph Waldo Emerson (Chapel Hill: University of North Carolina Press, 1960), v–xiii; Rusk, Introd., *L*, I, xlvii–xlviii. Steve Ellis, in *Dante and English Poetry: Shelley to T.S. Eliot* (Cambridge: Cambridge Universi-

ty Press, 1983), offers a useful perspective from which to interpret nineteenth-century American images of Dante.

33. Chandler, *A Dream of Order: The Medieval Ideal in Nineteenth Century English Literature* (Lincoln: University of Nebraska Press, 1970). For other discussions of English Medievalism, see Mark Girouard, *The Return to Camelot: Chivalry and the English Gentleman* (New Haven: Yale University Press, 1981); Charles Dellheim, *The Face of the Past: The Preservation of the Medieval Inheritance in Victorian England* (Cambridge: Cambridge University Press, 1982); Kevin L. Morris, *The Image of the Middle Ages in Romantic and Victorian Literature* (London: Croom, Helm, 1984); *Studies in Medievalism*, 1, No. 1 (Spring 1979), issue on Medievalism in England; *Browning Institute Studies*, 8 (1980), issue on Victorian medievalism.

34. Emerson was able to recognize, however, "How important an educator has Scott been!" (*JMN*, XVI, 114), and on the occasion of Scott's Centennial in 1871 Emerson called him "a benefactor of all civil nations, and through the light he has shed by his research as well as his imagination, on the history of the British races" (bMS Am 1280.213 [9]).

35. Charles J. Woodbury, *Talks with Ralph Waldo Emerson* (New York: Baker and Taylor, 1890), 147.

36. *Emerson in Concord*, 145. For similar intimations of decline, see *Autobiography and Correspondence, etc. of Lyman Beecher, D.D.*, ed. Charles Beecher (New York: Harper and Brothers, 1871), 18; also Michael Davitt Bell, *Hawthorne and the Historical Romance of New England* (Princeton: Princeton University Press, 1971), 20–27.

37. Frothingham, *Transcendentalism in New England: A History* (1876; repr. Philadelphia: University of Pennsylvania Press, 1959), 11; Miller, Introd., *The Transcendentalists: An Anthology*, ed. Perry Miller (Cambridge, MA: Harvard University Press, 1950), 8. T. J. Jackson Lears, in *No Place of Grace: Antimodernism and the Transformation of American Culture 1880–1920* (New York: Pantheon Books, 1981), provides a comprehensive and fascinating study of American Medievalism in the period immediately following Emerson's death.

38. "Chivalry" (1871), bMS Am 1280.211 (2).

King Arthur and Camelot, U.S.A. in the Twentieth Century

Valerie M. Lagorio

I<small>N HIS ESSAY ON AMERICAN MEDIEVALISM, HERWIG WOLFRAM STATES:</small>

> ... "Medieval Studies in America" as a field is in a position to inspire and integrate the popular and amateur interest in our subject. What might sometimes appear to a European as slightly comical is nevertheless an expression of astonishing vitality. And what many a dry pedant might dismiss as low-brow is in reality a kind of learning experience on a level different from that to which most Europeans are accustomed.[1]

In this same vein, he continues:

> The faculty engaged in medieval studies must never let their scholarship slide, and, on the other hand, they must not isolate themselves in ivory towers. They have to enlist the support of those who are amateurs, indeed to excite this interest. This is why the most disparate forms of activity vis-à-vis the Middle Ages belong to the phenomenon that Ernst Robert Curtius called "American Medievalism."[2]

One aspect of this phenomenon is the prominent place accorded to Arthur and Camelot in academia and popular culture in the United States. And, of course, Americans still recall the hopefulness and promise of the Kennedy era, with all of its Camelot associations. Many reasons have been given for this 20th-century Arthurian revival, such as the timelessness and, conversely, contemporaneity of the Arthurian myth, its meaningful adaptability to the age in which it appears, in the true spirit of Arthur, *Rex Quondam et Futurus*, and its setting forth of the full range of personal relationships, emotions, conflicts, aspirations, and other universals of the human condition. To the foregoing I would add one other dimension integral to the legend and its durability, and that is its essential apocalyptic thrust. Therefore, this study will deal with the academic Arthur, the popular Arthur, and the apocalyptic Arthur, particularly as he is depicted in twentieth-century literature.

The astonishing increase in Arthurian scholarship—and here I include not only the Camelot nexus, but also the Grail and Tristan legends—was either the cause or the effect of the foundation of the International Arthurian Society. This organization meets triennially, alternating between France and England, and publishes the *Bibliographical Bulletin* of the IAS, which is primarily medieval in its orientation. Not surprisingly, the largest and most active IAS group is the North American Branch, which benefits from a very vital newsletter, *Quondam et Futurus*, serving to link and inform NAB members and other Arthurians about meetings, research in progress, new books, and other current events. Moreover, there are two allied organizations, the International Courtly Literature Society, and the Tristan Society, both with their own journals. In addition to involvement in such professional bodies as the Medieval Academy of America, the Modern Language Association, and a number of regional conferences, these Arthurian entities participate actively in the annual International Congress on Medieval Studies at Western Michigan University. For example, at the May 1984 meeting, 33 Arthurian papers were presented, covering not only the medieval/modern spectrum, but extending to pedagogical presentations by TEAMS [Teaching Medieval Studies], then the Medieval Academy CARA [Centers and Regional Associations] Sub-Committee on Teaching Medieval Subjects. The University of Alabama in Birmingham has for the past two years sponsored a Conference on Arthurian Studies, and a brief overview of their 1984 program indicates the wide-ranging opportunities for research on Arthur. Complementing Geoffrey Ashe's plenary address, "The Convergence of Arthur Studies," sessions concerned "Malory and the *Morte Darthur*," "Place, People, and Problems in the Arthurian World," "Gawain and the Green Knight," "King Arthur and the Victorian Revival," "Geoffrey of Monmouth, Arthur's Knights and the 'Ideal,' " "The Grail in Modern Literature," "King Arthur's Women," and, reflecting the growing emphasis on pedagogy, "The Arthurian Legend in the Classroom."

There was also a concluding panel session on "Publishing Opportunities for Arthurian Studies," at which Mildred Day, editor of *Quondam et Futurus*, Geoffrey Ashe, James J. Wilhelm (Garland Library of Medieval Literature), Lewis Sumberg (editor of *Tristania*), and Freya Reeves Lambides (publisher of *Avalon to Camelot*), among others, participated. One can easily see from this list the typical and congenial mix of scholarly and popular Arthuriana noted and encouraged by Wolfram. With regard to publishing, scholarly journals are most hospitable to Arthur: in 1977 *Philological Quarterly* 56 published the proceedings of a Forum held at the Midwest Modern Language Association, entitled "Arthur of Britain and America: Camelot Revisited," thereby setting a precedent for special Arthurian issues, most recently in *Studies in Medievalism* and *Interpretations*. I am delighted to report that the latter publication, edited by Henry Hall Peyton at Memphis State University, has now become *Arthurian Interpretations*, a journal devoted entirely to Arthurian ideas, analyses, and criticisms.

Arthurian scholarly productivity in the past 25 years has resulted in book-length studies, articles, dissertations, and research tools, such as Charles and Ruth Moorman's *An Arthurian Dictionary* and the surveys of Nathan Starr (*King Arthur Today* [1954]), James Merriman (*The Flower of Kings* [1973]), Beverly Taylor and Elisabeth Brewer (*The Return of King Arthur: British and American Literature Since 1900* [1983]), and Raymond Thompson (*The Return From Avalon. A Study of the Arthurian Legend in Modern Fiction* [1985]), which, with a number of recent annotated bibliographies, chart the *de casibus* movement of Arthurian works from the fall after Malory until his resurrection in the Victorian Age and the twentieth century. Additionally, *The Arthurian Encyclopedia*, edited by Norris Lacy and written largely by North American scholars, is now in print. Complementing the foregoing are a number of new critical editions, among them Valerie Krishna's *Alliterative Morte Arthur* (1976), James Carley's edition of John of Glastonbury's *Cronica*, Mildred Day's *De Ortu Walwanii* (1985), Roger Dahood's *The Avowing of Arthur* (1984), David Lawton's *Joseph of Arimathea* (1983), James Spisak's *Caxton's Malory* (1983), and Carolina Eckhardt's *Fifteenth-Century English Commentary on the Prophetia Merlini of Geoffrey of Monmouth* (1982).

One of the landmarks for Arthurian scholarship is Roger Sherman Loomis's seminal *Arthurian Literature in the Middle Ages* (1959), which is devoted almost exclusively to medieval works, and which still remains the basic handbook of the discipline. Since ALMA's advent, neo-Arthurian scholarship has been on the rise, with a special focus on late nineteenth- and twentieth-century works, a long overdue development. This development has been encouraged by such publications as Leslie Workman's *Studies in Medievalism*, as well as by the desire of scholars to move from the well-tilled fields of Chrétien, Gottfried, Thomas, Wolfram, and Malory, and to recognize Arthur's ongoing literary domain. I am currently working on an anthology of critical essays covering Arthurian literature *through* the ages, which will concentrate on new avenues of research, medieval and modern, and incorporate intertextuality, semiotics, the Jewish, Italian, and Norse Arthurs, Christian mysticism and the Grail, the visual arts, Arthurian children's literature, popular culture, and modern fiction.

Arthur is also gaining in strength in the classroom, as can be seen from the TEAMS activities, and what I consider one of the most exciting and innovative academic programs, viz. the NEH Summer Institutes for Teacher and Curriculum Development in the Teaching of Medieval Civilization. These institutes feature Arthurian offerings, often providing a compilation of curriculum projects at nominal cost. There are, of course, the NEH Summer Seminars for College and Secondary Teachers. All of these special programs fill a definite need, given the popularity of Arthurian studies at all educational levels. Those of us who teach at colleges and universities know from happy experience that Arthur, the Round Table, and Camelot will pack a classroom, again manifesting the timeless appeal of the corpus, and permitting, in fact, demanding creative interdisciplinary and team-taught approaches. We are fortunate to have some excellent new teaching texts: *The Romance of Arthur* (1984), edited by James J. Wilhelm and Laila Gross, a survey of primary works; *The Legend of Arthur in the Middle Ages* (1983), edited by P. B. Grout, R. A. Lodge, C. E. Pickford, and E. K. C. Varty; *The Arthurian Legends: An Illustrated Anthology* (1979), by Richard Barber; and, complementing Vinaver's *Works*, the recent modernized editions of Malory by Michael Senior (*Tales of King Arthur* [1981]), Robert Lumiansky (*Le Morte Darthur* [1982]), the latter specifically directed toward non- specialized readers, and Nigel Bryant's translations of *The High Book of the Grail—Perlesvaus* and *Perceval: The Story of the Grail* (1978).

Nor is Arthur's modern realm limited to academia, as Norris Lacy, the IAS president, attests. In a recent article, "The Appeal of Arthur," he tells of receiving a continuing stream of inquiries from teachers of high school, junior high, and elementary school, asking about the availability of teaching materials, reading lists, and audio-visual materials for implementing courses on Arthur.[3] Recently, under the aegis of NEH and the Rockefeller Foundation, and directed by Dr. Claire Gaudiani (University of Pennsylvania), a new project, entitled "Strengthening the Humanities Through Foreign Language and Literature Studies" has been instituted to promote "Academic Alliances: School/College Faculty Collaboratives," whereby teachers of the same discipline at all educational levels and regardless of the age of their students, meet to improve the quality of their intellectual and professional lives, and to enhance educational programs. (Last year I formulated and implemented an interdisciplinary Arthurian venture for gifted junior high students in the Cedar Rapids area, and I encourage other academicians to join me in this outreach effort.) In this connection, *Avalon to Camelot*, the new Arthurian-centered journal, has instituted a regular column designed to encourage and aid in the teaching of the Arthurian corpus throughout the educational spectrum. I hope that the foregoing gives some indication of Arthur's reign in academia.

Turning to the popular Arthur, one sees that the vitality and creative force of the legend is manifest in the rich variety of literary, artistic, cinematic, musical, and quasi-historical works, as well as in such ephemera as comic strips and cartoons. To quote Freya Reeves Lambides,

> Each facet must be acknowledged and understood if one is to be concerned with the whole of the Arthurian tradition. Scholarly investigation provides new insight and popular interest promotes creative interpretations.[4]

Just who is the popular audience for Arthur? They come from all walks of life, and, more often than not, participate in a "confession syndrome," in that they are compelled to tell you how they came to know Arthur, and what he means to them. This was certainly the case when I presented three lectures on Arthur at the University of Iowa Hospitals, sponsored by the Department of Continuing Medical Education with the purpose of bringing the humanities and sciences together. When I asked the audience about their interest in Arthur, I learned that several had read Malory, T. H. White's *Once and Future King*, the Merlin trilogy of Mary Stewart, and similar fiction. Others had seen Lerner and Loewe's *Camelot*, *Monty Python and the Holy Grail*, and *Excalibur*. Still others cited Prince Valiant in the comics. At the end of the lectures, I asked them to analyze the appeal of Arthur, and found that, in addition to the elements of high adventure, magic, and romance, the audience responded to the ideals of loyalty, bravery, nobility, and justice invested in Arthur and his Round Table, the Golden Age of Camelot, and the tragedy of that dying world framing the destructive love affair between Lancelot and Guinevere, which, along with Modred's treachery, caused the end of Arthur's kingdom. Another factor was the mythic promise of Arthur, the once and future king, who will return again in mankind's hour of need.

Furthermore, there is a vocal and often *outré* segment of "individualists" who know the location or true nature of the Holy Grail, the zodiacal and earth current mysteries of Glastonbury, the secrets of Stonehenge, the actual site of Camelot, or occult and pagan antecedents of the Grail legend, and are anxious to share their arcane knowledge. These enthusiasts have often been dismissed as a "lunatic fringe," but they are very much a part of the twentieth-century Arthurian scene and should be given their just due. As an example, in 1976 Dr. C. Scott Littleton, a cultural anthropologist at Occidental College in Los Angeles, posited that Arthur and his knights were early descendants of a displaced military band of proto-Russians known as the Samaritans, who were commanded by one Lucius Artorius Castus of Roman Britain, giving impetus to the legend of the Narts of the Round Table. In 1983 one Derek Mahoney allegedly found the lead cross buried with Arthur at Glastonbury and was jailed in London when he refused to give it up. Here I would insert *Holy Blood, Holy Grail* (1982), a highly speculative accounting of Christ's marriage to Mary Magdalene, and the establishment of a line of Davidian descendants through the centuries who served and continue to serve in the esoteric Knights' Templar order of the Priory of Zion. The result has been attacks of high dudgeon on the part of European and British aristocrats, whom the book has identified as members of the bloodline (*Sangraal*) of Jesus, and cries of delight from booksellers in England and America, where it has been a best seller. On a somewhat more credible level, Debrett's Peerage is now counting Arthur among the sovereigns who actually reigned in Britain, and has commissioned Geoffrey Ashe to undertake this volume on Arthurian nobility, which undoubtedly will give pride of place to Prince William Arthur.

Arthur's twentieth-century *rex redividus* act has resulted in a number of societies, such as the Dragon Society, for people wanting to know more about Arthur, as well as the cultures of Britain in the Dark Ages, and the Pendragon Society, promoting Arthurian history, archaeology, mythology, and a number of Glastonbury-related esoteric topics. Here in the United States, we have the Society for Creative Anachronism, an enthusiastic group of amateurs throughout the country who strive for historical accuracy in their costumes, armor, weapons, and recipes, and, in the interests of enlivening the medieval tradition, engage in such activities as individual combat, jousts and tourneys, dances, fairs, crafts, musical performances, and banquets.

In Fall, 1983, *Avalon to Camelot*, as noted above, a Quarterly on Matters Arthurian, was launched by Freya Reeves Lambides and Debra Mancoff, with the express goals of traversing the Arthurian tradition, its evolution in history, art, archaeology, and fiction, and of presenting the world of Arthurian studies to a wider public. From its inception it has enjoyed an enthusiastic response from town and gown. It is informative and seriously committed to investigating and promulgating all dimensions of the Arthurian/Grail legend, so as to bridge the gap between ivory tower scholarship and popular appeal, as Wolfram urges, and it is achieving its purpose of encouraging an interchange between these two seeming polarities.

Another fairly recent development is the active pursuit of the historical Arthur of fifth- and sixth-century Britain, as first postulated by E. K. Chambers (*Arthur of Britain* [1927]), Kenneth H. Jackson, and others. In archaeology Leslie Alcock, author of *Arthur's Britain* (1971) and investigator of the South Cadbury/Camelot site, C. A. Ralegh Radford, who excavated at Glastonbury and Tintagel, and Richard Barber, in his *Figure of Arthur* (1972) have focussed attention on the possibility of a real King Arthur. Perhaps the greatest impetus comes from learned popularizers, such as John Robert Morris and his *Age of the British Isles, 350 to 650* (1973) and Geoffrey Ashe, whose numerous works, the latest being *The Discovery of King Arthur* (1984), reach a wide audience in America and abroad. This movement has resulted in a Dark Age Arthur, who is the protagonist in the majority of recent works of fiction, as I shall discuss below. Another ancillary effect, welcomed by travel agents, is the brisk business in tours of Arthurian Britain, where American tourists, as well as students taking the tour for credit, stream to Glastonbury Abbey, St. Michael's Tor, Chalice Well, Cadbury/Camelot, Tintagel, Stonehenge, Drustan's Stone, Caerleon, and Arthur's Seat near Edinburgh. Not to be outdone, Brittany/Armorica offers such attractions as the Magic Fountain of Barenton, Morgan's Pool, and the Broceliande Festival, which features a *son et lumière* presentation of a play about Lancelot du Lac. Indeed, the road to Camelot has many travelers and turnings.

The figure of Arthur in America is very visible in the novel, drama, poetry, musical, film, radio, television, cartoons, and comics, an unprecedented media sweep reaching untold numbers of readers, listeners, and viewers. Nor can one overlook the enormous popularity of the Dungeons and Dragons game, which has challenged Monopoly and Trivial Pursuit as a leading national pastime.

Most recently, Michael Jackson's highly heralded Victory Tour opened with "one of the gaudiest, most grandiose spectacles in the history of pop music," a reenactment of *The Sword in the Stone* featuring large Muppet-like monsters, a magically glowing sword, and Michael as a visored knight in shining armor—"King Arthur meets Luke Skywalker," amid lasers, strobe lights, smoke bombs, fireworks, and an over-voice crying "Behold your kingdom!"[5] Camelot may never be the same again. This was not Arthur's first sortie into the world of rock, for in 1975 A & M Records of Beverly Hills, California, produced an album by Rick Wakeman, entitled *The Myths and Legends of King Arthur and the Knights of the Round Table*, which contained the following songs: "Arthur," "Lady of the Lake," "Guinevere," "Sir Lancelot and the Black Knight," "Merlin the Magician," "Sir Galahad," and "The Last Battle," with its haunting refrain, "Gone are the days of the knights."

In the world of film, there have been 14 movies on Arthur since 1945, ranging from the third remake of *A Connecticut Yankee in King Arthur's Court* (1949), in which Bing Crosby joined the Round Table; *Prince Valiant* (1954), inspired by the comic strip; the musical film *Camelot* (1967), which broadcast the Arthurian message of T. H. White and Lerner and Loewe's stage play; and John Boorman's surrealistic *Excalibur* (1981), to 1983–84 science fiction spinoffs like *The Dark Crystal, Krull*, and the amazing *Knightriders*, which imposes Camelot's chivalric royalty and code on jousting motorcycle gangs, to the patent absurdity of *Monty Python and the Holy Grail* (1974). In the near future, the silver screen will spotlight Mary Stewart's Merlin series and Marion Zimmer Bradley's *Mists of Avalon*. An Arthurian structure has been imputed to the *Star Wars* trilogy, in that Arthur and Luke Skywalker are ignorant of their real parentage, but pursue their heroic destiny; both have a wise mentor, thereby equating Merlin with Obi-Wan Kenobi and the 900-year-old Jedi Master Yoda; Modred and Darth Vader are *Doppelgängers*; and the Force is a galactic chivalric power for good, with strong overtones of the Grail. The influence of Jesse Weston's theories on the Grail quest and wasteland has been ascribed to Francis Ford Coppola's *Apocalypse Now* and John Boorman's *Excalibur*, while *The Natural* (1984), based on Malamud's novel, has been hailed as a Parsifal/Grail allegory. In a lighter vein, Disney's imaginative hand is present in *The Sword in the Stone* (1963) and *The Spaceman and King Arthur* (1979), both clarion calls to juvenile audiences. In 1982 television produced *Mr. Merlin*, an engaging albeit shortlived series featuring a twentieth-century "with it" Merlin *redivivus* who ran a garage, and, with his sorcerer's apprentice Zac, brought a touch of Camelot magic to the small screen. CBS has filmed a made-for-TV saga entitled *Arthur the King*, with Malcolm McDowell as the noble Arthur and Candice Bergen as Morgan le Fay, in her own words, "a New Wave witch without warts"; while BBC has just presented a critically acclaimed version of the *Morte Darthur*, narrated by the knight/prisoner/author Sir Thomas Malory, with all of the action conveyed in pantomime amid visually arresting sets. Both should attain high Nielson ratings, while gladdening the hearts of Arthurian viewers.

Other popular spheres of Arthurian influence in America are comics and comic books. The best known and most important vehicle is Harold R. Foster's *Prince Valiant, In the Days of King Arthur*, which first appeared in February, 1937, and continues today, although Foster died in 1982. In one sense, its inclusion in the Arthurian canon parallels that of many medieval and modern works, where, if the hero is going to or coming from Arthur's court, or happens to meet one of his knights *en passant*, the work is labeled Arthurian. Prince Valiant, however, has a stronger claim in that Valiant is first a squire for the gregarious, brave Sir Gawaine, and then a knight of the Round Table, and his numerous ongoing adventures are punctuated with frequent visits to Camelot. The illustrations are nonpareil, the story line and spirit Maloryan, and justly Prince Valiant has dominated the comic strip field since its inception. Foster's Arthurian world also informs many of the comic book versions of Arthur, such as *The Shining Knight* and *Parsifal*. Two of the more extraordinary series which center around time-travel fantasies on the *Artus redivivus* theme are: *Mage*, in which one Kevin Matchstick, the latest manifestation of an Eternal Hero who once was King Arthur, and Mirth, a reincarnated Merlin, battle forces of darkness and prevail, but just; and *Camelot 3000*, written by Michael W. Barr and illustrated by Brian Bolland. This series is subcaptioned "Continuing Legends Chronicled by Sir Thomas Malory," and each issue contains an appendix, giving the medieval backgrounds of, as well as the Arthurian *raison d' être* for, this fantasy venture of Arthur and his followers against alien invaders of the earth. Not only are Arthur, Excalibur, and Merlin at hand, but also Guinevere, commander of U.S. defense forces, her secret lover Lancelot, cast as a jet-set leader, Percival, Galahad as a samurai, Gawain, and, most surprisingly, Tristan as a beautiful woman, owing to some mistake in the time warp. While Arthur and Merlin look and speak like their medieval counterparts, *Camelot 3000* is a far remove from Foster's Arthurian vista, with Morgan Le Fay a fitting amalgam of Sheena the queen of the jungle, and the Dragon Lady, and visual sound effects of "zap, kaboom, pow" reverberating throughout Camelot. Not to be outdone, the Marvel Comics Group, featuring Iron Man and Dr. Doom, has invaded Arthur's kingdom of Logres, with the aforementioned supersonic heroes becoming enmeshed with Arthur and his Round Table knights, and entangled, inevitably, with Morgan Le Fay. Yet the Arthurian message of the triumph of right over might, and hope for mankind invested in the fulfilled promise of Arthur's return in these works make a significant contribution to Arthurian popular culture.

Since 1900 there have been over 400 British and American works on the

Arthurian Grail legend, including the Tristan saga. Out of this total, 84 were written for children, among them the well known works of Howard Pyle and Jane Curry, indicating that Arthurian children's literature is an important genre that merits scholarly attention. Of the 115 works since 1950, only nine concern Tristan and Isolt, which is a reversal of the ratio in the early twentieth century in America. There is a similar diminution of Arthurian drama.

As it is impossible to assess all of this corpus, I am limiting remarks to selected British and American works which have been influential or popular in the United States. Admittedly, all too many of the modern works have characters courtesy of Malory, plots out of Harlequin romances, and close links with the wizard-and-warriors, sword-and-sorcery syndrome, often with a neo-Gothic, occult overlay. Moreover, their treatment of love provokes a wistful recall of Sir Thomas Malory's statement on unstable love:

> But the olde love was nat so. For men and women coude love togydirs seven yerys, and no lycoures lustis was betwyxte them, and than was love trouth and faythefulness. And so in lyke wyse was used such love in kynge Arthurs dayes.[6]

Such *opera*, however, pay tribute to Arthur's indomitable ability to survive, and to retain the "et futurus" in his epithet. Lest I appear to be Pen-draconian, a number of these works have artistic merit, and the entire output proclaims Arthur's prominence in modern America.

There are several general tendencies in twentieth-century Arthurian literature, which are especially evident in works written since World War II:

1) Striving for historical realism, authors depict Arthur as a sixth-century British *dux bellorum* or king in post-Roman Britain, fighting the Saxons and other foreign invaders. As a corollary, there is a pragmatic rejection or rationalization of magical and supernatural wonders, including the Grail. This results either in naturalistic tales, like John Gloag's *Artorius Rex* (1977), Peter Vansittart's *Lancelot* (1978), and David Drake's *The Dragon Lord* (1979), or in the idealized presentation of Arthur which marks Rosemary Sutcliff's *Sword at Sunset* (1963), Mary Stewart's *Merlin* trilogy (1970–79), Victor Canning's *The Crimson Chalice* (1976–78), Catherine Christian's *The Pendragon* (1979), and Gil Kane and John Jakes's *Excalibur* (1980).

2) An intensification of the psychological depth and moral problems of the characters, caught up in a dying world, again in the interest of 20th-century realism. Edwin Arlington Robinson's *Merlin* (1917) and *Lancelot* (1920), along with Parke Godwin's *Firelord* (1980), Arthur's deathbed retrospective autobiography, best exemplify this treatment.

3) A de-emphasis on the Christian religion in the legend, and a corresponding emphasis on pagan religions, their mysterious rites, and sacerdotal figures of the Druidic or Mother Goddess persuasion. Marion Zimmer Bradley's *The Mists of Avalon* (1982) capitalizes on this Dark Age, very old-time religion nexus.

4) A shift in point of view from Malory's omniscient narrator to a subordinate character, and allowing for example, Merlin, or Modred, to share the center stage with Arthur. Thus we have Vera Chapman's *Three Damosels* (1978), in which, like *The Mists of Avalon*, a bevy of Arthurian women tell the tale, Catherine Christian's *The Pendragon* (1979), narrated by Bedivere, and Dorothy James Roberts's *Lancelot My Brother* (1956), told by Bors. In addition to making Merlin the protagonist of her trilogy, Mary Stewart casts Modred as the central figure in *The Wicked Day* (1982), treats him sympathetically, and, to some extent, necessarily denigrates Arthur. Similarly, Sharon Newman's *Guinevere* (1981) creates a prenuptial history of Arthur's queen-to-be, while Parke Godwin's *Beloved Exile* (1984) relates a post-Arthur history of Guinevere's campaign to reestablish the Round Table.

5) Parodic, satiric, or ironic treatments abound. T. H. White's *Once and Future King* (1958), John Steinbeck's unfinished *The Acts of King Arthur and His Noble Knights* (1977), Walker Percy's *Lancelot* (1977), and Thomas Berger's *Arthur Rex. A Legendary Novel* (1979) are literary accomplishments that distill and stress the essential strengths of the legend. *Monty Python and the Holy Grail* (1974), on the other hand, represents the nadir of Arthurian burlesque.

6) Arthur's immersion in the realms of science fiction and fantasy gives rise to Sanders A. Laubenthal's *Excalibur* (1973), H. Warner Munn's *Merlin's Ring* (1974) and *Merlin's Godson* (1976), André Norton's *Merlin's Mirror* (1975), and Richard Monaco's *Parsival* trilogy (1977–80). This movement parallels the above-mentioned development in films and comics.

7) A participation in the Arthurian apocalyptic tradition, which has its origins in the great medieval histories and romances on Arthur, written in the mid-twelfth and thirteenth centuries, and also informing ensuing works. This was a chiliastic age, obsessed with the medieval conviction of the end of the world, a conviction sustained by such Last Signs as rampant moral laxity in the Church, heresies, widespread social disruptions, recurring wars, and pagan oppression. Geoffrey of Monmouth's *History of the Kings of Britain* chronicles the rise and fall of Arthur's kingdom and people, as prophesied by the Sybil and Merlin, and ends on a messianic note, with the implicit Breton hope of Arthur's return. The authors of the Vulgate romances, expanding on Geoffrey

and adding the Grail, modelled their history of the Arthurian world on the *Heilsgeschichte* patterning of medieval history, which, like the Bible, viewed the continuum of human experience and the rise and fall of empires as God's divine plan unfolding in *chronos*, and which ended with a *de ultimis temporibus* epilogue, stressing the coming Armageddon and the immanence of *kyros*.

I have elsewhere dealt with the Vulgate as an Arthurian apocalypse, holding up the end of Arthur's world as a warning speculum for its own perilous times.[7] I now want to discuss the apocalyptic paradigm found in ensuing Arthurian works: the messianic figure of Arthur, cast as the puissant *Last World Emperor*, whose reign will be a Golden Age until its end, and who will return to conquer mankind's enemies; Modred as the awesome Antichrist, the evil correlative of the messiah; and the "abomination of desolation" heralding the Arthurian Armageddon. There is, moreover, according to Frank Kermode, the recurring historical sequence of empire, decadence, hope of renovation, progress, a period of transition, and final catastrophe which was and continues to be invoked in times of crisis.[8] And finally, there is a concomitant message on the destructiveness and futility of war.

Wace's *Roman de Brut* (1155), Layamon's *Brut* (c. 1200), the Alliterative *Morte Arthure* (c. 1365), the Stanzaic *Morte Arthur* (c. 1400), and Malory graphically depict the carnage of Arthur's final battle which decimated the Round Table, and all of these works, with the exception of the Alliterative *Morte Arthure*, uphold or imply Arthur's return in Britain's time of need. *Artus redividus* also appears in Etienne de Rouen's *Draco Normannicus* (c. 1169), an account of the reigns of Stephen, Henry II, and Richard I, with Arthur warning Henry II not to war against the Bretons, and threatening a cosmic disaster if he persisted.

Malory's *Morte Darthur* (1470), like its sources, and particularly the Vulgate, enlarges this apocalyptic patterning to include Arthur's coronation as Holy Roman Emperor, the messianic Galahad, and the Grail as a katechon, the force restraining the coming of the Antichrist and the End of the World. Malory's apocalypse and theodicy not only unfolded the ways of God to his contemporary Englishmen, but warned them to adhere to the good and avoid the evil of Arthur's world and their own, and thus achieve terrestial and celestial worthship. It also offered a *consolatio* by reaffirming the human spirit's capacity to surmount the inescapable limitations and failures of a timebound and transitory world. And it must be remembered that Malory is the source for Arthuriana in the late nineteenth and twentieth centuries. In this regard, Beverly Taylor and Elisabeth Brewer note:

The tumult and torment of life in the twentieth century . . . give a deeper understanding of Malory than was possible before. Thus we are enabled to realise the symbolic potential of the myth of Arthur to an extent impossible in the nineteenth century, but also impossible in the Middle Ages and for Malory himself. Limited by his historical situation, Malory only partially appreciated "The inwardness of the astonishing material at his disposal."[9]

British and American works in this century increasingly used the Arthurian apocalyptic not only to express anti-war sentiments following World Wars I and II, but also to reflect the millenialism of our own age, the "Boom in Doom" aroused by the advent of the year 2000, the omnipresent "Last Signs," and the threat of the End by nuclear annihilation. The anti-war moral dominates Edwin Arlington Robinson's *Merlin* and *Lancelot*, and *Tristram*, which won the Publitzer Prize in 1927, Archibald MacLeish's *Destroyers* (1942), and T. H. White's works. In point of time, T. S. Eliot's *Waste Land* not only deplores the devastation of the first World War, but also the resultant moral and spiritual sterility of this age. Lawrence Binyon's *Arthur: A Tragedy* (1923) is both pacifist and millenarian, lamenting the waste of war and articulating the hope for a better future, to be effected by coming generations imbued with the Arthurian spirit. The poet David Jones's *In Parenthesis* (1937) and *The Anathemata* (1952) draw heavily on the Arthurian Grail legend and the theme of Arthur's return. This same theme is paramount in Richard Cammell's "The Return of Arthur: A Ballad Written Under the Threat of Invasion" (1944), a morale-booster during World War II, and Clarence Dane's *The Saviours: Seven Plays on One Theme* (1942), in which Arthur revives as King Alfred, Robin Hood, Elizabeth I, Horatio Nelson, the Unknown Warrior of World War I, and the indomitable spirit of Britain at the onset of World War II. Martyn Skinner's two poems on *The Return of Arthur* (1951, 1955) and John Heath-Stubb's *Artorius* (1973) depict Arthur's return to a terrible and terrifying modern world, while John Badger's *Arthuriad* (1970) hails Arthur as "The Once and Aquarian King" who will transform the world from a wasteland into a Golden Age Camelot. Jean Markale ends his propagandistic *King Arthur, King of Kings* with a call for a new classless Celtic/Marxist society:

The world is on the brink of a major upheaval. The times of darkness are done. For centuries we have been waiting for Arthur. We have given him the title of king because, according to the Celts, the king maintains the balance of the world, his presence is required before anything can happen. We have made him the symbol of an ideal society such as was promised to us by the prophets and the poets. One day their prediction must come true. It is our right and our duty now to waken King Arthur.[10]

C. S. Lewis gives a different treatment of the ongoing spirit of Arthur in *That Hideous Strength* (1945) by placing the responsibility for defending Arthur's idealistic Logres against the attacks of materialistic, nihilistic Britain, in the charge of a line of Arthur-delegated Fisher Kings. In this way, Lewis communicates his view that life, and particularly modern life, is a series of minor apocalypses, of recurring Antichrists battling messianic forces of good, which fittingly reside with Arthur's Pendragon heirs.

I would like to conclude with Edwin Arlington Robinson's *Merlin* and *Lancelot* and T. H. White's *Once and Future King*, which have been hailed almost unanimously by scholars and critics as the finest Arthurian works of this century. This accolade is well merited, for, in addition to their literary worth, they mirror forth the Arthurian apocalyptic as a warning to contemporary society.

Robinson wrote his two poems during and shortly after World War I, which he saw as the end of a civilization that, like Camelot, was built on rotten foundations. In *Merlin*, the mage is in Broceliande, the lover and beloved of Vivian, and only returns to Camelot to aid a demoralized, broken Arthur, beset by disloyalty, treachery, war, and the imminent fall of his kingdom. As in the Vulgate and Malory, Merlin is the founder of the kingdom, seer, and apocalyptic prophet, saddened by Arthur's plight. Even more, he is Robinson's surrogate as he reflects:

> All this that was to be is what I saw
> Before there was an Arthur to be king,
> And so to be a mirror wherein men
> May see themselves and pause....
>
> (VII, 119)[11]

He continues:

> I saw too much when I saw Camelot;
> And I saw further backward into Time
> And forward, than a man may see and live,
> When I made Arthur king....
>
> (VII, 95)

Trying to console a despondent Arthur, he says:

> But say not you have lost, or failed in
> aught
> Your golden horoscope of imperfection
> Had held in starry words that I have read.
>   (III, 26–27)

Modred is described as a satanic "worm," "serpent," "mongrel son and nephew," the "last of terrors," "And a most precious reptile in addition— / To ornament his court and carry arms, / And latterly to be the darker half / Of ruin..." (VI, 82). Merlin's vision of dying Camelot provides a cosmic frame for its failed lives and loves:

> ... There came
> Between him and the world a crumbling sky
> Of black and crimson, with a crimson cloud
> That held a far-off town of many towers,
> All swayed and shaken, till at last they fell,
> And there was nothing but a crimson cloud
> That crumbled into nothing, like the sky
> That vanished with it. ...
>   (V, 64–65)

Merlin, justifying his return to Camelot as a call to duty, says to Vivian: "This time I go because I made him king, / Thereby to be a mirror for the world" (V, 73), but he wonders somewhat dejectedly:

> If his avenging injured intellect
> Might shine with Arthur's kingdom a twin mirror,
> Fate's plaything, for new ages without eyes
> To see therein themselves and their declension.
>   (VI, 77–78)

Vivian, furious at Merlin's planned departure, taunts him mercilessly:

> ... You made him king
> Because you loved the world and saw in him
> From infancy a mirror for the millions.
> The world will see itself in him, and then
> The world will say its prayers and wash its face,
> And build for some new king a new foundation.
>   (VI, 89–90)

This ironic pronouncement is echoed positively by Bedivere near the poem's end:

> We pass but many are to follow us,
> And what they build may stay; though I believe
> Another age will have another Merlin,
> Another Camelot, and another King.
>
> (VI, 103)

But this hopeful prophecy cannot lift the darkness that engulfs Camelot.

Lancelot, occurring during and after the siege at Benwick, is a jeremiad against the folly of war. Moreover, like its Maloryan source, it explores the moral reasons for Camelot's fall: the illicit love of Lancelot and the queen; Gawain's monomaniacal desire for revenge; Arthur's impotence, so that he is "Like a sick landlord shuffling to the light / For one last look-out on his mortgaged hills" (IV,37); and Modred campaigning as Antichrist:

> God made him as He made the crocodile,
> To prove he was omnipotent. Having done so,
> And seeing then that Camelot, of all places
> Ripe for annihilation, most required him,
> He put him there at once, and there he grew.
> . . .
> His evil it was that grew, the King not seeing
> In Modred the Almighty's instrument
> Of a world's overthrow.
>
> (VIII, 101)

Dying, a penitent Gawain articulates the poem's moral: "The World has paid enough for Camelot" (VIII, 104), which Robinson considered the most significant line in the two works.[12] The poem ends with Lancelot beginning again his quest of the Grail, which Robinson "interpreted universally as a spiritual realization of Things and their significance":[13]

> He rode on in the dark, under the stars,
> And there were no more faces. There was nothing.
> But always in the darkness he rode on,
> Alone, and in the darkness came the Light.
>
> (VIII, 129)

Thus Robinson, captures the moral realism, spiritual dimensions, and ultimate consolation of Malory's *Morte Darthur* apocalypse.

Like Robinson, T. H. White used *The Once and Future King* to convey his apocalytpic message.[14] In one sense, the work is a mirror for magistrates, showing the making of Arthur into a good king, who, doing what he thinks is best for mankind, rejects the old chivalry based on Might is Right, for his Round Table chivalry, which uses Might only for the Right. Despite his well-intentioned efforts, his plan fails, and Arthur, as White's persona, laments:

> If something is not done ... the whole Table will go to ruin. It is not only that feud and open manslaughter have started; there is the bold bawdry as well. ... Morals are difficult things to talk about, but what has now happened is that we have invented a moral sense, which is rotting now that we can't give it employment. And when a moral sense begins to rot, it is worse than when you had none. I suppose that all endeavors which are directed to a purely worldly end, as my famous Civilization was, contain within themselves the germs of their own corruption. ... What I mean is that the ideal of my Round Table was a temporal ideal. If we are to save it, it must be made into a spiritual one. I forgot about God. ... If our Might was given a channel so that it worked for God, instead of for the rights of men, surely that would stop the rot and be worth doing. (434)

The moral rot did not stop, and, facing his last battle with Modred and his force of Thrashers, a discouraged Arthur ruminates on man's venality, the seeming inevitability of war, and the sad finale of his Round Table. Yet, cheered by a conversation with his young page, Tom Malory, Arthur reaffirms his idealized vision of humanity and Camelot, and reaches this consolation:

> There would be a day—there must be a day—when he would come back to Gramarye with a new Round Table which had no corners, just as the world had none—a table without boundaries between the nations who would sit to feast there. (639)

The book closes on a similar note of consolation and hope: "Here ends the book of The Once and Future King," followed by the words: "THE BEGINNING."

Consonant with the Arthurian apocalyptic, White has cast Arthur as a sincere *rex justus*, Mordred as the *Antichristus pessimus*, the Round Table and the Grail as the katechon or force holding back Armageddon, and the entire work, as an exemplum of the Arthurian Glorious Imperfect.

In 1941, at the height of the Battle of Britain, White wrote *The Book of*

Merlyn, which, possibly owing to its anti-war polemic, was not published until 1977.[15] Yet the *Merlin* is a fitting coda, ending the entire saga where it began, with a discourse between Arthur, Merlin, and the Council of tutelary animals on the subject of man and the folly of war. The Council concludes with T. natrix, the Grass Snake's parting words to Arthur:

> You remember the story of St. George, and *Homo sapiens* is like that still. You will fail because it is the nature of man to slay, in ignorance if not in wrath. But failure builds success and nature changes. A good man's example always does instruct the ignorant and lessen their rage, little by little, over the ages, until the spirit of the waters is content: and so, strong courage to Your Majesty, and a tranquil heart. (178)

That Arthur is and will be that good man is implied by the hedgehog's "Say not Farewell," but "Orryvoyer ... Orryvoyer" (179).

Speaking of Arthur's fate and possible return, White encapsulates the Arthurian apocalyptic:

> As for myself, I cannot forget the hedgehog's last farewell. ... For I am inclined to believe that my beloved Arthur of the future is sitting at this very moment among his learned friends, in the Combination Room of the College of Life, and that they are thinking away in there for all they are worth, about the best means to help our curious species; and I for one hope that some day, when not only England but the World has need of them, and when it is ready to listen to reason, if it ever is, they will issue from their wrath in joy and power; and then, perhaps, they will give us happiness in the world once more and chivalry, and the old medieval blessing of certain simple people—who tried, at any rate, in their own small way, to still the ancient brutal dream of Attila the Hun. (192–93)

NOTES

1. Herwig Wolfram, "Medieval Studies in America and American Medievalism," *Journal of the Rocky Mountain Medieval and Renaissance Association* 2 (1981): 10.
2. Wolfram, 11.
3. *Avalon to Camelot* 1, no. 2 (Winter, 1983): 10–12.
4. *Avalon to Camelot* 1, no. 1 (Fall, 1983): 1.
5. *Newsweek*, 17 July, 1984, 66; *Time*, 16 July, 1984, 64.

6. Sir Thomas Malory, *Works*, ed. Eugene Vinaver (London: Oxford University Press, 1976), 649.

7. Valerie M. Lagorio, "The Apocalyptic Mode in the Vulgate Cycle of Arthurian Romances," *Philological Quarterly* 57 (1978): 1–22.

8. Frank Kermode, *The Sense of an Ending: Studies in the History of Fiction* (London: Oxford University Press, 1966), 28–29.

9. Beverly Taylor and Elisabeth Brewer, *The Return of King Arthur: British and American Literature Since 1900* (Cambridge: D. S. Brewer; Totawa, NJ: Barnes and Noble Books, 1983), 268.

10. Jean Markale, *King Arthur, King of Kings*, trans. Christine Hauch (London and New York: Gordon and Cremonesi Publishers, 1977), 220.

11. Edwin Arlington Robinson, *Merlin, Lancelot, Tristram*, in *Collected Poems*, vol. 3 (New York: The Macmillan Company, 1927). All citations in this study, identified by book and page number, are taken from this edition.

12. Edwin Arlington Robinson, *Selected Letters*, ed. Ridgely Torrence, et al. (New York: The Macmillan Company, 1940), 113.

13. Hermann Hagedorn, *Edwin Arlington Robinson. A Biography* (New York: The Macmillan Company, 1938), 112.

14. T. H. White, *The Once and Future King* (New York: G. P. Putnam's Sons, 1965; Berkley Books, 1966). All citations by page numbers are taken from this edition.

15. T. H. White, *The Book of Merlyn* (New York: Berkley Publishing Corporation, 1978). All citations by page numbers are taken from this edition. Also published as "The Book of Merlin: The Passing of Camelot," in *Harper's*, September, 1977, 49–64.

Part Three: Architecture

The Medieval Heritage in American Religious Architecture

Peter W. Williams

HE SUBJECT OF THE RELATIONSHIP OF THE ARCHITECTURAL HERITAGE OF THE Middle Ages to the material culture of the religion of the United States is an extraordinarily rich one, in part because American religious architecture has never received systematic exploration or interpretation. A good deal has been written, especially during the last decade or two, about the Gothic Revival in its various phases, and also in studies of the work of some of its more distinguished exponents, but the question of what American religious building can tell us about the nature of religion in America has hardly been touched. This may in part owe to what Sacvan Bercovitch has identified as the *logocentric* character of American religious life, that is, the preoccupation of Americans with the Word in literal, verbal form, as written or as preached (but only incidentally as sung).[1] This is an insightful characterization, but it does not take into account the obvious fact that American Christians from the days of Jamestown and Plymouth have *built* as well as spoken. In addition, the bias which Bercovitch's term indicates towards accepting the Puritan formulation of Christianity as normative for all of American culture also skews interpretation towards novelty, innovation, and even revolutionary change, to the neglect of what seems to be a deeply significant stratum of continuity with the medieval past. Still further, attention to American Gothic as the revival rather than, at a perhaps deeper level, the survival of medieval patterns, also has produced distortion. It is this deeper stratum of cultural continuity and survival in American religious building that I would like to discuss in this paper.

From the point of view of the historian of art and architecture, the development of the medieval church and cathedral from the earliest basilicas of the Constantinian epoch through the extended career of the Romanesque into the varied glories of Gothic is an extraordinarily complex story. From the point of view of the religionist, however, details of ornament and construction yield in significance to some more fundamental considerations, especially when they are studied with an eye to their relevance to the American scene. At the risk of vast oversimplification, let me suggest some features of medieval religious space and place that we can regard as normative for our descriptive and comparative purposes.

In the beginning was the basilica, the basic spatial form from which Romanesque and eventually Gothic emerged. It is significant first that the basilica was originally a Roman secular building, a place of civic assembly and judicial proceedings, which lacked the connotations of imperial cult from which Christians desired to dissociate themselves.[2] The Christianized basilica thus became the *domus ecclesiae*, the house of the congregation, who could now assemble publicly rather than in small secret assemblages in private homes and catacombs.[3] This public character of post-Constantinian worship is the first feature of medieval worship structures we should note.

Secondly, the Christian public house of worship was a place of assemblage, but obviously no longer a secular or profane space. Its very purpose was to provide an appropriate and convenient setting for the celebration of the Christian liturgy. In the pre-Constantinian era, this congregation for worship presumably had to assemble wherever it was possible to do so. What now emerged as distinctive, however, was the association of worship space with the physical remains of saints, and specifically of martyred saints.[4] Both churches themselves and a specialized structure, the martyrium, were built in early years over the burial sites of martyrs, but the spread of Christianity throughout Europe and beyond made it impossible to insure such a siting for every church. Eventually the architecturally distinctive martyrium was absorbed into the church, and the latter acquired part of its sacral quality from its association not with a distinctive site but rather with its possession and sheltering of relics. The seemingly miraculous proliferation of relics which later evoked the sardonic hilarity of Mark Twain in his *Innocents Abroad* was certainly one of the decadent aspects of later medieval piety that helped to hasten the drive to extirpate sacrality, a drive which was a principal characteristic of the puritanical impulses of the Reformation.

The sacrality of medieval churches did not derive entirely from their possession of martyrial and saintly remains, but also from the uses to which these were put. The church, of course, was the ordinary site for the celebration of the sacraments, particularly the Mass, and the restructuring of the secular basilica for liturgical purposes was necessary for the proper performance of these sacred acts. The increasing aura of mystery which the sacraments acquired, and the corresponding distancing of the clergy who alone were privy to the arcana needed for their proper performance, resulted in a separation of clergy and laity which was reflected in physical arrangements as well. The latter and larger class of the faithful were thus confined to the nave, while only the clergy had free access to the sanctuary. Thus did the site for Christian worship increasingly acquire the character not only of the *domus ecclesiae*, the house of the publicly congregated faithful, but of the *domus dei*, the temple or house of God, as well. As Harold Turner has pointed out in his exhaustive phenomenological study of Western worship, *From Temple to Meeting House*, the tension between these two types has run through the history of Western religion from the days of the Jerusalem Temple to the present.[5] As a distinctively medieval Christianity developed, however, the emphasis on mystery and sacrality was clearly on the rise.

With the coming of the Gothic style, still further elements developed and accentuated the notion that the church and especially the cathedral were sacred places. The influx of light, which Gothic methods of construction permitted, created an ethereal atmosphere that many centuries later could still haunt that imperfectly secularized American visitor, Henry Adams.[6] Gothic sculptural programs reflected an understanding that the cathedral was a recapitulation in microcosm of the sacred cosmos.[7] Complex numerical symbolism also reinforced the notion of the cathedral's sacral quality.[8] It thus seems probable that entering and participating in the worship conducted in the Gothic cathedral was for the medieval believer a distancing of the self from the profane and an entry into, an anticipation of, the experience of paradise.[9]

All medieval Christian religious buildings, however, were not cathedrals or churches. The Church was a much more comprehensive institution in medieval society than in the post-Reformation era, and many of the functions now performed by governmental or other secular agencies were then relegated to the Church as its appropriate province. This province included education, eleemosynary activities, hospitality for travellers, institutional complexes for religious communities, and shrines. Sacred geography and its accompanying architecture therefore had a number of layers or levels. First, it frequently paved the way, especially during the earlier centuries, for the expansion of settlement and civilization through monastic foundations. Secondly, it sanctified or legitimated the ordinary course of life, serving the religious needs of town and country folk, and marking with special structures, i.e., cathedrals, the foci of the political and social order. Thirdly, it provided institutions parallel to those of the "secular" world for classes of people who fell outside the quotidian norm, e.g., scholars, monks and nuns, travellers, orphans, and the sick and dying. Fourthly, it marked irregular eruptions of the sacred—alleged scenes of heroic martyrdoms, epiphanies or theophanies, or particularly potent collections of relics with supernatural powers—in the form of shrines, which served as loci of pilgrimage activity.[10] The medieval world, then, was characterized by a quest for cosmos rather than chaos or its present-day equivalent, secularity; no ground within Christendom was entirely neutral ground, but all was provided symbolic focus by edifices which gave it structure and meaning.[11] Medieval Christianity, in short, was incorporated into a *church* in the classic sense developed by Troeltsch and Weber.[12] It was a comprehensive institution co-extensive with the boundaries of the society which recognized its exclusive claims, and on which it in turn bestowed legitimacy as well as religious and social service.

With all of this in mind, we can proceed to a typology of medieval religious building which need not take into account the various stylistic shifts and developments that characterized these centuries. In doing so, we sacrifice a great deal of the complexity of artistic and technological understanding, but gain a useful tool of socio-religious analysis. Therefore, we may say that the typical medieval house of worship (as opposed to other structures with religious functions) from the early Constantinian to the late Gothic period in the West generally possessed the following characteristic features:[13]

1. It was a place of public assemblage for worship.

2. It was a sacred space, with the focus of sacrality in the sanctuary.

3. It was literally oriented in space, with the altar facing east and the principal entrance at the west.

4. Its plan was horizontal, with the altar and sanctuary at one short end and the narthex at the other. (Religious buildings of other shapes existed, but usually had special functions.)

5. Its vertical component was manifested in the height of the structure itself and frequently also in adjoining or attached domes, towers, and/or spires.

6. It was a monumental public structure, prominently sited, and an in-

trinsic material expression of the social fabric in its symbolic dimension.

7. Both its structure and its iconographic content often incorporated specifically religious symbolism.

Many of these qualities, of course, could be attributed to houses of worship in other traditions and cultures, but this particular concatenation seems unique to medieval Christendom.

It is an historical commonplace that, with the coming of the Reformation, the medieval effort to mold a religiously-grounded universal civilization came to an effective end, as did, as a common principle, the notion that the most appropriate house for public worship was one that constituted a sacred space. The Anglican and Lutheran branches of the Magisterial Reformation represented modifications rather than root-and-branch abolition of the medieval tradition. It is the more radical, even revolutionary, thrust of Calvinism to which we must look not only for a dramatic alternative in religious architecture, but also as the most immediate source of the religious culture that would set the tone for the development of Christianity in what eventually was to become the United States.

Although Calvin and his followers attempted to purge the churches of Geneva of the allegedly pagan excesses of medieval Catholicism, it was only in New England that the new ideal of an appropriate place of worship could be realized free from the accumulated detritus of the previous centuries. Just as the Christians of Constantine's time had found themselves free to create an appropriate style of public building for worship, and turned to secular rather than sacred Roman precedent in choosing the basilica, so did the Puritan founders of New England look to late medieval English town-halls or market-halls rather than to the traditional parish church for their model.[14] The Puritan meeting-house was self-consciously intended as a radically new form of religious building, one in which an authentically biblical worship could be conducted. Its inspiration was not only positive but negative, since it was intended to be the direct antithesis of the medieval church. Where the church had been rectangular, the meeting-house was frequently square. (When rectangular, its entrance was on one of the long sides.) Where the church was monumental, the meeting-house was domestic, as its name implies and as the ordinary table-ware used in its communion services emphasizes. Where the church and especially the cathedral were adorned with representational works of art, the meeting-house was austere and iconoclastic in conception, with occasional indulgence in its more ornate manifestations in non-representational wood-carving. Finally, and perhaps of most importance, where the church constituted a sacred space, the meeting-house was deliberately erected, regarded, and utilized as a secular building.[15] In the earliest days of the Bay colony especially, the meeting-house was used for a wide variety of public functions, including political, military, and educational endeavors. Humanity encountered the Divine solely through the Word of God, and the meeting-house was erected to provide a place where the proclamation and exposition of the Word could fittingly take place. God, however, did not reside in the meeting-house. The space itself was indifferent and purely functional; to imply that the Divine could in any way be confined or contained within the realm of the mundane was idolatrous and blasphemous.

An issue that continually arises in Puritan studies is whether that singular group was more medieval or modern, reactionary or revolutionary. In juxtaposition to early generations of historians who celebrated the Puritans not only as the scourge of Popish superstition but as the forerunners of modern democratic institutions, a more recent school of historiography has tended to stress the continuities between the first white New Englanders and their late medieval forebears in the ways especially in which they transplanted the "deep structures" of English material culture to the New World.[16] When examined from this point of view, the meeting-house seems somewhat less dramatically revolutionary than it might at first appear. To begin with, late medieval English parish churches were hardly islands of undisturbed sanctity in the midst of the hurly-burly of the profane world, but were used for a wide variety of secular purposes. Secondly, the symbolic character of the meeting-house as an ontological center for the community was certainly a mark of continuity with medieval practice, even though the Puritan method of meeting-house placement seems to have been more systematic and rationalized than in most medieval instances. As the archaeologist Colin Platt observes with regard to both of these points: "The church, ceasing to be private property, took on a variety of public roles. With the castle and the market, it completed the third essential element of medieval settlement, a natural focus for the life of the community."[17] Thirdly, early New England town-planning may have been influenced by biblically-based mystical numerological symbolism, as demonstrated in John Archer's study of New Haven.[18]

A fourth major point of continuity between medieval and early New England patterns lay in what might be called "the parochial principle." To this day, the Roman Catholic, Anglican, and other churches organize their jurisdictions territorially, with ecclesiastical units corresponding to geographical and political division. The implication, of course, is that church and society are working in co-ordination, and that the religious and social realms are fundamentally coextensive. Although Puritanism began as a basically sectarian movement in Old England, its character, once it was transplanted to the New World, rapidly changed, in Perry Miller's phrase, from a reformation to an administration.[19] Church and state, though never merged, were still coordinate and cooperative in their character, and quite naturally the parochial principle of territorial organization for religious purposes persisted. A major part of the scandal of the Great Awakening of the 1730s and 40s, once it had entered into its more radical phases, was the shambles which the practice of itinerant preaching made of the deeply ingrained notion that one church and one minister should serve one discrete social unit; any challenge to that principle was feared as a challenge to the social order itself.

Even before the Awakening was challenging the hegemony of the established churches, both Puritan and Anglican, along the entire seaboard, an equally significant change was taking place in the realm of church design. In the Southern colonies, especially Virginia, this development was slow and organic. The earliest Anglican church in the English-speaking colonies was St. Luke's, Isle of Wight County, Virginia, a genuine survival of the popular tradition of church building, in which a basically Gothic structure showed signs of increasing knowledge of neo-classical conventions in its ornament.[20] Subsequent Anglican churches in the South demonstrated the rapid triumph of the classicism which had swept England after Christopher Wren's rebuilding of the ecclesiastical fabric of London following the great fire of 1666. These rural churches were built in a wide variety of shapes, sizes, and degrees of elaborateness, but all embodied Wren's concern that a proper place be provided for both preaching and the sacraments, the two sides of the Anglican *via media*.[21]

In New England, the increasingly noticeable Anglican presence, which came with the installation of a royal governor in Boston (1689), led to the rapid introduction there of this new church form. Christ, or Old North Church, later of Paul Revere fame, was built in 1721 along the lines of Wren neo-classicism, and provided one of the first distinctive models for the nascent American imagination of "what a church ought to look like." (Bruton Parish Church in Williamsburg was a notable Southern analogue.)[22] In Christ Church we can see a thorough-going repudiation of the principles for which the meeting-house stood, even in the name itself, which combined direct reference to the deity with the rejected term "church." Here also we have a return to the traditional rectangular form with the entrance at one of the short ends, a tower and steeple which added a vertical thrust at least vestigially reminiscent of the Gothic, and a return to prominence of the altar/table at the east end.

Well, one might ask, what should one expect of Anglicans, whom the Puritans had from the beginning accused of showing only the most lukewarm interest in the abolition of Popish idolatry. The answer was soon provided by the Puritans themselves, who began to construct structures such as Boston's Old South meeting-house in 1729, which were virtually indistinguishable on the exterior from their neighboring Anglican prototype.[23] The precise reasons for this shift in style among the Congregationalists are not clear, but the possibility of an increasing dis-ease among the latter as to their social standing in a progressively more pluralistic community certainly needs to be considered. Also, with the erosion of political power occasioned by the loss of the original charter, the Puritan leadership was no longer able to enforce the regulation of prices, conspicuous consumption, and other behavior which had routinely come under communal supervision during the previous century. And Old North was not an isolated instance. From that time onward, the meeting-house was defunct as a viable building form for all but the most radical sectarians such as the Friends. Baptists vied with Congregationalists in erecting churches or remodelling meeting-houses to conform with the new fashion, and neither Old nor New Light seemed tempted following the Awakening to revert to the old ways. A genuinely American style of church-building, albeit one derived from an English model, seems to have emerged in this period, just as the English Grand Itinerant George Whitefield provided the colonists with their first example of an American celebrity whose fame transcended local boundaries.

What had therefore emerged by the early eighteenth century were two distinct types of American Christian religious building. The first, the meeting-house, which had gone into a temporary eclipse within a century of its inception, was essentially a functional structure on a domestic plan renouncing any sacral character. On the other hand, the church, repopularized by the Anglicans and rapidly adopted by erstwhile iconoclastic sectarians, was in its fundamental character a medieval structure that could trace most of its basic elements back to the Constantinian period. The main question was, how far one could say that the church-type possessed that quintessentially medieval ingredient, sacrality? Answers to this question differed, and informed much of the controversy over church-building that would characterize nineteenth- and much of twentieth-century American religious dialogue.

Religious building in the nineteenth century may be interpreted as a dialectic between the two paradigms of church and meeting-house. On the one hand, the notion of religious space as fundamentally functional continued through the tradition of revivalism, from the open-air camp meetings of Cane Ridge through the vast built-to-order "tabernacles" of Moody and Sankey in post-Civil War days.[24] Most of the explicitly Evangelical denominations, such as Baptists and Methodists, were either oblivious to considerations of liturgics and aesthetics beyond the needs of simple practicality, or, especially among Baptists in the South, looked with suspicion upon architectural display as a manifestation of worldliness.[25] The Southern Baptist insistence on local autonomy also placed them squarely in the sectarian camp, and therefore at odds with what we have been delineating as the medieval norm. Methodists, however, were schooled in another, less rigorously nonconformist heritage, and were thus moved not to reject but to transform the parochial principle into an intricate pattern of circuits which, with the passing of the frontier, would eventually be normalized into a system of territorial exclusiveness not very different from its sister churches with which it shared some form of episcopal polity.

In terms of architectural style, Methodists of sufficient means to erect full-scale architect-designed churches tended to adopt the Greek and Roman revival styles that were popular among virtually all Christian denominations during the National Period.[26] Even the fledgling Roman Catholic community joined this celebration of an iconography of democratic virtue, and Bishop John Carroll of Baltimore chose a Roman Revival design for his cathedral over the alternative Gothic plan offered by his architect, Benjamin Henry Latrobe.[27] The unalleviated horizontality of the Greek temple, however, apparently proved unacceptable to American churchpeople, as the imposition of steeples or towers in such diverse cases as the Congregational Church in Madison, Connecticut, and St. Peter in Chains Roman Catholic Cathedral in Cincinnati both illustrate. The basic scheme of a horizontal hall for public assembly with the entrance at one of the short ends and with at least a vestigial vertical thrust had now become sufficiently fixed in American religious iconography so that any radical departure could hardly hope for general acceptance. It was only such marginal groups as Swedenborgians or, later, Christian Scientists, that felt free enough to depart very far from this norm; even Latter-Day Saints' experiments with exotic symbolism need to be balanced against the essentially traditional external patterning of their houses of worship, as the vaguely Gothic Salt Lake City Temple commissioned by Brigham Young himself demonstrates.[28]

The dominant interpretation of the character of religious structures which predominated in antebellum American Protestantism oscillated between an idea of civic assembly in virtuously classical structures—a sort of civil religiosity—and a sectarian suspicion of aesthetics or symbolics which transcended the purely functional. A new element—or, perhaps, a very old one—was introduced into this religio-cultural matrix via the Romantic Revival—most particularly, of course, in the form of the Gothic Revival. As we have already noted, the first appearance of the Gothic style in the colonies (Old St. Luke's) was an authentic medieval survival rather than a conscious revival. The later revival, in which medieval forms were adopted self-consciously rather than matter-of-factly, extended in several phrases from the earliest toying with Gothic ornament in the England of Horace Walpole through its last days in pre-World War II American domestic Protestantism. Early nineteenth-century attempts by such prominent architects as Latrobe, Bulfinch, and Ithiel Town at churches in a Gothic mode are interesting more as examples of taste rather than as serious aesthetic or liturgical reform.[29] These attempts consisted primarily of Gothic elements grafted onto what was basically the rectangular box into which the American Wren tradition had evolved, with little attention to structural or iconographical considerations. The evolving American tradition of church building was sufficiently similar to medieval church-form that the grafting of Gothic features into a Neo-classical frame was not perceived as particularly incongruous (until sufficient sophistication could develop to permit a purist revulsion). Also, the Puritan suspicion of Popery had by the "Era of Good Feeling" sufficiently subsided to permit a sympathetic interest in medieval themes.

The main impetus to a systematic interest in and revival of medieval church-building, however, did not arise until the impact of the theological and liturgical revivals at Oxford and, particularly, Cambridge began to be felt in America.[30] In place of the dilettantish and aesthetic Gothicism of the earlier decades of the century, a drive that was at once programmatic and theological launched one of the most decisive shifts in religious architectural patterns in our history. St. James the Less near Philadelphia was one of the first and finest examples of this campaign to revive what the Ecclesiologists regarded as an authentic Christian understanding of symbolism, as derived from the thirteenth century French bishop Durandus.[31] This campaign involved a "high" ecclesiology and doctrine of sacraments, and a correspondingly appropriate house of worship for which the English "middle" or "Decorated" style of Gothic was viewed as ideal.

Americans were spared the damage that this narrow theological approach to architecture wrought in England by ill-conceived attempts to restore churches that had developed through several stylistic eras to what the Camden Society considered an authentically Christian style. In both England and America, however, the Ecclesiologists were afforded an opportunity to engage in the construction of new churches for Anglican worship on an extensive scale. In our own country, a number of factors converged to make possible this Gothic efflorescence. In the first place, the Episcopal Church, which had fallen into a profound state of demoralization during the decades following the Revolution, had now regained its vigor, and was beginning to emerge as a suitable church particularly for that segment of the population which possessed the greatest means to invest in new construction. This appeal to the Anglophilia of the newly wealthy would reach its peak later in the nineteenth century, but even before the Civil War it seems to have acquired a considerable momentum. Secondly, American Episcopalians were becoming increasingly, almost violently, divided along High and Low church alignments. The first party frequently followed the lead of the English Ecclesiologists in a sometimes precious concern with the details of church building, and a branch of the movement became institutionalized in New York City, where the General Theological Seminary became the seedbed of the American High Church party.[32] Thirdly, the Gothic Revival as the expression of a theological and liturgical movement found a forceful exponent and practitioner in the person of Richard Upjohn, whose subsequent impact on the development of the American vocabulary of material religious expression was to be incalculable.[33] Upjohn was responsible not only for such monumental structures as New York's Trinity Church, which he was compelled to construct with less fidelity to Gothic principles than he would have liked, but also, directly or indirectly, for the myriad of "carpenter Gothic" churches that burgeoned from Maine to Wisconsin to Florida during the middle and later parts of the century. Although Upjohn preferred (as did his successor Ralph Adams Cram) to confine his practice to Anglican churches, the Congregationalists of Brunswick, Maine, for example, managed to inveigle him to design their splendid hammerbeam arabesque, and the influence of his designs rapidly spread through what we might now begin to describe as the "middle Protestant" denominational spectrum.

Had this first phase of what we might call an "authentic" Gothic revival been sponsored solely by an audience committed to the ecclesiology of the Cambridge Camden Society, its impact on the American scene would doubtless have been rather limited. However, the movement flourished both within and beyond Anglican boundaries because of its harmoniousness with a much broader cultural drift in which Americans became eager disciples of their British and Continental mentors. Romanticism was such a vast and complex movement that no reasonably well educated person could have avoided some contact with it, and its appeal was so various that it seemed to offer something for everyone.

To begin with, the Puritan impact on American culture had become so attenuated within the religious sensibility of the cultural elite, many of whom had now become Unitarian or Episcopalian, that a Romantic flirtation with medieval or later European Catholic themes became virtually a commonplace in the writings of such widely-read figures as Channing, Longfellow, Prescott, and Parkman.[34] The culture of the Middle Ages, as expressed in its heroic legends, its reputedly "organic" Church and society, and especially in its great cathedrals, seemed to be closer to the "natural" human condition than was the rapidly modernizing life of contemporary England and America. The Romantic notion that Gothic architecture derived its characteristics from the natural forms of the forest was one expression of this fancy, an idea which has immediate resonances with Emerson's search for religious and cultural truth in Nature and especially Horace Bushnell's theory that human language ultimately derives from deep-seated resonances between words and the realities they organically reflect.[35]

Significantly, these themes suggest that popular American Romanticism was fundamentally a force for the resacralization of nature and society, a repudiation of the Puritan estrangement of the spheres of divinity and creation. Some excellent examples of this cultural reversal are, first, the rehabilitation of Christmas, in part through the writings of Irving and, later, Dickens, with considerable emphasis on the "natural" elements of seasonal joyousness;[36] secondly, the "garden cemetery" movement, which advocated the burial of the dead in pleasant parklike grounds such as Cambridge's Mount Auburn, New Haven's Grove Street, and Cincinnati's Spring Grove;[37] and, thirdly, as Clifford Clark has argued, the vogue of the Gothic cottage among the middle class, based on the notion that the home could take on a religious character as an appropriate setting for Christian nurture.[38] This character could be enhanced through the proper set of visual architectural associations, namely, domestic Gothic. All of these can be construed as a sort of natural sacramentalism, much more diffuse and even sentimentalized than anything with which Aquinas would have cared to claim intellectual kinship, but nevertheless representing a coming together of the realms of a rehabilitated nature and a reconceptualized grace, which would have chilled John Winthrop's bones to their very marrow. The coziness of Carpenter Gothic and its later modifications into Stick and Shingle modes fit in extremely well with this new mood, even though the latter frequently led to liturgical expressions far too lax for Upjohn and his Ecclesiological contemporaries.

The second phase of the Gothic Revival in America (as well as England, which generally set the pace in these matters) needs to be considered with its contemporary medievalistic counterpart, H. H. Richardson's resuscitation of the Romanesque. In both of these cases, the Episcopal Church frequently took the lead in commissioning many of the best examples of these styles, but it by no means could claim a monopoly on their adoption. Even within the Episcopal church itself, medievally-inspired churches could be put to very different uses. Richardson's Trinity Church at Copley Square, Boston, was originally designed not for High Church liturgical usage but rather as a preaching platform for the enormously popular Phillips Brooks, who was associated with the emergent Broad Church party; only later did it take on its current and more ornate interior.[39] However, within a few years and a few blocks of the erection of Trinity, John H. Sturgis's Church of the Advent was designed and built to reflect a very different sort of churchmanship, one closely aligned with the revival of Anglican monasticism then taking place in both England and America. (Cram's chapel for the Cowley Fathers in Cambridge is a good example of this interaction.)[40]
The nature of the Medievalism involved in this phase of the Gothic (and fundamentally the only real phase of the Romanesque) revival was thus rather complicated. First, as the case of the Church of the Advent illustrates, a genuine interest in the revival of medieval religious institutions could provide part of the context for a Gothic which, in its fanciful polychromy and other novel aspects, would have hardly been acceptable to the earnest purism of the Ecclesiologists. Secondly, medieval exteriors could shelter liturgical usages thoroughly Protestant and unmedieval, as in the case not only of Boston's Trinity but of the countless Methodist, Presbyterian, Baptist, and other "middle Protestant" churches that were erected in Gothic and Romanesque (or, perhaps more evocatively, generic Victorian Medieval) exterior form during the latter decades of the nineteenth century and the earlier ones of the twentieth. Finally, the popularity which Victorian Gothic and Richardsonian Romanesque achieved in the broader public realm — e.g., in such disparate structures as Harvard's Memorial Hall and Cincinnati's City Hall and Music Hall — can be read as an indication that the iconography of the religious and civic spheres were beginning (again) to blend into one another, betokening the emergence of a Christian Commonwealth transcending not only denominational lines but also those of church and state. Another noteworthy development that began to accelerate during the later nineteenth century was the extraordinary campaign of institutional expansion undertaken by the Roman Catholic Church, whose numbers were being

increased by the thousands upon thousands of immigrants making their way
to American shores primarily from southern and central Europe. Since public facilities for assistance were in short supply, and since the hierarchy was
concerned that these newcomers and their offspring not be lost to the Faith
through exposure to Protestant and secular influences, a building campaign
of unprecedented dimensions commenced for the construction not only of
Catholic churches but of rectories, convents, schools at all levels, hospitals,
orphanages, and a whole host of structures serving religious and charitable
needs. The style of these buildings, especially churches, included but was
by no means confined to the Gothic and Romanesque. Even more significant
than style, however, was the attempt to create a material infrastructure for
what amounted to a Catholic American counter-culture. This counter-culture
provided an alternative to the Protestant-dominated but rapidly secularizing
social order in those facets, ranging from foundling hospitals to cemeteries,
where religious or symbolic goals were manifest. Many of these structures
were monumental in scale, and incorporated both the "total institutional" approach of other nineteenth century American "asylums" as the penitentiary
or the madhouse on the one hand as well as such typically medieval institutions as the monastery (which now began to appear both in Roman and Anglican form in the New World) on the other.[41] Whether the external form
was specifically medieval revival or generic Victorian institutional, the goal
of domination of the landscape with structures at once functional and symbolic was certainly reminiscent of the pre-Reformation epoch.

The third phase of American Gothic which, like the earlier phases, was
roughly contemporaneous with a number of other stylistic revivals, was again
closely associated with though not confined to the Episcopal Church. It was
also associated with one dominant figure, Ralph Adams Cram. Since this
volume contains a detailed study of Cram by Richard Guy Wilson, I shall
write in detail here neither of Cram's thought and work nor of the specifically
architectural characteristics of this phase, but would like to make some observations about its social context.

In the first place, the late nineteenth and early twentieth centuries were
the apogee of the association of the Episcopal Church with individuals and
families of almost undreamt of wealth. Gothic—especially good Gothic—is
expensive, and in this epoch of great new fortunes and the absence of a gradu-
ated income tax the superfluity necessary for its creation coincided with the
required social and theological motivations as well as the availability of the
requisite theoretical and practical talent. Secondly, the same families that
were joining and supporting the Episcopal Church so lavishly were also con-

cerned with the creation of schools of an appropriately elite and, preferably, English sort for their offspring.[42] This was, in consequence, the era of the flourishing of the great "prep schools" of the Northeast, many of them Episcopalian in affiliation and Gothic in fabric, as well as the era of the construction of the Gothic phases of the Yale and Princeton campuses. (Duke, a Southern relative in the Wesleyan tradition, would follow suit, along with many others.)

Thirdly, rivalries among several religious camps for social prestige engaged in architectural as well as other, more covert forms of status warfare. The American Catholic Church, which through the Civil War years had no real architectural idiom of its own, now began to reappropriate its authentic Gothic heritage. The magnificent St. Patrick's Cathedral on Fifth Avenue was the work of an Episcopalian architect, James Renwick, Jr., but its lineage was Continental Catholic, and its presence was an unmistakable sign that the Roman Church was a force to be reckoned with on the American social, political, cultural, and economic as well as religious scene.[43] Later Charles D. Maginnis and others would provide specifically Catholic leadership in the profession, and prove capable of providing their Church with both a philosophy and a fabric in the realm of building. It was the presence of St. Patrick's, however, which allegedly was one of the major spurs to the Episcopal Church's undertaking of one of the most dazzling projects in the history of religious architecture, the Cathedral Church of Saint John the Divine, at the crown of Central Park. The later vicissitudes of that still unfinished structure are an instructive testimony to the relationship between church building, economics, and the still unresolved question (as also illustrated in the controversy over Manhattan's St. Bartholomew's) of religious stewardship in the post-urban age.

The revival of Gothic on a monumental scale was not confined to those denominations that could legitimately lay claim to it on historical grounds. Methodists, whose tradition was primarily functional, began to adopt this fashion in churches whose Akron-Plan interiors were camouflaged with Romanesque or Gothic facades designed by the Plan's prophet, George Kramer.[44] During the 1920s, after that denomination had become sufficiently bureaucratized to permit the creation of a Bureau of Architecture, its indefatigable director, Elbert W. Conover, used his influence to promote the Gothic as the favored style.[45] (The Duke University Chapel and the Highland Park Methodist Church in Dallas are some of the more impressive examples of the Methodist quest for Gothic monumentality.)[46] The allure of the tradition for Presbyterians can perhaps be best illuminated in Woodrow Wilson's commissioning of Ralph Adams Cram as Princeton's official architect, which resulted in his design of the Graduate College and, after Wilson's day, the splendid Princeton chapel.[47] In addition, Wilson's remains ultimately found repose in Washington's National – and Episcopal – Cathedral. (It might be mentioned parenthetically here that the medieval idea of church as sepulchral monument is something of a rarity in the United States, although commemorative plaques, as opposed to actual tombs, are not infrequent.)

The National Cathedral,[48] designed by the Anglican Henry Vaughan and others, leads naturally into a question that has already surfaced periodically in this paper. This is the question of an American public iconography. In his seminal and much-discussed essay on the "American Civil Religion," the sociologist Robert Bellah pointed to Washington, DC, the location of the National Cathedral as well as a number of other public buildings, as the center of the putative civic cult, the existence of which he was seeking to establish.[49] Bellah, previously a student of Japanese Shinto, explicitly used the category of "shrine" to characterize such structures as the Washington and Lincoln Memorials; in this connection, it is also useful to recall Lloyd Lewis's study of the myths that grew up around Lincoln after his assassination, and their parallel to those which had long ago focussed on King Arthur.[50] American civic monumentality has generally favored some version of neo-classicism for these enterprises, which transcend the functional in their provision of the social order with some sense of coherence and of civic cosmos. At times medievally-inspired styles, such as the Richardsonian Romanesque and Victorian Gothic cited earlier, have enjoyed brief popularity for these purposes, and it can be argued that such privately endowed creations as the Yale Colleges or St. Patrick's Cathedral serve an essentially public function in their contribution to the imageability (in Kevin Lynch's term) of their respective cityscapes, as material projections of the *res publica* broadly understood.[51] Whatever the style, however, each points to a deep-felt need in this allegedly ahistorical nation, this *nova respublica*, for the sacralization of the common life. As James P. Walsh argued in a provocative article in the *American Quarterly*, even the Puritans were unsuccessful in their ostensible goal of stripping times, places, and buildings of their sacramental meaning, and ultimately (and ironically) converted the land of New England itself into a holy ground as well as its people into a holy commonwealth.[52] In the longer run of our history, this impulse, which in the Middle Ages took more explicitly and uniformly religious dress, has continued to resurface in our public material life, whether in medieval or classical garb, both through public and private funding.

Although some forms of Gothic church construction may have survived the ravages of the Depression and the distractions of the Second World War, those two calamitous events brought an effectual end to its adoption for truly monumental projects such as cathedrals and campuses. It was during the decades following the War also that two intellectual currents with origins in the earlier part of the century began to converge within American Christianity to put what may have been a definitive end to explicitly medieval motifs in church building. On the one hand, Frank Lloyd Wright's functionalism, as expressed in religious form in Oak Park's Unity Temple, proved enormously influential in creating a revulsion against the lavish ornamentation that is so intrinsically connected with the Gothic idiom.[53] Simultaneously, and also in the Midwest, the American Benedictines at Collegeville were laying the groundwork for a liturgical revolution that would take as normative not the elaboration of medieval (not to say Tridentine) worship but rather the relative simplicity and commonality of the pre-Constantinian Church.[54] By the late 1950s, Protestants of a liturgical bent would be turning away from their earlier liturgical revival, as exemplified in Elbert Conover's Wesleyan appropriation of the Gothic, to join in a common Christian quest for the kind of worship to which the constitutions of Vatican II gave definitive form for their Catholic counterparts. The now commonly accepted and essentially medieval model of the longitudinal church, which increased in sacred intensity as one advanced from narthex to sanctuary, was scrapped in favor of new (or very old) forms which diminished rather than exacerbated the distinction between clergy and laity. And, even had one wanted to turn again to the Gothic, the dearth of qualified craftspeople, whose collective skills Cram had decades earlier co-ordinated to such rich effect, and the immense costliness both of materials and workmanship, would render such an undertaking nearly impossible.

Is our contemporary age, then, one from which the medieval patterns of church structure and societal sacralization have been forever banished? Have even the great Gothic and Romanesque revival churches of previous decades become so definitively overshadowed by neighboring skyscrapers that they remain only as impotent symbols of a vanished authority? Even the Catholic Church, the most systematic institutional force for the religious structuring of the landscape, has yielded much of its educational and charitable mission to secular agencies, and its abandoned seminaries and refuges are giving way to urban renewal efforts on their sites. Have the Christian churches retreated in their visual and material aspect to the private sphere, except as they might occasionally remain as anachronistic reminders of a sacral past? Do high school senior classes even make "pilgrimages" to the nation's capital anymore?

In a search for possible clues to the contrary, the contemporary observer may be driven to the current Evangelical resurgence which was so conspicuously manifest in the 1984 presidential campaign. Where the "mainline" denominations, both Catholic and "middle Protestant," have been forced to retrench in their once vigorous building campaigns, our urban interstate beltways and the "strips" on the fringes of our cities and towns are now effloresing with humble Pentecostal churches, still rectangular, with vestigial plastic spires affixed to their roofs, as well as vast temple-like edifices in the most dazzling array of geometrical shapes, proudly surrounded by fleets of school buses. Religious theme parks and other latter-day shrines abound in the South, patronized by tourists equipped no longer with scallop shells but rather with Shell credit cards. Schools that characterize themselves as "Christian," with no further qualifications (perhaps in both senses of that phrase), no longer bent so much on avoiding racial integration as on resacralizing the social order, have displaced the Catholic parochial schools as the "growth industry" of the private educational sector. And Jerry Falwell stands poised, eager to abandon his role as revivalist and prophet to assume, as did Billy Graham before him, the status of de facto bishop, a not-so-gray eminence alongside the princes of the State; he and his colleagues seem ever-ready to summon another crusade against the infidels of secular humanism and godless Communism, the "evil empire" which has taken over the role once enjoyed by Islam (or, perhaps, now shared with the Ayatollah). If nothing else, the Middle Ages was an epoch in which the social order was infused, even saturated, with symbolic expression. Even our allegedly secularized society seems to abhor a symbolic vacuum, and we scarcely lack for those ready to leap into the breach.

NOTES

1. See Bercovitch, "The Biblical Basis of the American Myth," in Giles Gunn, ed., *The Bible and American Arts and Letters* (Philadelphia: Fortress Press; Chico, CA: Scholars Press, 1983), 221–32.

2. Jeannette Mirsky, *Houses of God* (Chicago and London: University of Chicago Press, 1976), 136.

3. Harold W. Turner, *From Temple to Meeting House: The Phenomenology and Theology of Places of Worship* (The Hague: Mouton, 1979), 12.

4. Ibid., 166–68.

5. Ibid., 11–12.

6. Pre-eminently in *Mont-Saint-Michel and Chartres* (Boston: Houghton, Mifflin, 1913).

7. See, *inter alia*, Erwin Panofsky, *Gothic Architecture and Scholasticism* (Cleveland and New York: Meridian, 1957).

8. Emile Mâle, *The Gothic Image* (New York: Harper and Row, 1958), 5–14.

9. Otto von Simson, *The Gothic Cathedral* (New York: Harper and Row, 1962), 8.

10. See Jonathan Sumption, *Pilgrimage: An Image of Medieval Religion* (Totowa, NJ: Rowman and Littlefield, 1975).

11. I am using here concepts articulated by Mircea Eliade, e.g., in his classic *The Myth of the Eternal Return or, Cosmos and History* (Princeton: Princeton University Press, 1971).

12. See Thomas F. O'Dea, *The Sociology of Religion* (Englewood Cliffs, NJ: Prentice-Hall, 1966), 66–68.

13. See Turner, *Temple to Meeting House*, Chapter 10, especially 178–94.

14. Marian Card Donnelly, *The New England Meeting Houses of the Seventeenth Century* (Middletown, CT: Wesleyan University Press, 1968), 94.

15. Ola Elizabeth Winslow, *Meetinghouse Hill 1630–1783* (New York: Norton, 1972), 51.

16. See, *inter alia*, Sumner Chilton Powell, *Puritan Village* (Garden City, NY: Doubleday, 1965).

17. Colin Platt, *The English Medieval Town* (London: David McKay, 1976), 155.

18. John Archer, "Puritan Town Planning in New Haven," *Journal of the Society of Architectural Historians*, 34, no. 2 (May 1975): 140–49.

19. Perry Miller, *The New England Mind: From Colony to Province* (Cambridge, MA: Harvard University Press, 1953), 11.

20. William H. Pierson, Jr., *American Buildings and Their Architects: The Colonial and Neoclassical Styles* (Garden City, NY: Doubleday, 1970), 34–45.

21. See G. W. O. Addleshaw and Frederick Etchells, *The Architectural Setting of Anglican Worship* (London: Faber and Faber, 1956), 54–56.

22. *American Buildings*, 94–100.

23. Ibid., 102–05.

24. See plates between pp. 246–47 in James F. Findlay, Jr., *Dwight L. Moody: American Evangelist, 1837–1899* (Chicago and London: University of Chicago Press, 1969), and in Bernard Weisberger, *They Gathered at the River* (Boston and Toronto: Little Brown, 1958), between pp. 114–15.

25. Mary Josephine Sellers, "The Role of the Fine Arts in the Culture of Southern Baptist Churches" (Ph.D. diss., Syracuse University, 1968), chapter II, 57–97.

26. For a wide variety of illustrations of Methodist churches in these and other popular styles, see Elmer Talmage Clark, *An Album of Methodist History* (New York: Abingdon-Cokesbury, 1951), *passim*.

27. *American Buildings*, 360–72.

28. See Laurel B. Andrew, *The Early Temples of the Mormons* (Albany: State University of New York Press, 1978).

29. William H. Pierson, Jr. *American Buildings and Their Architects: Technology*

and the Picturesque, the Corporate and the Early Gothic Styles (Garden City, NY: Doubleday, 1978), 116–34. Hereafter cited as Pierson (1978).

30. See especially James F. White, *The Cambridge Movement* (Cambridge: Cambridge University Press, 1962).

31. Pierson (1978), 184–90.

32. See George E. DeMille, *The Catholic Movement in the American Episcopal Church* (New Brunswick, NJ: Church Historical Society, 1941).

33. Pierson (1978), chapter IV; also Everard M. Upjohn, *Richard Upjohn, Architect and Churchman* (New York: Columbia University Press, 1939).

34. See Peter W. Williams, "A Mirror for Unitarians: Catholicism and Culture in Nineteenth Century New England Literature" (Ph.D. diss., Yale University, 1970).

35. E.g., in John Henry Hopkins's *Essay on Gothic Architecture* (Burlington, VT, 1836). See also Horace Bushnell, "Preliminary Dissertation on the Nature of Language..." (1849), in Sydney E. Ahlstrom, ed., *Theology in America* (Indianapolis and New York, 1967), 319–70.

36. James H. Barnett, *The American Christmas, A Study in National Culture* (New York: Macmillan, 1954), 1–18.

37. Thomas Bender, "The 'Rural' Cemetary Movement: Urban Travail and the Appeal of Nature," *New England Quarterly* 47, no. 1 (June 1974): 196–211; Stanley French, "The Cemetery as Cultural Institution: The Establishment of Mount Auburn and the 'Rural Cemetery' Movement," *American Quarterly* 26, no. 1 (March 1974): 37–59.

38. Clifford E. Clark, Jr., "American Architecture: The Prophetic and Biblical Strains," in Giles Gunn, ed., *The Bible and American Arts and Letters* (Philadelphia: Fortress Press; Chico, CA: Scholars Press, 1983), 105–27, esp. 112–13.

39. Henry-Russell Hitchcock, *The Architecture of H. H. Richardson and His Times* (1936; repr., Cambridge, MA and London: MIT Press, 1966), 136–44; Bettina A. Norton, ed., *Trinity Church, The Story of an Episcopal Parish in the City of Boston* (Boston: Wardens and Vestry of Trinity Church, 1978), 52–59.

40. See Douglas Shand Tucci, *Church Building in Boston 1720–1970* (Concord, MA: Rumford Press, 1974), on Boston Church architecture in general and Cram's role in particular.

41. See David J. Rothman, *The Discovery of the Asylum: Social Order and Disorder in the New Republic* (Boston and Toronto: Little Brown, 1971).

42. See James McLachlan, *American Boarding Schools* (New York: Scribners, 1970).

43. Pierson (1978), chapter V, 206–69.

44. See George W. Kramer, *The What and How of Church Building* (New York: n.p., 1897), for a description and rationale of the Akron Plan, together with a plethora of line drawings and diagrams.

45. Among Conover's many publications were *Building the House of God* (New

York and Cincinnati: Methodist Book Concern, 1928), and *The Church Builder* (New York: Interdenominational Bureau of Architecture, 1948).

46. William Blackburn, *The Architecture of Duke University* (Durham, NC: Duke University Press, 1936); Doris Dowdell Moore, *Signs of His Presence* (Dallas, TX: Highland Park United Methodist Church, 1975).

47. On Cram's relationship with Wilson, see Arthur S. Link, ed., *The Papers of Woodrow Wilson* (Princeton: Princeton University Press), volumes 17 (1974), 18 (1974), and 19 (1975), *passim*.

48. William Morgan, *The Almighty Wall: The Architectures of Henry Vaughan* (New York, Cambridge, MA, and London: MIT Press, 1983), 73–86.

49. Robert N. Bellah, "Civil Religion in America," in Bellah and William G. McLouglin, eds., *Religion in America* (Boston: Beacon, 1968), 3–23.

50. Lloyd Lewis, *Myths After Lincoln* (New York: Press of the Readers Club, 1929).

51. Kevin Lynch, *The Image of the City* (Cambridge, MA: MIT Press, 1960).

52. James P. Walsh, "Holy Time and Sacred Space in Puritan New England," *American Quarterly*, 32, no. 1 (Spring 1980): 79–95.

53. Robert C. Twombly, *Frank Lloyd Wright* (New York, Evanston, San Francisco, and London, 1974), 80–82; Frank Lloyd Wright, "Designing Unity Temple," in Edgar Kaufmann and Ben Raeburn, eds., *Frank Lloyd Wright: Writings and Buildings* (New York, London, and Scarborough, Ont., 1974), 74–83.

54. Colman J. Barry, S.J., *Worship and Work: Saint John's Abbey and University 1856–1956* (Collegeville, MN: St. John's Abbey, 1956); Howard Vincent Niebling, "Modern Benedictine Churches: Monastic Churches Erected by American Benedictines Since World War II" (Ph.D. diss., Columbia University, 1973); Ronald William Roloff and Brice Howard, *Abbey and University Church of St. John the Baptist, Collegeville, Minnesota* (St. Paul, MN: A. G. Muellerleile and North Central Publishing Co., 1961).

Ralph Adams Cram:
Dreamer of the Medieval

Richard Guy Wilson

A
RCHITECTS AS ARTISTS MUST DREAM; THEY IMAGINE MAGICAL WORLDS OF
their making: Broadacre Cities, White Cities, Walled towns, and
vast naves capable of sheltering thousands. The conviction by which
an architect can bring these visions or fantasies to the physical reality of form,
space and image is one of the distinctions between great architects and those
who simply build. The dream or vision is the irrational, which is then fitted
to a function, the rational, which will hopefully make a lasting piece of art.
Ralph Adams Cram dreamed, he imagined: "magnificent activity, manly
fighting, chivalrous ideals," "Chartres Cathedral and its glass, the sculpture
of Rheims, The *Dies Irae*, Aucassin and Nicolette, the Song of Roland, the
Arthurian Legends"[1] (Fig. 1). Mont-Saint-Michel exerted a hold on Cram as
it did on Henry Adams, whose book he greatly admired, and in some of Cram's
drawings the building takes on the image of an island—towers, pinnacles,
crockets, and spires—offering a refuge from a barbarian world.[2]

Of course, Cram was not simply a dreamer; he was a dominant architectural presence in America from the 1890s into the 1930s with hundreds of
buildings scattered across the country and abroad. An acknowledged eclectic who based his designs upon the past, Cram creatively adopted and modified
traditional styles, forms, and details, creating in the end his own personal-
ized vision—the Cram Medieval. The overt archaeologizing or direct copying

1. Cover of *Knight Errant*, 1892, Bertram Goodhue, delineator, Ralph Adams Cram, editor.

of specific models in Cram's own work is always loose; he drew from the past, but changed and made for the present. Cram felt at ease in abandoning buttresses, in reversing the traditional eastern orientation of the altar, in creating one great nave and very thin aisles as well as a great cave for the chapel,

2. Rice University, Houston Texas, 1909+, Cram, Goodhue & Ferguson, Architects
(Author's collection).

and in using French flamboyant tracery on a permanently unfinished facade
on New York's Fifth Avenue. While specific features such as the proportions
of the clerestory windows can be traced to the Cathedral at Troyes—and some
of the ideas for the interior arcade came from the Cathedral at LeMans, still
Saint Thomas in New York (1905–13) is basically a creative whole of balanced
asymmetrical voids and solids, enlivened by Bertram Goodhue's exuberant
ornament.[3] Similarly, at Rice University in Houston (1909 onwards), the

main complex of buildings was not based upon northern European Medieval Gothic as was so much of Cram's work but on southern or Mediterranean Medieval (Fig. 2), or as Cram explained: "I reassembled all the elements I could from southern France and Italy, Dalmatia, the Peloponnesus, Byzantium, Anatolia, Syria, Sicily, Spain," and made them into a "new style."[4] The result was an extravaganza, layer upon layer horizontally and vertically, of color, detail, and mass, that echoed ancient civilizations but certainly not in a mimicking or archaeological manner. Rice University is eclectic, but the stylistic confection has principles: climatic reference in the arcades and deep windows, regional associations in the coloration of the natural landscape, and cultural resonance in that the great styles of the hot south—the Mediterranean—have an affinity with the Texas Gulf. And, finally, though the university is new, the associations with the great cultures of the past are appropriate for a university that seeks to know the past but lacks indigenous traditions.

With Ralph Adams Cram the dreamy visionary quality and the creative eclecticism of his built work are always important to keep in mind because the public persona of Cram could frequently appear at odds, denying this dream. There were many "Ralph Adams Crams." There was "Doctor" (an honorary degree) Ralph Adams Cram, a leading scholar of the Middle Ages, a founder of the Mediaeval Academy of America, and a consort of individuals such as Arthur Kingsley Porter and Kenneth Connant. There was a preachy Cram who advocated Anglo-Catholicism or High Episcopalianism and who wrote books such as *Church Building* (1901) and edited journals such as *Christian Art* (1907–08). There was a cynical Cram, the social critic, who despaired of the machine and capitalism, and wrote constantly for journals such as *The American Mercury, Commonweal,* and others, proclaiming that a return to medieval forms and virtues was the only solution. Altogether, Ralph Adams Cram is a very formidable figure with 22 books to his credit, another 15 or so which he either edited or wrote introductions for, at least 150 articles, and too many public lectures even to begin to count. Indeed Cram's career is so extensive and has so many facets that merely listing his accomplishments and citing instances of his importance, e.g., from the cover of *Time* for December 13, 1926 to the public pronouncements at his death in 1942, can be a task in itself.[5] While all of these activities combine to make the "total man," the fact remains that Cram's primary importance and his own self-definition was as an architect. It is not that the different activities are mutually exclusive, since the writing and commentary did promote his architectural practice. Yet this public persona hid the real Ralph Adams Cram, the "hot eyed" Bohemian who could write in 1892:

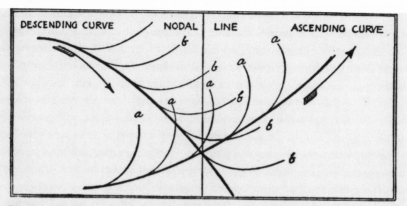

DIAGRAM No. 3. The reactions thrown off by (*a*) the descending line of vital force, (*b*) by the ascending line.

3. Ralph Adams Cram, Diagram on medieval civilization, from Cram, *Towards the Great Peace* (Boston: Marshall Jones Company, 1922), 261.

The Abbey is all dim and shadowy: a fickle light flickers vaguely on the vast stone piers that gather themselves mistly out of the darkness below and vanish in the cavernous night overhead. In the choir the monks are chanting their Vespers: Slowly, solemnly. It is as though the mouldering stones found voice, singing and laughing our Lady *Ave Maria, gratia plena, Dominus tecum.*

The cantor stands before an oaken lectern fashioned with craft and cunningly of grinning griffins and slim angels: the flaming candles on either hand flaunt and flare restlessly, and the monk drops his tonsured head over the beaviary splendid with scarlet, and azure and fine gold.[6]

The public persona of Cram shielded Cram the dreamer, for he knew that if his visions would have any reality, they needed the guise of a Yankee realist – after all he was born a Unitarian. At the risk of being branded a cultural heathen, I suggest that Cram's writings have overpowered the man as an architect, and in a sense have done him a disservice. If his writings are taken without the context of his architecture, they are "harebrained," such as his solution to the world's ills advanced in 1919 that everybody should retreat to Puginesque fifteenth-century walled towns to be built from New England to South Dakota.[7] In another book at the end of World War One he claimed medieval society was the wave of the future, drawing Toynbee-esque graphs (Fig. 3) to show the various energy levels and the inevitability of the coming medieval restoration.[8] These are nutty on their own, unless they are taken with reference to Cram's ultimate source, William Morris and the Arts and Crafts movement, which inspired him, as it did Frank Lloyd Wright's own solutions to America's problems. In common with many architects who write, Cram's writings were promotional—they brought in clients—and also explanatory—they showed how his buildings fit into the cosmic scheme, at least as he saw it. Cram wrote with style and vigor, he was facile with words (he had been a critic for the Boston *Transcript* for a few years in the mid–1800s), but perhaps he was his own worst enemy, for he appears at times verbally extravagant and pompous.[9] As is common with many architects when they write and make the leap from designing a single building to the role of social critic, Cram could envision the vast landscape filled with his architecture, but he offered no reasonable means by which the walled town, or the modern feudal society would come into being. He despised modern mechanical civilization, he thought Protestantism wrongheaded and felt that the peak of world civilization had been reached in the fifteenth century before Henry VIII and the reformation began the downhill slide. The world and civilization were seen architecturally, for as he wrote about his first major church commission, All Saints' Ashmont, Dorchester, Massachusetts (1891–95), the purpose was "to take up English Gothic at the point when it was cut off during the reign of Henry VIII and go on from that point, developing the style England had made her own, and along what might be assumed to be logical lines, with due regard to the changing conditions of contemporary culture." To Cram, "Gothic as a style ... was not dead but only moribund."[10]

Still another way in which Cram's writings undercut his architectural reputation was in admitting the creative quality of his design and eclecticism. Of course, the cult of originality was not as strong in the first third of this century as it has subsequently become; Cram also found modernism repugnant. In his writings he claims he was "archaeological" while his partner, Bertram Goodhue was more modern.[11] Cram implies in his autobiography that this difference led to their separation in 1914. Evidence, however, indicates the split came primarily from Goodhue's insecurity and craving for recognition rather than fundamental disagreements on modern versus traditional.[12] Goodhue was a very talented designer and one of America's truly great ornamentalists and draftsmen. Initially, Cram had been the main designer producing the overall plan, form, mass and proportions of a project with Goodhue providing the more intricate detail.[13] This only lasted for the first few years of the partnership and ultimately both Cram and Goodhue did their own projects, in consultation with each other.

While Cram was archaeological, this did not mean an exact replication of the past, and constantly he noted that he and his colleagues were picking up lost threads, not copying. Such disclaimers are easy to overlook, especially with Cram's powerful scholarly persona and his constant recitation of the glories of the medieval period. Consequently, he became to many—especially those who did not know the medieval firsthand—an archaeologist and not a creative eclectic.[14] Certainly not archaeological is Saint Stephen's, Cohasset, Massachusetts, 1899 (Fig. 4). The building is molded to the rocky outcropping overlooking both the town and the green: the church grows effortlessly upward. The plan as in many of Cram's churches is a creative departure from the normally rigid program; it has one side aisle and a large nave (Fig. 5). The different functional elements are clearly spelled out in both form and materials. Detail is simple and sparse, reduced to a bare minimum.

Cram's dreams of an architecture for America based on medieval forms—an architecture drawing upon the Old World and yet of the New—began in his youth, and were given substance during crucial years in Boston in the 1880s and 1890s. The "figure in the carpet" is not the rational elder spokesman for correct historicizing design, but a "hot eyed" Bohemian decadent.[15]

Ralph Adams Cram was born in 1863 in rural New Hampshire. His father, "a mystical philosopher," became a Unitarian minister during Cram's youth, while his mother held "keen rationalist convictions."[16] He records in his autobiography, *My Life in Architecture* (1936), a genteel, monetarily skimpy but intellectually rich upbringing with reading in the usual books, especially Ruskin and Walter Scott. His youthful interest in buildings and towns was given some outlet in the construction of models, which he then burned up. Freudian psychoanalysts would certainly have a field day with such activity, especially in light of Cram's later condemnation of most modern cities and towns. Unable to afford a college education for him, his family shipped Cram off to Boston in 1881 for apprenticeship with the architectural firm of Rotch and Tilden. Arthur Rotch and George Tilden had attended M.I.T. and the Beaux Arts, though their work of the 1880s when Cram was a member was more in the Aesthetic Movement—Colonial Revival, aspects of which blend in imperceptibility into the New England Arts and Crafts of the 1890s and 1900s. Cram worked for Rotch and Tilden for 5 years, made two trips to Europe, wrote some art and literary criticism, and in 1889 founded, with Charles Francis Wentworth (1841–97), the firm of Cram and Wentworth. Bertram Grosvenor Goodhue (1869–1924) joined in 1892, and the firm became Cram, Wentworth and Goodhue. With Wentworth's death, Frank Ferguson (1861–1926) became a partner, and the firm remained Cram, Goodhue

4. Saint Stephan's, Cohaset, 1899, Cram, Goodhue and Ferguson, Bertram Goodhue, delineator (courtesy, AIA Foundation, Washington, D.C.).

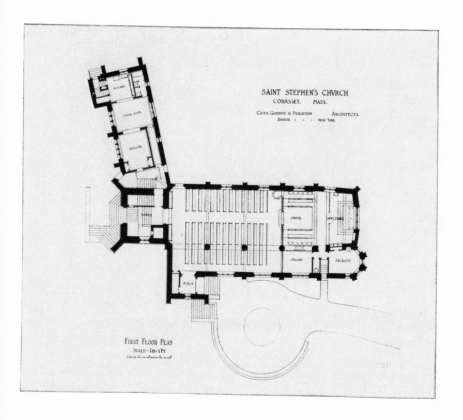

5. St. Stephan's, plan. Source: Cram, *Church Building* (Boston: Small, Maynard & Co., 1906).

and Ferguson until 1914 when Goodhue left. From 1914 to Cram's death in 1942 the firm's name was Cram and Ferguson.

As important as Cram's architectural activity is, the cultural milieu in Boston in which he immersed himself, and which forever colored his architectural proclivities, proved equally significant. Photographs of Cram from the 1880s and 1890s, for example, show him looking like a character from Gilbert and Sullivan's *Patience* or like Oscar Wilde; Cram admired both the opera and the author. Cram became a member of a Bohemian group which emphasized artistic, literary, and religious ideas; such activity was *de rigueur* in the *fin de siècle* (or Decadent) movement.[17] In fact Cram's first book, entitled *The Decadent* (1893), is filled with the usual world-weary, heavy symbolism

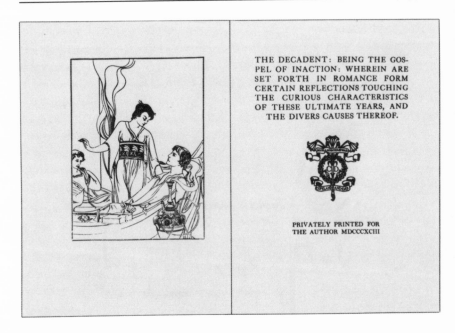

THE DECADENT: BEING THE GOS-
PEL OF INACTION: WHEREIN ARE
SET FORTH IN ROMANCE FORM
CERTAIN REFLECTIONS TOUCHING
THE CURIOUS CHARACTERISTICS
OF THESE ULTIMATE YEARS, AND
THE DIVERS CAUSES THEREOF.

PRIVATELY PRINTED FOR
THE AUTHOR MDCCCXCIII

6. Ralph Adams Cram, *The Decadent* (Boston: Copeland & Day, 1893), frontispiece by Bertram Goodhue.

common to most of the Decadent literature, along with some passages on depravity, drugs, and sex (Fig. 6).[18] Essentially "Aesthetes," Cram and his group took clues from books such as Walter Pater's *Marius the Epicurean* (1885) and rapturized continuously about ideal and complete beauty, pure sensation, and symbolic religion. Cram discovered the Pre-Raphaelites and their later work at the Museum of Fine Arts, became a "besotted Wagnerite," and went to Europe in 1886 on his first trip, principally to attend the Bayreuth festival.[19] In his autobiography Cram self-deprecatingly notes this Decadent period, playing down some of the more lurid features. The photographs of Cram's close friend F. Holland Day with male nudes, as Pan, caressing statues, or reenactments of the *Crucifixion* are American soft-focus equivalents of Aubrey Beardsley.[20] Later in life Cram passed off as "the way of Youth" his Monarchist or Royalist sentiments with the passage "we had our services of mourning and expiation on the Feast of Charles the Martyr and on the other Loyalist days, drank our seditious toasts, sang our Jacobite songs...."[21] But as late as 1900, when Cram was in his mid-thirties, he was the "Prior" of the Order of the White Rose, an English-based organization which advocated the restoration of the Stuarts to the throne of England, and of monarchy world wide, including the United States. Cram wrote that the Order believed in "loyalty, chivalry, honour, the defense of lawful government and legitimate Princes, denial of the heresy of popular sovereignty, the upholding of the Divine source of power, belief in a monarchical system of government as having Divine sanction. . . ." In his article, Cram, who signed himself Ralph von Cram, did allow that the American Revolution had occurred and that for the near future the best course would be to work for a replacement of the "democratic follies of Jefferson" with a Hamiltonian constitution.[22] On the other hand Cram also experimented with socialism, not the Karl Marx variety, but the softer William Morris style; he and friends even founded a "Church of the Carpenter," which "could but appeal to the working classes — which it conspicuously did not."[23]

Much of this activity provides the background of the American Arts and Crafts movement in New England. In his youthful writings Cram frequently invoked Morris, as in a mid 1880s article: "Morris is without doubt, the most wholly and roundly great man that the century can show."[24] *The Knight Errant*, a lavish magazine that appeared for four issues in 1892 and was edited by Cram, was consciously intended and indeed, seen as an American version of the English *Hobby Horse*.[25] It was named for a poem by Cram's close friend Louise Imogene Guiney, inspired by Donatello's Saint George (which was the subject of Goodhue's cover design as well):

> Spirits of old that bore me,
> And set me, meek of mind,
> Between great dreams before me,
> And deeds as great behind,
> Knowing humanity my star
> As first abroad I ride,
> Shall help me wear with every scar
> Honour at eventide.[26]

The Knight Errant's contents and contributors were eclectic: Bernard Berenson, Ernest Fenollosa, Walter Crane, F. Holland Day, and others on Japanese art, Renaissance paintings, the "Restoration of Idealism" by Cram, along with his own poems, such as "Ave Maria."[27] Bertram Goodhue contributed a number of articles, including critical notice on William Lethaby's *Architecture, Mysticism and Myth*, a book that would become very important to both Cram and Goodhue in outlining the lineage between tradition and symbolism and the unity of the Middle Ages.[28]

Another part of this activity was Cram's religious wanderings and conversion to Anglo-Catholicism in 1889. While I do not intend to disparage Cram's religious convictions, which were obviously sincere, one must nevertheless point out that Anglo-Catholicism was part of the *fin de siècle* and Arts and Crafts atmosphere. In his autobiography Cram admits to an infatuation with Madame Blavatsky's Oriental occultism, and he did investigate other mystical strains.[29] Letters to the editor of the *Boston Transcript* from the mid–1880s indicate his already High-Anglican propensity before he experienced a revelation at a Christmas midnight mass at a Catholic Church in Rome in 1888.[30] Significantly, he returned to Boston and joined not the Roman Catholics but the High Episcopalians or Anglo-Catholics at Saint John the Evangelist and the Church of the Advent. The choice of High Anglicanism has several reasons. Elitism and snobbery certainly played a part, since in Boston in the 1880s – and elsewhere in the United States as well – Catholic meant Irish and poor European immigrants, an association to avoid at all costs. Secondly, the Anglo-Catholic movement in the United States, and in Boston in particular, was a rebellion against the dominant Puritan, Congregational, Unitarian, Transcendentalist lineage. It replaced preaching and intellectual prayer with liturgy and ritual, and was still considered in the 1890s suspect and *outré*.[31] High Episcopal worship is a spectacle: the colorful vestments, the incense, the ritualistic dance of the priests, the "mystery" of the preparation of the elements, the chanting and singing are distinctly exotic and at times erotic. Cram clearly gloried in the pageant of worship. Finally, there is Cram's extreme anglophilia, very strong in the 1880s and 1890s, which would continue though somewhat diminished throughout the remainder of his life and in his architecture. In spite of William Morris's agnostic or areligious attitudes, most of the English Arts and Crafts participants, and their roots back through Street (with whom both William Morris and Philip Webb studied), Butterfield, the Cambridge Camden Society and the Ecclesiological Society were High Anglican, and, in a very fundamental way, the English design revolution which culminates in the Arts and Crafts Movement has a religious component. The architectural aspect of High Anglicanism attracted many followers, including Ralph Adams Cram.

The architectural consequences of Cram's Boston Bohemianism and Anglo-Catholicism were to make him an Arts and Crafts designer, knowledgeable and interested in symbolic eclecticism, and with a strong – though not complete – propensity to the medieval and the Gothic in particular. The Aesthetic Movement and its continuation, the Arts and Crafts Movement, did not have one specific style. The Queen Anne most associated with the 1870s and 1880s Aesthetic Movement was a combination of 1680s English classicism and medieval with elements of North European and English vernacular, and here and there Japanese features. In the United States it became nationalized as the "modernized" "colonial" or the Shingle style, and later in the more formal Colonial revival. Fundamentally though, both the Aesthetic Movement and the Arts and Crafts were astylistic; the designers were eclectic and chose whatever was suitable or struck their fancy and included Gothic, Romanesque, Byzantine and various forms of classicism.[32] So while in spite of Cram's propaganda for the Gothic in print, his firm could use the Colonial or Georgian revival for Sweet Briar College in Virginia and the Second Church (Congregational) in Boston. Also, Cram did a proposal in 1897–98 for the Japanese parliament house in a style based upon the Ashikaga and Fujiwara periods, and later in 1905 wrote a book, *Impressions of Japanese Architecture*. And there are buildings of the firm which are openly Beaux Arts in spite of Cram's very public antagonism to the École.[33] This knowledgeable eclecticism was common to most architects of the turn-of-the-century. Even a firm such as McKim, Mead and White, known particularly as classical rivals, could produce knowledgeable Gothic, as with St. Peter's in Morristown, New Jersey, a building which Cram admired.[34] Within Cram's firm a division existed between those draftsmen who were assigned to the more mundane, non-medieval projects and those, known as the "Saints," who were considered expert enough to handle Gothic and other medieval designs.[35] Cram's sympathies were with the medieval, but in the same way that he created a public persona at odds with his "hot eyed" Bohemian, the firm did very creditable work in styles far removed from what he publically advocated.

Cram's architecture is fundamentally of the Arts and Crafts Movement, and while the movement is generally seen as dying out in the United States with World War One, there were continuations after the war that merge into 1920s decorative design known as Art Deco. This is the work of Cram and his partners; they stood for high quality craftsmanship, and Cram, along with Goodhue, were founders of the Boston Society of Arts and Crafts, the first such organization in the United States. The firm Cram, Wentworth and Goodhue exhibited furniture, and Goodhue showed drawings, in the first major exhibition held in the United States, which took place at Copley Hall in April, 1897, prior to the formation of the Arts and Crafts Society. Both as a firm and as individuals they continued to show in subsequent years.[36] As noted earlier, Cram admired William Morris, and much of Cram's rabid anti-industrialism, hatred of the machine, and dislike of capitalism was influenced by Morris, as was his solution, viz., a Morris-inspired return to a feudal-medieval society with artisan guilds and handicraft reigning supreme. One result was Cram and partners integrated artisan-produced crafts in their buildings, such as the stained glass of Charles Connick and Nicola D'Ascenzo, the sculptural carvings of John Evans and Lee Laurie, the metalwork of Henry Wilson, the woodwork of Johannes Kirchmayer, Irving and Casson, and A. H. Davenport, and the tile work of Henry Chapman Mercer.

Cram's interest lay with creating symbolic structures, and this led him almost inevitably to medieval and Gothic architecture. The heart of the philosophy advocated by Morris and his followers was basically medieval, both socially and aesthetically. The medieval period and its artifacts were seen as ethically pure, uncontaminated by the egocentric, capitalist artist who emerged in the Renaissance. The division of labor between the designer and the craftsman did not exist. Medieval (and Gothic) architecture was seen as moral; it was honest structurally, organic in both form and relation to society, spontaneous, and functional. In many architects and critics' minds the Gothic or the medieval contained the only avenue to aesthetic freedom and a new architecture.[37] Cram wrote: "Gothic was neither a temporary phase nor yet a sequence of episodes; it was a tendency, a progress, a development. . . . [By] a violent and sudden revolution, its wonderful career was terminated, half its possibilities undeveloped."[38] Medieval was also Christian (in spite of the barbarian name of Gothic), and true Catholic (before the Reformation and Counter-Reformation), and uncontaminated by pagan associations as were the various forms of classical. Symbolically, the medieval offered a much richer line of exploration. Cram and his partners reacted against the High Victorian willful synthetic eclecticism that seemed to take motifs from anywhere and mangle the forms and details. While Cram did admit admiration for Richardson, he could see no relevance for the Southern French Romanesque, or in most cases for Ruskin and Butterfield's usage of the Italian Gothic.[39] These styles—except in specific instances such as Rice University—lacked the appropriate symbolic connections. Some of Cram's earliest unbuilt church designs have a Richardsonian heaviness, but his reliance on more appropriate medieval prototypes is already evident.

In England by the late 1870s and early 1880s the heavy High Victorian church design had given way to a new moderation of lightness, delicacy, and more fidelity to original sources. Architects such as Bodley and Garner, Leonard Stokes, and J. D. Sedding tossed out the aggressive and crude juxtapositions of the High Victorian, and sought a balanced composition, where the parts fit as a whole. Cram greatly admired their work, writing favorable reviews comparing "Good and Bad Modern Gothic."[40] In the Boston area

Henry Vaughan, an English emigré from Bodley's office, did substantial work in this new mode, especially for the High Episcopal church. Vaughan influenced Cram to turn towards this new more knowledgeable medieval revival.[41] While the designs of Bodley and Vaughan were at times more definitely within a certain style and not of the heterogeneous mixture of the earlier High Victorians, still these men were not strict archaeologists. Cram claimed that they embodied a "medieval spirit vitalized by modern conditions."[42]

Cram's brand of eclecticism was creative and yet academic or scientific in that there are obvious correspondences with older buildings, forms, styles and details, but they were always modified and reintegrated. Details are generally studied with an intensity and fetishness in an attempt to create a harmony of style, scale, proportion and weight, but they are never archaeological copies. The attention given to "correct" details and their replication has a certain scientific element.[43] Cram's buildings are generally of one stylistic period or expression, and seldom juxtapositions. He rarely tried to create the unconscious accidents of vernacular builders; he saw the building as one whole, and not a series of parts. The vernacular was for inspiration, not copying. Similarly the buildings were not designed to be old, or imitate age through either self-conscious additions or worn stone. The details are new, whether capitals, rood carvings, or moldings. There is a tightness and repetitiveness about each of Cram's designs; they do not contain designed accidents. Geometry is a ruling element in the repetitive details and a reminder of the abstraction in much of Beaux Arts work. There is always a sense of an underlying geometry and module.

All Saints' Ashmont, Dorchester, Massachusetts (1891–95) was Cram's first total church (Fig. 7). The irregular, random, seam-faced Quincy granite used for the walls gives a texture, but the dark color is pollution and not integral. Against this rough texture the Nova Scotia sandstone trim provides a regularity and a crisp newness. Similarly on the interior of All Saints' Ashmont and many other churches, the walls are a smooth plaster finish and very plain. These with time could be embellished, but at the beginning they would look new.

What Cram wanted to do in his medieval churches was, as he claimed, to create a mood: "Length and loftiness, mystery gained through dark roofs and shadowy aisles and chapels; dimness and solemnity, powerful masses, lofty columns, arches that curve into the dark, infinite richness of detail on a basis of perfect simplicity."[44] Cram stressed the need for a sense of mystery; he intended not to brighten the interior too much, but create areas of

7. Cram and Wentworth, All Saint's Ashmont, Dorcester, Mass., 1891–1895. Source: *The Churchman* 79 (April 15, 1899).

darkness, and so the contrast is frequently dramatic between light and dark. He would not widen a church out, or create wide aisles, but lengthen it. At All Saints' Ashmont, the seating is in a very unorthodox way—at least for medieval examples—pushed out under the tower, to avoid a too wide nave and aisles (Fig. 8).[45]

Detail in Cram churches is concentrated. Typically on the exterior Cram likes to start with relatively plain and solid bases and continue the wall with strength and small penetrations. Foliation and picturesqueness would appear only at openings and the top. When possible and appropriate, large towers would dominate the composition and on their tops might be set back, or cut back, and crested with pinnacles.

With the interior, detail, color, and richness are concentrated at one major point, the chancel and the altar. Dark roofs, dark aisles with repetitive points of light, simplified arcades, columns and capitals lead to the chancel. Cram's success was such that very early in his career he began doing churches for Protestant denominations, cloaking them in Anglo-Catholic garb. Preaching stands in Presbyterian and Unitarian churches become altars, and many of his richest and most complicated designs appear for the offspring of the Reformation.

In some of Cram's work there appears an element of geometrical reductionism, a severity of composition. All Saints' Peterboro, New Hampshire

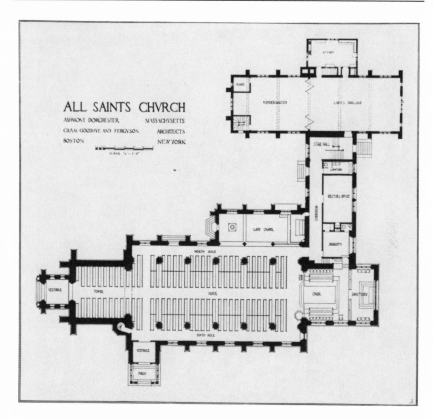

8. All Saint's Ashmont, plan. Source: Cram, *Church Building.*

(1912) (Fig. 9), Saint James's, Lake Delaware, New York (1919), and Church of our Savior, Middleborough, Massachusetts (1897) are exercises in reductivist geometry. Each of the parts, the nave, transepts, chancel, and crossing is given its own uncomplicated basic form; detail is minimal and applied to the openings. The textured stone in all cases provides some relief to the harsh astringent geometrical forms. Exterior detail, as is to be expected, is concentrated at the openings, the entrances, and windows, but it is not lavish. This concentration was appropriate at the parish church level, while for cathedrals and larger buildings, such as the chapel at Princeton, more richness was in order.

The medieval culture that Ralph Adams Cram envisioned for America was one of words and one of physical reality. Words, even carefully chosen and beautifully composed as prose or poetry, still remain on the printed page; they can create visions and fantasy and dreams, but still these dreams must

9. Cram, Goodhue and Ferguson, All Saint's Peterboro, N.H., 1912. Source: Author's collection.

disappear under the light of day. Cram's achievement was more than words: it was stone, and it was more than an archaeological recreation, a fun park or Disneyland—rather it was a creative interpretation that could only be American. It was possible to be born in a house, go to the library, to school, to the university, and to worship in buildings all designed by Cram and reflecting his belief in the moral and aesthetic superiority of the medieval civilization.

NOTES

1. Ralph Adams Cram, *The Gothic Quest* (New York: The Baker and Taylor Company, 1907), 69, and Ralph Adams Cram, "Introduction" in Henry Adams, *Mont-Saint-Michel and Chartres* (Boston: Houghton Mifflin, 1913), vi–vii.

2. Ralph Adams Cram, *My Life in Architecture* (Boston: Little, Brown, 1936), 226–29, recounts Cram's efforts to have Adams's 1904 privately published book represented with a commercial publisher.

3. The attribution of the responsibility for the design of Saint Thomas has been disputed; however, most of the evidence seems to indicate that Cram had primary responsibility for the overall appearance, and that Goodhue did the decoration and the interior fittings. See Harold E. Grove, *Saint Thomas Church* (New York: Saint Thomas Church, 1965); and Richard Oliver, *Bertram Grosvenor Goodhue* (Cambridge: The MIT Press; New York: Architectural History Foundation, 1983), 61–64.

4. *My Life*, 126. See also: Stephan Fox, *The General Plan of the William M. Rice Institute and Its Architectural Development*, Architecture at Rice, monograph 19 (Houston: School of Architecture, Rice University, 1980).

5. For the study of Cram there are his many writings, some noted above and below. Major bibliographies of his writings can be found in: Ann Miner Daniel, "The Early Architecture of Ralph Adams Cram, 1889–1902," (Ph.D. diss., University of North Carolina at Chapel Hill, 1978); and Douglas Shand Tucci, *Ralph Adams Cram, American Medievalist* (Boston: Boston Public Library, 1975). A consideration of Cram as a writer and thinker can be found in: Robert Muccigrosso, *American Gothic: The Mind and Art of Ralph Adams Cram* (Washington, DC: University Press of America, 1980). For other recent scholarship see, Douglas Shand Tucci, *The Gothic Churches of Dorchester* (Ann Arbor: Xerox University Microfilm, 1974). I am indebted to the above studies, but I differ significantly in many points of interpretation.

Major research materials on Cram can be found at: Boston Public Library, Cram and Ferguson Collection: National Cathedral, Washington, DC; Letters of R.A. Cram, Isabell Stewart Gardner Museum; MIT Libraries, Rotch Architectural Library, Cram Collection; and in the archives of the many buildings he designed.

6. Ralph Adams Cram, "An Ave Maria of Arcadelt," *Knight Errant* 1, no. 3 (April 1892): 72.

7. Ralph Adams Cram, *Walled Towns* (Boston: Marshall Jones, 1919).

8. Ralph Adams Cram, *Towards the Great Peace* (Boston: Marshall Jones, 1922), 253, 260–61.

9. Charles D. Maginnis, "Introduction" in *The Work of Cram and Ferguson, Architects* (New York: Pencil Points Press, 1929), n.p., noted Cram was a "master of crisp and arresting phrase, of witty and scathing invective [who] has written and preached his Gothic thesis with the zeal of an apostle."

10. *My Life*, 73, 72.

11. Ibid., 78.

12. Ibid., 79; and Oliver, *Goodhue*, 120–25.

13. *My Life*, 77–78.

14. See for example, Paul Goldberger's review of Walter Kidney, *The Architecture of Choice: Eclecticism in America, 1880–1930* (New York: George Braziller, 1974), in *The New York Times Book Review*, 28 July 1974, 4. See also the negative assessment of Cram's later work in Marcus Whifen and Frederick Koeper, *American Architecture, 1607–1976* (Cambridge, MA: The MIT Press, 1981), 289.

15. "An Ave of Arcadelt," 72.

16. *My Life*, 58.

17. Photographs of Cram can be found in Estelle Jussim, *Slave to Beauty: The Eccentric Life and Controversial Career of F. Holland Day* (Boston: D.R. Godine, 1981), 52–56. For general background on the Decadent movement see Van Wyck Brooks, *New England: Indian Summer, 1865–1915* (New York: E.P. Dutton, 1940), chap. XXI, "The Epigoni"; Gustave L. Van Roosbroeck, *The Legends of the Decadents* (New York: Institut des Études Françaises, Columbia University, 1927); and Holbrook Jackson, *The Eighteen Nineties* (New York: Alfred Knopf, 1922).

18. Ralph Adams Cram, *The Decadent* (Boston: Privately Printed for the Author, 1893; repr., Boston: Copeland and Day, 1901).

19. *My Life*, 7.

20. Jussim, *Slave to Beauty*, 120, 135, 168, and plates 17, 18, and 53.

21. *My Life*, 19–20.

22. Ralph von Cram, "Letter of the Prior of the Order of the White Rose in North America," *The Royal Standard* 1 (September, 1900): 16, 15; Cram Collection, Boston Public Library.

23. *My Life*, 19.

24. Ralph Adams Cram, Letter to the Editor, "William Morris, Poet, Artist, Socialist," from *Boston Evening Transcript*, undated but c. 1883, in "Journal, 1881–1885," Cram Collection, Boston Public Library.

25. "*The Knight Errant* of course, suggests *The Hobby Horse* and Mr. Morris and his coterie"; unidentified clipping in Cram Collection, Boston Public Library. See also, Walter Crane, *An Artist's Reminiscences* (New York: MacMillan, 1907), 371.

26. Louise Imogen Guiney, "The Knight Errant," *The Knight Errant* 1 (April 1892): 3; reprinted in Cram, *My Life*, 87–88; and Louise Imogen Guiney, *Happy Ending* (Boston: Houghton Mifflin, 1899), 11–12.

27. See note 6. Ralph Adams Cram, "Concerning the Restoration of Idealism," *The Knight Errant* 1 (April 1892): 10–15; reprinted in his *The Gothic Quest*, 17–30.

28. Bertram Grosvenor Goodhue, review of William Lethaby, *Architecture Mysticism and Myth* (New York: MacMillan, 1891), in *The Knight Errant* 1 (April 1892): 31. William Lethaby's *Medieval Art, from the Peace of the Church to the Eve of the Renaissance, 312–1350* (New York: Charles Scribner's Sons, 1904), was very important to both Cram and Goodhue.

29. *My Life*, 46.

30. "Journals," Cram Collection, Boston Public Library; and *My Life*, 58–59.

31. George E. DeMille, *The Catholic Movement in the American Episcopal Church* (Philadelphia: The Church Historical Society, 1941); and Edward D. Chorley, *Men and Movements in the American Episcopal Church* (New York: Charles Scribner's Sons, 1946). See also, Douglas Shand Tucci, *Church Building in Boston, 1720–1970* (Concord, N.H.: The Rumford Press for the Trustees of the Dorchester Savings Bank, 1974), part II.

32. See Elizabeth Aslin, *The Aesthetic Movement, Prelude to the Art Nouveau* (London: Alek, 1969); Mark Girouard, *Sweetness and Light: The Queen Anne Movement, 1860–1900* (Oxford: Clarendon Press, 1977); Robin Spencer, *The Aesthetic Movement: Theory and Practice* (London and New York: Studio Vista Dutton, 1972); and Vincent Scully, Jr., *The Shingle Style* (New Haven: Yale University Press, 1955).

33. Ralph Adams Cram, "An Architectural Comment," *The Architectural Review* 6 (January 1899): 18; and Cram, "The Case Against the École des Beaux Arts," in *The Gothic Quest*, 295–319.

34. Ralph Adams Cram, *Church Building* (Boston: Small, Maynard, 1901), 47.

35. Harold Bush-Brown, *Beaux Arts to Bauhaus and Beyond* (Cincinnati: Watson-Gupton, 1976), 21.

36. The Boston Public Library holds the records of the Boston Society of Arts and Crafts. See *First Exhibition of the Arts & Crafts, Copley Hall, Boston, April 5–16, MDCCCXCVII*. See also May R. Spain, *The Society of Arts and Crafts* (1924); Karen Evans Ulehla, comp., ed., *The Society of Arts and Crafts, Boston, Exhibition Record, 1897–1927* (Boston: Boston Public Library, 1981); and Editorial, *The Architectural Review* 6 (April 1899): 54–55.

37. In addition to Lethaby cited above, see Montgomery Schuyler, "The Works of Cram, Goodhue and Ferguson," *The Architectural Record* 29 (January 1911): 89; and Claude Bragdon, "The Gothic Spirit," *Christian Art* 2 (January 1908): 165–72, in which Cram, Goodhue and Ferguson are seen as part of the same movement with Louis Sullivan, H. H. Richardson, and Wilson Eyre.

38. Ralph Adams Cram, "All Saints' Church, Dorchester (Boston), Mass.," *The Churchman* 79 (15 April 1899): 560.

39. *My Life*, 31–34.

40. Ralph Adams Cram, "Good and Bad Modern Gothic," *The Architectural Review* 6 (August 1899): 115–19; and Ralph Adams Cram, "John D. Sedding, Some Considerations of his Life and Genius," *The Architectural Review* 1 (14 Dec. 1891): 9–11.

41. *My Life*, 36. See also, William Morgan, *The Almighty Wall: The Architecture of Henry Vaughan* (Cambridge: The MIT Press; New York: Architectural History Foundation, 1983); Edward Prioleau Warren, "The Work of Messrs. G. F. Bodley and T. Garner," *The Architectural Review* 6 (February 1899): 25–34, and David Verey, "G. F. Bodley" in Jane Fawcett, ed., *Seven Victorian Architects* (London: Thames and Hudson, 1976), 84–101.

42. "Good and Bad," 116.

43. Richard Guy Wilson, "Scientific Eclecticism," in Richard Guy Wilson, Dianne Pilgrim, and Richard Murray, *The American Renaissance, 1876–1917* (Brooklyn and New York: The Brooklyn Museum and Pantheon, 1979), chap. 4.

44. Cram, "Good and Bad," 119.

45. *Church Building*, 53, mentions the problem of seating. At All Saints' Dorchester he had conflicts with the vestery seating as related in Tucci, *The Gothic Churches of Dorchester*, 87– 91. Nobody seems to have realized that Cram's solution was to extend the seats, in a very unorthodox manner, into the tower.

Louis Sullivan's Use of the Gothic: From Skyscrapers to Banks

Narciso G. Menocal

L OUIS SULLIVAN IS WIDELY ACKNOWLEDGED AS ONE OF THE CREATORS OF THE skyscraper and as the designer of very beautiful Midwestern rural banks. These two kinds of buildings take up a very sizable portion of his production and are central to his *oeuvre*. Possibly because these building types are very different from each other a cause-and-effect stylistic relationship between them has never been established. This article proposes to make evident that such a connection does exist and that Sullivan's conception of the Gothic serves as a link.

Before analyzing this relationship as a result of Sullivan's concept – and use – of the Gothic, some of his sources must be surveyed to understand the peculiar meaning he gave to certain stylistic terms, such as Gothic. One must turn for this question to the relationship of architecture and nature, and to the different interpretations of that relationship throughout the nineteenth-century. Some of these he accepted, others he made a partial use of, and others he rejected outright.

I. Sullivan's Romantic Conception of Architecture

Hegel and Schopenhauer are a good starting point. In spite of their differences in other matters, both endorsed a typical early nineteenth-century classicist attitude towards architecture. The post-and-lintel system was the best expression of the relationship of architecture and the law of gravity.[1] Such purely classicist opinions soon became outmoded, however. By the mid-century, Romantic ideas of associationism and the belief that a building should reflect the function it serves modified earlier stricter views. A second generation of transcendentalists argued in favor of the accidental and of the typical, creating an insoluble conflict. Functional and essential realities were to produce individual solutions proper to each design, but at the same time architecture was to express universal objectivity. In short, Romanticism and Transcendentalism had been brought together into a marriage of strange bedfellows.

Paradoxically, it was a philosopher not widely read, Friedrich Vischer, who stated best the problem. A follower of Hegel in his youth, Vischer brought into use a self-contradicting term, *subjective idealism*, to denote a simultaneous portrayal of the typical and of the universal in a synthesis Hegel would have probably disavowed.[2] In design, beginning with the late 1860s, an evocation of tectonics became the means of joining these mutually exclusive ideas. Protruding and receding volumes indicated the relative importance of each part of a building, while massive compositions standing for the universal idea of matter aroused the idea of geomorphism. As Vischer himself explained it, architectural elements until then considered as inert came to have dynamic characteristics they shared with the observer's life, vertical lines now "soared upwardly," and horizontal ones "broadened out." This notion of dynamic expression is at the core of Vischer's idea of *Einfühlung*, or empathy. This was an act of inner imitation, of the lending of our humanity to forms without souls, of the reading of ourselves into inorganic nature.[3] Architecture, besides expressing the universal idea of matter, as well as the individual characteristics of each building, also became symbolic of the movements of man, and by extension, of man himself. In the opinion of the day, this identification was the highest degree of poetry architecture could achieve.

By Sullivan's time these ideas were widespread and available to anyone from a large variety of sources. To him, as well as to many of his contemporaries, buildings were to appear as products of nature – of *Natura naturans* – not of human intelligence. Sullivan moved from the theory implied in these notions to practice by applying an eclectic method. He turned a number of widely-held views on architecture, borrowed mainly from the writings of Ruskin, Viollet-le-Duc, and Leopold Eidlitz into a personal amalgam.

Among John Ruskin's contentions close to Sullivan's beliefs there are those proposing that excellence in architecture depended not on planning and structure but on ornamentation and artistic composition, that decorative details are to copy the most common forms of vegetal and animal life, and that the design and application of ornamentation were to follow the organic principles of its models.[4] Sullivan further agreed with Ruskin that "as nature adorns earth so should man adorn buildings" to contribute "to his mental health, power, and pleasure."[5] But unlike Sullivan, who was an agnostic, Ruskin saw a profoundly religious connotation in the linking of the good, the true, and the beautiful. For him imitating forms of nature in architecture was not only the only means of creating beautiful buildings, but more importantly an act of thanksgiving to God for having created nature for the service of man.[6] To Ruskin, man stood superior to and distinct from nature,[7] a notion Sullivan would have never agreed with.

Sullivan did not believe he had invented a new architecture as much as he was certain he had discovered the method nature had prescribed for the creation of architecture since the beginning of time. He saw himself as a sort of new Prometheus. In spite of these views, one must continue with Ruskin, as well as turn to Emerson, for two important expressive roles ornamentalism was to play in Sullivan's work: one was Ruskinian, relating to *Natura naturata*; the other was Emersonian, pointing to *Natura naturans*.

In his "Lamp of Beauty" Ruskin had pointed out how architecture was to mirror the gorgeousness of nature. "All most lovely forms and thoughts are directly taken from natural objects," he wrote, and conversely, "forms which are *not* taken from natural objects *must* be ugly."[8] These natural objects were to be lovely in themselves, and color was to Ruskin one of the sources of their loveliness. Rendering an organism beautiful through color was nature's way; architecture had no choice but to follow suit.[9] "I cannot consider architecture as in any wise perfect without colour," he stated,[10] inasmuch as a building was "a kind of organised creature."[11]

Sullivan went beyond Ruskin in his mimetism. Reflecting nature's gorgeousness in architecture had to him a reason beyond rendering a building lovely. By echoing the productions of nature he hoped to help humanity—through its observation and use of architecture—to realize the advantages of becoming one with nature. This was to be done not out of moral duty, as Ruskin had posited, but because such a surrendering of the self was rewarded by a state of constant ecstasy, as Emerson had explained it.[12] Sullivan relied on the instincts nature had given him for designing like nature, or so he believed. He could not accept like Ruskin that modern architects had to turn to specific historical periods to learn to imitate nature on the contention those periods offered the best examples of an imitation of nature.[13] Ruskin was wrong; his precept implied substituting an imitation for nature. His advice was historicist, dogmatic, and unfeeling; better to take instinctively from a myriad sources whatever was needed at the moment, and combine it best to promote gorgeousness. At times Sullivan mixed in his ornamentation Islamic and Celtic motifs with naturalistic renditions of foliage, and perhaps used a pattern loosely derived from the Gothic as background.

Combinations of motifs from different periods were not to be read taxonomically to identify the style of a building or of an ornamental piece. *Style*, to Sullivan, had nothing to do with evoking or imitating past periods of architecture. In a typically Transcendentalist vein he identified *style* as the portrayal of essential character through outward appearance, and recommended young architects to make note of the integrity of the *style* "of running water, of a pine tree, of a cow grazing in a meadow, of the sweeping eagle in his flight or [of] the open apple blossom, the toiling work-horse [or] the branching oak."[14] Like Viollet-le-Duc, Sullivan could have said, "Proceed as nature does in its productions and everything your brain may conceive will have style."[15]

This notion of style as an unchanging entity—existing beyond the reach of taxonomy and of archaeology—was possibly the most important lesson Sullivan learned from Viollet-le-Duc. Style was for Viollet-le-Duc an intimate relationship of efficiency among a number of things, such as function, the form that serves it, the materials out of which the object or building is made, and the methods of construction with which it is built. As in nature, from which he took his model, such a relationship in design had to yield a *natural beauty*.[16]

Sullivan's concept of style—in spite of its close similarity with Viollet-le-Duc's—never went as far as accepting technology and the serving of material needs as the bases of a modern architecture—and of its style. Neither would he approve of Viollet-le-Duc's attempts to formulate a style by applying Cartesian logic to understand the uses of past architectural forms. (Out of a merging of logic, erudition, and engineering, Viollet-le-Duc believed, architects would derive a method similar to the empirical one French Positivists endorsed for the sciences, philosophy, and the arts.)[17] This notion of *l'architecte savant* could not be further removed from Sullivan's Transcendentalist ideals. Neither had his ideas on architecture much in common with the more widespread nineteenth-century mechanicalist notion of functionalism, and of the proper way to express it in buildings. "C'est notre maître, mon cher Sullivan, qui roulairait de gros yeux s'il te voyait commettre de telles hérésies, de pareils mensonges!" Thus Jacques Hermant, a former fellow student of Sullivan's at Emile Vaudremer's *atélier* in Paris, voiced his shock when he saw Sullivan had covered metallic structures with brick and terra cotta, that he had clad those same buildings internally in granite, onyx, plaster, or marble, but that iron supports were nowhere visible.[18] Presumably both Hermant and his teacher Vaudremer agreed with Viollet-le-Duc in that the first condition of good architecture was not to deceive, "ni dans la composition de l'ensemble, ni dans celle des moindres details de l'édifice à construire."[19] Indeed, perhaps, Viollet-le-Duc might have well dismissed Sullivan as another gifted *architecte dessinateur*, had he lived long enough to know his work.[20] Moreover, in one of their rare agreements, both Viollet-le-Duc and Ruskin rejected the notion that art may serve to express the metaphysical.[21] This issue, above all, separates Sullivan from both Ruskin and Viollet-le-Duc.

Sullivan's ideas are much closer to Leopold Eidlitz's.[22] Born in Prague in 1823, Eidlitz arrived in New York twenty years later, finding that Emerson and his followers—Horatio Greenough among them—had created a sympathetic intellectual climate for beliefs he had acquired in Germany and in Austria.[23] Eidlitz soon became prominent in architecture circles, was one of the founders of the American Institute of Architects in 1857, and published around that time a series of articles in *The Crayon*, presenting his views on architecture. Those articles served him later as the basis for his 1881 book *The Nature and Function of Art, More Especially of Architecture*.

No archival evidence has shown Sullivan owned a copy of Eidlitz's book, nor did he ever mention Eidlitz's name in any of his writings, but it is hard to imagine Sullivan had not read Eidlitz's book carefully, as even some of his metaphors seem to have been borrowed from it. Eidlitz, like Sullivan later, referred to nature to establish a connection between a building and the transcendental idea from which its design emanates.[24] According to Eidlitz:

A work of art, like a work of nature, is a realized idea, and the ideal is the essence of architecture. It is the godlike attempt to create a new organism, which, because it is new, cannot be an imitation of any work of nature, and, because it is an organism, must be developed according to the methods of nature. It is this fact which places architecture ... above all other arts. If a building can express no idea, as ideas are expressed in the works and through the laws of nature, then architecture never was an art.[25]

The relation of form and function was also important to Eidlitz, but he did not make it as central to his scheme of things as Viollet-le-Duc did. To Eidlitz "natural organisms serve the purpose of teaching the relation of form to function, but the majority of men are by the process of so-called civilization removed from nature, and surrounded by creations of art." For Eidlitz, as well as for Sullivan, the word *art* had a pejorative meaning, signifying sophistry in the handling of form, while poetry, to both, was "the expression of an idea in matter," or in other words, of the transcendental.[26] To Sullivan and to Eidlitz the kinship between composition and decoration determined the characterization of a building's image—that is, of its *style*—more than planning, construction, and structure, as it was for Viollet-le-Duc. As the student expressed it in Sullivan's *Kindergarten Chats*, "a building, to be good architecture, must first of all, clearly ... be its image, as you would say."[27]

In relation to *style*—as he understood it—Eidlitz believed the highest attainment of any art was to reproduce emotions, and noted how painting and sculpture achieved this aim by arresting motion.[28] Architecture was handicapped in this respect; it had a limited capacity to express emotion; it lacked the representational range of painting or of sculpture, and it could only hope to express emotions associated with stress and strain; its expressive possibilities began and ended with the relationship existing between architectural masses and the law of gravity. Yet, inasmuch as the human body is the noblest of all natural organisms, architecture—according to Eidlitz—should recur to the human form to suggest feelings, as painting and sculpture do. In that respect, he wrote:

> The human frame does mechanical work, sometimes with the labor of a carrier of burdens, and then again with the ease of an athlete. It is these gradations of ease, grace, directness, and expression with which ... mechanical work is done by the human frame, which furnish the architect the elements of art expressions in his structures.... Every structure, like the human body, that assumes to be a work of art, must also be possessed of a soul.[29]

Eidlitz's fundamental contribution to Sullivan consisted of making him aware of architectural anthropomorphism as the best method for representing the characteristic essence of a building, for giving it *style*. "It is the problem of the architect," Eidlitz wrote, "to depict the emotions of the structure he deals with; to depict, as it were, the soul of the structure."[30] Through Eidlitz Sullivan came to consider buildings as paradigms of athletic virility. Describing Richardson's Marshall Field Wholesale Store in Chicago, Sullivan wrote in *Kindergarten Chats*:

> Here is a *man* for you to look at. A man that walks on two legs instead of four, has active muscles, lungs and other viscera; a man that lives

and breathes, that has red blood; a real man, a manly man; a virile force—broad, vigorous and with a whelm of energy—an entire male.... I call it, in a world of barren pettiness, a male; for it sings the song of procreant power, as others have squalled of miscegenation.[31]

This description is but one example illustrating a general architectural principle. In *Kindergarten Chats* Sullivan also stated:

The architecture we *seek* shall be as a man, active, alert, supple, strong, sane. A generative man. A man having five senses all awake; eyes that fully see, ears that are attuned to every sound; a man living in his present, knowing and feeling the vibrancy of that ever-moving movement, with heart to draw it in and mind to put it out.... To live, wholly to live, is the manifest consummation of existence.[32]

Sullivan revealed much of his thought in this passage. "The vibrancy of that ever-moving movement" refers to nature's constant recreation of the universe. He turned Herbert Spencer's mechanicist conception of the universe—where force produced motion, motion determined the diffusion of matter, and concentration of matter slowed down motion—into the awesome transcendent rhythm all art was to echo.[33] "The heart to draw it in" in Sullivan's passage refers to man's intuitive understanding of nature's process of creation; "the mind to put it out" alludes to his intellectual ability to express it in art. This process of "drawing in" and "putting out" is another expression of how man is part of nature, "for all [of nature] is rhythm."[34] When man's creative force mirrors the creative force of nature, the result is "wholly to live," and the ultimate reward, a state of perpetual ecstasy is attained.

II. The Skyscrapers:
Sullivan's First Use of the Gothic

Sullivan found the skyscraper the building type revealing best that "permanent Dionysian quality" at the heart of the American drive for progress.[35] Its vertical thrust gave it its basic characteristic, its *style*. Emphasizing its height would convey best its transcendental essence. Presumably Sullivan remembered Viollet-le-Duc's advice and drew lessons applicable to modern work from the Gothic, transformed its principles of design into personal ones, and avoided copying medieval styles verbatim.

Out of a very personal interpretation of the "tall and lofty Gothic" he created his universally praised version of the modern skyscraper. Accordingly, he translated the spirit of the Gothic structure from cut stone into metal and terra cotta.

By suffusing Viollet-le-Duc's teachings with Eidlitz's Transcendentalism, Sullivan surpassed the Frenchman's theories as much as he had surpassed earlier Ruskin's counsel in ornamentation. The skyscraper was to "be tall, every inch of it tall. . . . [T]he glory and pride of exaltation must be in it."[36] To achieve this aim, the interior elevation of a Gothic cathedral served him as a basis for his definition of the skyscraper. The Romantic notion that a Gothic interior was like a grove provided him with an organic basis for the style. This idea may have come to him through Eidlitz, who in his book not-ed how eighteenth- and nineteenth-century romantic writers had often com-pared the interior of Gothic cathedrals with forests because of the similarity of their piers and vaults with tree trunks and branches interlacing high above the ground. (Eidlitz quoted at length an excellent example of such a simile from Thomas Hope's *A Historical Essay on Architecture*, a two-volume work published posthumously in 1835.)[37]

To Sullivan the skyscraper was to be like a new and organic Gothic cathedral jetting forth out of the earth like an exultant being, rising to remind man of the joy of being one with nature. But the skyscraper performs two actions. One is subjective, it soars; the other is objective, it bears down on the soil. Sullivan solved this conflict by going to the original Romantic simile, and compared the pier to the trunk of a tree, to the primeval column that grew tall at the same time it was borne down by the weight of the branches. The transfer of this duality into construction created a paradox that Sullivan justified with Transcendentalist arguments. In a pier, as in the trunk of a tree — its counterpart in nature — there should be a constant rhythm of pulling up and pushing down (which Sullivan expressed later in design through manipula-tion of architectural elements.) He identified the subjective component of growth in the pier (the upward pull) with the "Rhythm of Life." The objective down-bearing compression became the "Rhythm of Death." In an ambiguity Sullivan sought passionately, the objective became subjective and the sub-jective objective at the will of the observer and according to his frame of mind. This capacity Sullivan granted architecture for being in a constant state of flux echoed the perpetual rhythmic becoming in the cosmos,[38] but his ar-chitectural metaphor went beyond a Spencerian model. In its downward pres-sure, in its recognition of the law of gravity, the skyscraper was geomorphic; in its growth, like the trunk of a tree, it was phytomorphic; its gesture, its leaping aloft, was anthropomorphic. The tall office building became an image of the unity of all that exists – mineral, vegetal, and animal – in the oneness of the cosmos. Sullivan made the images of the geomorphic, of the phyto-morphic, and of the anthropomorphic interchangeable; they were like facets of the same crystal; in the end, all sang the same anthem. Not bound by strict academic stylistic rules, Sullivan suffused Viollet-le-Duc's lessons on the modern use of the Gothic with a goodly dose of Transcendentalism. The result was a conception of subjective elasticity in structures creating admirable possibil-ities for symbolizing the transcendent. It is in that Sullivanesque sense that the word Gothic will be used in this paper, one that implies that the words *dynamic* and *Gothic* are almost synonymous when applied to architecture.

Sullivan did not apply, nor did he mature, all of these ideas at once. His architecture evolved from a stylistic adaptation to an eventual personal inven-tion. For the facade of his first skyscraper, the Wainwright Building, St. Louis (1890), he relied heavily on his recollections of the interior of the west wall of the Cathedral of Reims and of the interior elevation of Notre Dame in Paris, yet he also made use of piers and mullions to suggest an effect of slim trees standing close together to create an illusion of growth, of the building being "tall, every inch of it tall." On the inside of the west wall of Reims a system of horizontal and vertical moldings determines alternating rows of vertical panels and of smaller horizontal rectangles under them. The large vertical panels frame cusped niches, and the horizontal ones contain a decoration of naturalisti-cally rendered foliage (Fig. 1). If one imagines the large rectangles enclosing windows instead of niches, the similarities between the Reims walls and the Wainwright facade become evident (Fig. 2). The ambiguity of the interior ele-vation of Notre Dame of Paris, where all the piers are alike instead of there being a succession of major and minor supports to correspond with the struc-tural behavior of the sexpartite vaults, is mirrored in the Wainwright facade, where alternating piers and mullions have the same design (Figs. 3–4).

The interior elevation of Sullivan's Transportation Building for the World's Columbian Exposition, designed only five months after the Wainwright, and consisting of a ground-floor opening, a gallery above it, a circular window at the triforium level, and a clerestory, was also a very close adaptation of Viollet-le-Duc's bays in the transepts and nave of the Cathedral of Paris (Fig. 5).[39] Moreover, in the Transportation Building only alternate piers support-ed the roof, a structural ambiguity that echoed the designs of Paris and of the Wainwright Building. Viollet-le-Duc had finished restoring Notre Dame as late as 1864, and Sullivan, a student at the École des Beaux-Arts shortly thereafter, more than possibly paid close attention to Viollet-le-Duc's work in particular and to Notre Dame in general. The chapter of a direct influence

1. Reims Cathedral, detail of interior west wall.

2. Wainwright Building, St. Louis, detail. Adler and Sullivan, 1890–91.

3. Wainwright Building.

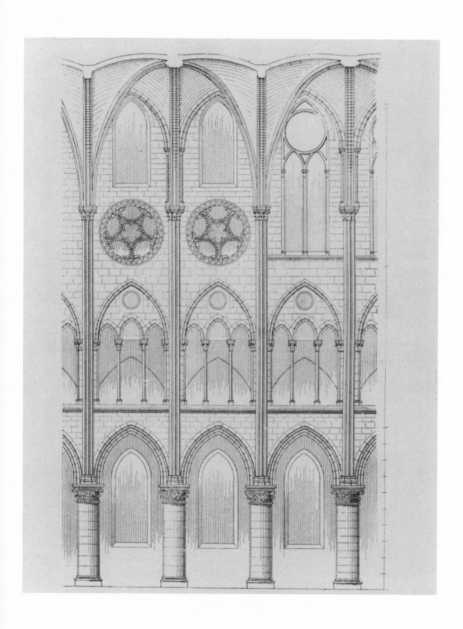

4. Notre Dame, Paris. Nave elevation.

5. Transportation Building, World's Columbian Exposition, Chicago, interior. Adler and Sullivan, 1891–93.

of the Cathedral of Paris on his skyscraper architecture did not close until 1894, with the design of the Guaranty Building, Buffalo, where as in the Wainwright, piers and mullions are alike, and where differentiated first and second floors follow closely a similar disposition in the Transportation Building (Fig. 6).

In subsequent facade designs Sullivan added anthropomorphic meanings to the standard romantic conception of the vegetal origins of the Gothic. Eventually he came to a full expression of his transcendentalist idea of the skyscraper through intimation of organic life and by suggesting that certain structural elements were capable of movement.

The facade of the Bayard Building, New York (1897–98), which Sullivan considered to be his best, serves admirably as an example of how he applied these ideas to design (Fig. 7).[40] The building may be compared to an enormous Gothic clerestory, complete with plate tracery and elongated colonnettes. It also reveals a kinship with the organic. The idea of an eternal becoming, of the "Rhythms of Life and of Death," is evident in the polarities he ascribed to the symbolic rhythm of the piers, of this building. In them death supported life and evolution issued out of dissolution.

The piers of the Bayard Building make clear this idea by establishing a closed circuit with the moldings that decorate them. Beginning at any point, one can follow the design down, then, with no interruption, across the second floor sill, up the next pier, and finally, closing the cycle, across the top through the arch beneath the attic. As this circuit may be established clock- or counter-clockwise, neither the subjective expression of upward movement nor the objective statement of physical pressure is compromised. The piers seem to give the impression that while carrying the weight down to the floor, they are also capable of leaping, like limbs in a human frame. This anthropomorphic scheme is further reinforced visually by the opposing character of the design of the first floor, where the supports show no ambiguity. Structural elements at the street level express only their supporting function; their design reveals no evidence of Sullivan wishing them to evoke a feeling of growth. The lintel works as a summer beam in its etymological sense of *sagma*, or pack saddle, carrying visually the weight of the superstructure. The squat columns below it translate into architecture the muscular strain of an Atlas-like feat, supporting the colossal weight of the building. To create an even greater contrast between the supportive character of the base and the soaring ascension of the piers, Sullivan decreased the height of the floors as the building rises, establishing an optical correction that increases the vertical perspective.[41] As one looks up at the building, it appears to be taller than it actually is.

6. Guaranty Building, Buffalo. Adler and Sullivan, 1894–95.

7. Bayard Building, New York. Louis Sullivan, 1897–98.

8. Farmers' National Bank, Owatonna, Minnesota. Louis Sullivan, 1906–8.

III. The Banks:
Their Relation to the Gothic

Sullivan designed his last skyscraper after the turn of the century and after 1906 rural bank buildings became his most important commissions. In
that year he designed for Owatonna, Minnesota, a bank that became for him
the model of a subsequent series of rural banks of load-bearing construction. These commissions became the largest and most important component
of his remaining *oeuvre* (Fig. 8). Because of the abrupt change, shifting from
designing skyscrapers with free-standing structures to load-bearing one- and
two-story brick buildings, it took Sullivan some time to bring to the banks
what he had learned from the skyscrapers. As such, there is little in the design of his first bank to remind one of the Gothic-derived esthetic of the
skyscrapers; its antecedent was the Golden Doorway of the Transportation
Building of the Columbian Exposition, 1891–93 (Fig. 9). In each case a
monumental panel capped by a strong cornice framed a bold arch supported by a plinth. Since Sullivan was experimenting with a new esthetic, there
were fundamental differences between the two designs. For the Golden Doorway he had established a picturesque program associated with Islamic architecture; in Owatonna he related the design of the bank to the rhythms
of impressionist music and of French symbolist poetry. At the same time the
bank was to evoke the colors of the Midwestern landscape of early spring
or of late autumn.[42] Neither the new esthetic program nor the new type of
construction allowed room for including the Gothic, as Sullivan reinterpret-
ed it in his designs for skyscrapers.

New constructivist concerns derived from his earlier French training and
from his knowledge of Viollet-le-Duc eventually became apparent in the new
architecture. These sources, in turn, establish a link with his earlier uses of
the Gothic. Sullivan's new interest in construction as an esthetic entity in architecture is evident in *Suggestions in Artistic Brick* (1910).[43] Reviving lessons on architectural rationalism he had learned at the École des
Beaux-Arts,[44] he concluded that the appearance of a new building material
on the market had exerted sufficient influence to help create the new Midwestern movement of progressive architecture. Thanks to the new tapestry
brick, he wrote, the architect "began to feel more sensible of the true nature
of a building as an organism or whole." He also stated that "this new material, brick, has led to a new development."[45] Facts become simpler when
divested of the rhetoric Sullivan used to justify them to himself. Tapestry brick
was merely a means to bring new poetry into a building type with which he

9. Transportation Building, Golden Doorway.

had not worked previously. On the other hand, the economic and programmatic realities of his new buildings forced him to seek a fresh connection between architecture and nature.

His new ideas differed from statements he had made during his skyscraper period. In "The Tall Office Building Artistically Considered" (1896), he had established a link between architecture and nature almost exclusively through composition and ornamentation. Physical functions, the properties of methods of construction, and the needs of the client had been pedestrian matters for him fourteen years earlier; an architect dealt with them by means of judicious selection. "These things," he had written, "and such others as the arrangement of elevators, for example, have to do strictly with the economics of the building, and I assume them to have been fully considered and disposed of to the satisfaction of purely utilitarian and pecuniary demands. Only in rare instances does the plan or floor arrangement of the tall office building take on an esthetic value."[46] Believing otherwise in 1910, he stated in *Artistic Brick* that "all the functions of a given building are allowed to find their expression in natural and appropriate forms—each form and the total shape making evident, instead of hiding, the working conditions of the building as exhibited in plan."[47] Proclaiming the expression of plan in volume as a law of nature implied not only a new intellectual attitude towards composition, but also an endorsement of the new progressive Prairie Style of the Midwest.

A typically French rationalist manner of thinking helped Sullivan to understand why the new architecture insisted on an intimate relationship between plan, volume, and function. Paraphrasing Viollet-le-Duc to explain the reasons for making obvious through exterior composition how a building worked inside, he wrote: "This law is not only comprehensive, but universal. It applies to the crystal as well as to the plant, each seeking and finding its form by virtue of its working plan, or purpose, or utility."[48] In his newly held opinion, treating each element of design as a discrete entity nobly expressing its own mechanical, and therefore functional, reality was an important aim of the new organic architecture.

The People's Savings Bank in Cedar Rapids, Iowa (1911), is chronologically the closest to the statements of *Artistic Brick*. Hence it is the most rational and least lyrical among Sullivan's larger bank designs (Fig. 10). With a minimum of ornamentation, it comes closest to his conception of the Prairie Style, one in which geometry rendered in tapestry brick played a very important role. It has a simple shape: a central oblong of double height reinforced with corner pylons is surrounded by a single-story rectangle of offices, all in tapestry brick. Remarking upon its stark appearance, Montgomery

10. People's Savings Bank, Cedar Rapids, Iowa. Louis Sullivan, 1911.

Schuyler pointed out that this bank had been "clearly designed from within outward," and that "Mr. Sullivan had denied himself all the opportunities of doing what he can do as much better than any other living architect," namely creating "fantastic decoration."[49]

Sullivan could not sustain for long such a style. In 1913 he had a change of heart and brought lyrical ornamentation back into his design. At the same time he attempted to recapture the anthropomorphic quality of his skyscrapers of the turn of the century, which owed so much to his conception of the Gothic as a paradigm of forces in equilibrium.[50] In many ways this stylistic change paralleled an earlier one of 1890. Then, after three years of unornamented buildings that in his own words had been "comely in the nude"–as was the Walker Warehouse–he turned to importantly stated exterior ornamentation. The Getty tomb (1890) was the first of his buildings "clad in a garment of poetic imagery" to satisfy his urge for the "romanticism . . . [he] crave[d] to express."[51]

But results in 1913 and 1914 were not of the quality of those of 1890–92. In his attempt to recapture the anthropomorphic quality of the skyscrapers, Sullivan allowed lyrical sentimentality the upper hand. In the Van Allen Store, Clinton, Iowa (1913–15), he applied three thin, pier-like decorations to only one of the facades of a corner building, giving the impression of an incomplete program (Fig. 11). In the Home Building Association, Newark, Ohio (1914), both the anthropomorphic program and its scale seem excessive for the size of the building (Fig. 12). A one-to-one translation of the Gothic-derived anthropomorphic effects of the skyscrapers simply did not work on small buildings, and Sullivan had to find new ways to express his esthetic interests.

In the bank in Grinnell, Iowa (1914), he gave a new dimension to what he once had learned from the Gothic. There he mastered a dynamic composition of upward-thrusting and downward-bearing forces, symbolic and real (Fig. 13). Showing caution about his expression of anthropomorphism in load-bearing construction, he concentrated his dynamic effects exclusively on the ornamentation around the door and the rose window above it. The new effect was perfectly proper to the characteristics of terra cotta. Moreover, it established a clear distinction between construction and ornamentation. His bank style came to maturity, and three reasons come to mind: 1) through tapestry brick he stated once more his desire to associate his buildings with the Midwestern landscape through polychromy; 2) a sharply defined box-like shape did no violence to his interests to express construction and to reveal the plan of a building in its volumetric composition; and 3) his new use of terra cotta ornamentation made his small buildings rich with an anthropomorphic pro-

11. Van Allen Store, Clinton, Iowa. Louis Sullivan, 1913–15.

12. Home Building Association Bank, Newark, Ohio. Louis Sullivan, 1914.

13. Merchants' National Bank, Grinnell, Iowa. Louis Sullivan, 1914.

gram that linked the esthetics of the banks with the Gothic-derived esthetics of the skyscrapers.

In his two last executed banks, the one in Sidney, Ohio (1917–18), and the one in Columbus, Wisconsin (1919), Sullivan took the final logical step beyond his achievements of Grinnell and involved whole facades in anthropomorphic programs instead of depending exclusively on ornamentation, but prudently limited himself to the tectonic possibilities of load-bearing construction.

This is evident in the Sidney bank (Fig. 14). There the great arch seems to carry the weight of the spandrels to nothing more substantial than a pair of windows. The composition establishes a wonderful exercise in ambiguity by making ornamentation above an opening seem to support one of the most ponderous masses of the facade. On further analysis one realizes that the mechanical reality is different, that at each of the lower sides of the elevation a marble base and the masonry flanking the windows rise up to receive the downward thrust of the arch. To paraphrase one of Sullivan's earlier statements, "the subjective becomes the objective" and are interchangeable in this composition, which, at the same time, calls attention to the entrance to the building, the focus of the facade. To emphasize that effect, pillars flanking the door shoot up to support heraldic lions that become symbolic buttresses, propping up visually, rather than supporting physically, the mosaic of the tympanum.

The anthropomorphic program of the Columbus bank is even richer, and depends for its success, mainly, on economy of means, on good proportions, and on the dynamic qualities of the composition (Fig. 15). The facade consists of three principal items: a set of three piers, one very large lintel, and a tapestry brick panel framing a telescoping arch decorated with terra cotta archivolts. The openings—windows and door—are visually less important, and read like spaces left in between these elements. The loveliness of the facade depends in no small measure on symmetry and balance enriched by harmonious proportions between the parts. By way of example one may notice that the top of the lintel divides the facade in half, that the radius of the arch is equal to one-sixth of the height of the building, which is also the height of the rectangular window and of the marble panel of the lintel, that the lintel itself may be divided into four equal parts, the one at each end being a square, and that the terra cotta archivolt rises from the central axes of those squares. Besides symmetry and balance, there is also a mannered treatment of form that prepares the elements of architecture for their anthropomorphic roles; each element of the composition proclaims more than reveals its own entity and its particular function. The thickness of the lintel is exaggerated; the relationship of the arch and the lintel is more important than that of the arch and the window; and the piers hold up the lintel at the ends rather than at the points supporting the arch. Needless to say, had Sullivan chosen the latter solution, there would have been no need for a central pier; the door would have been on center, the lintel could have been thinner, and the facade would have been static, academic, and banal. Finally, there is the anthropomorph-

14. People's Savings and Loan Association Bank, Sidney, Ohio. Louis Sullivan, 1917–18.

15. Farmers' and Merchants' Union Bank, Columbus, Wisconsin. Louis Sullivan, 1919.

ic program itself. The observer comes away with the impression that the building has been the result of masses surging from below while others pressed from above. What one witnesses as architecture is the final dramatic moment of equipoise on the all-important lintel, which now justifies its thickness. One also realizes that the anthropomorphism of the Columbus bank springs out of the essential tectonic characteristics of load-bearing construction and that it finds consonance with the Gothic-derived anthropomorphic and phytomorphic effects of the skyscrapers of the 1890s.

We have seen how the Gothic had always for Sullivan a broad connotation, and similarly as the French Romantic architects had made use of classical form in unclassical ways, he translated into his own Transcendentalist language what he considered to be the essence of the Gothic as a system of forces in equilibrium. On the other hand, copying Gothic as a style was to Sullivan as much of an aberration as the imposition of any other historicist allusion on a building; nature required all human creation to parallel her own process rather than to establish associations with the past. "The American architecture of today is the offspring of an illegitimate commerce with the mongrel styles of the past," he once wrote.[52] Hence his insistence on a design that would evoke the movement of the anthropomorphic, the growth of the phytomorphic, and the stress and strain of the geomorphic, all at the same time. Nature also demanded each design to express its essence. Sullivan learned this truth in stages. In the early 1890s he stopped designing large commercial buildings of load-bearing construction like the Chicago Auditorium and began working with skyscrapers. He then changed his style from the downward-bearing Romanesque of Richardsonian derivation to a soaring Gothic inspired by Viollet-le-Duc. This change implied translating his American Transcendentalist ideas into compositional programs where some of the structural elements of a facade expressed their mechanical behavior, while others mirrored the essential characteristic of their archetypes in nature. Endorsing to the last the Romantic conception that Gothic architecture was essentially a paradigm of stresses, he chose to reinterpret that notion in terms of combinations of real and symbolic forces that responded to his Romantic fervor. This position was far removed from Viollet-le-Duc's Positivist attitude, from which, nevertheless, he had learned much. The Gothic, as he saw it, served Sulllivan to relate his architecture to the fundamental unity of the cosmos, to an everlasting, ever changing flow. In the late 1890s, with the design of the Bayard Building, he finally had a clear vision of the style he had been attempting to define since his youth. Because of the kind of commissions coming to him, his style became intimately linked to the skyscraper as a building type. When orders for tall commercial buildings ceased and his only jobs dealt with load-bearing construction, it took him years to re-adapt that earlier vision, which he considered to be the most truthful to his beliefs as well as the closest to his esthetic sensibilities. Among his later build-ings, the bank in Columbus makes available to us his conception at its most vivid. Ironically, his use of academic forms in that design underscores the ex-pression all the more clearly. That contradiction reveals three things: how little Sullivan depended stylistically on the Gothic for his banks; how much his con-ception of it contributed to his Transcendentalist programs; and how his later skyscrapers and his later banks are like two different sides of the same thing.

His first bank, the one in Owatonna, had been an expensive and irreproduc-ible *tour de force* recalling the colors of the landscape and establishing rhythms that made architecture come close to music and poetry. For about four years after it, and under the influence of Prairie School ideas, he experimented with stark, naked masses of which he eventually tired, bringing about the facile lyricism of the Van Allen Store and of the bank in Newark, Ohio. Finally, the bank in Grinnell, and above all, those in Sidney and Columbus, reveal how he finally came to a rich and stable conception. As had been the case with the skyscrapers, he worked progressively and laboriously to master the idea of the bank as a building type in which he could represent images of dark and light, of action and reaction, of the subjective and the objective, of the ambiguous and the concrete, of life and earth, and the portrait of a lyrically rural landscape that was also the expression of the awesomeness of the cos-mos. To the last, Louis Sullivan referred his buildings back to an ideal arche-type pulsating with the tension of opposites; made them stand as images of his teleological idea of architecture; and incidentally made them serve as the best expressions of the ideas of Leopold Eidlitz, which he followed closely, and of Friedrich Vischer, of whom he never heard.[53] To achieve all of that his conception of the Gothic served him well, be it for designing banks or for building skyscrapers.

NOTES

1. For Hegel, see his *Philosophy of Art*, 4 vols., trans. F. P. Osmaston (London: G. Bell and Sons, 1920), especially Part III. For Schopenhauer, see his *The World as Will and as Representation*, 2 vols., trans. C. F. J. Payne (New York: Dover, 1969) I: 214–18; and II, "On the Aesthetics of Architecture," 411–18.

2. Friedrick Vischer, *Aesthetik oder Wissenschaft des Schönen*, 3 parts in 4 vols. (Reutlingen and Leipzig: Carl Mäcken, 1846–51; Stuttgart: Carol Mäcken, 1852–54). See especially the section devoted to architecture, III.1: 173–338.

3. Ibid., "Die untergeordnete Tektonik," III.1: 331–38. Vischer was responsible for systematizing ideas on empathetic architecture. According to his theory, the principal esthetic aim of architecture was to evoke shapes of inorganic nature and to idealize them by means of an anthropomorphic association. This notion was at the base of his theory of *Einfühlung*. On this respect, see mainly his *Vorträge*, published posthumously by his son (Stuttgart: J. B. Gotha, 1898), especially the section entitled "Das Schöne une Kunst."

4. For these ideas of Ruskin, see *The Seven Lamps of Architecture*, 2nd ed. (London: Smith, Elder and Company, 1855), "Lamp of Sacrifice," I: 7–8; "Lamp of Beauty," II: 94–95; XII: 104; XV: 106–07.

5. Ibid., "Lamp of Sacrifice," I: 7–8.

6. Ibid., II–VI: 8–15.

7. Ibid., "Lamp of Power," II: 64.

8. Ibid., "Lamp of Beauty," III: 96. Emphasis in the original.

9. Ibid., XXXVI: 126–27.

10. Ibid., XXXV: 125.

11. Ibid., XXXVI: 126.

12. Ralph Waldo Emerson, *Complete Works*, ed. James Elliot Cabot, (Boston: Houghton Mifflin, 1903) I: 214.

13. In the "Lamp of Obedience," VII: 192, Ruskin argued that the four best styles of architecture were the Pisan Romanesque, the Early Gothic of the Western Italian Republics, Venetian Gothic "in its purest development," and English Decorated because these were the periods when architecture best imitated nature and consequently they furnished architects with the best lessons on how to design a building.

14. Louis Sullivan, "Style," *Inland Architect* 11 (1888): 59–60.

15. Eugène Viollet-le-Duc, *Entretiens sur l'architecture* (Paris: A Morel, 1863) I: 184.

16. In the *Entretiens*, I: 183, Viollet-le-Duc wrote: "Dans tout ce qu'elle produit, la nature a toujours du style, parce que, si variées que soient ses productions, celles-ci son toujours soumises à des lois, à des principes invariables. Une feuille d'arbuste, une fleur, un insecte, ont du style, parce qu'ils croissent, se développent, se conservent par des lois essentiellement logiques. On ne peut rien enlever à une fleur, car dans son organisation chaque partie accuse une fonction en adoptant la forme qui convient à cette fonction."

17. In that respect Renan had said: "La seule fonction de la science est de connaître la réalité, non de réaliser l'idéal. Comment, d'ailleurs, le pourrait-elle? La réalité est une, l'idéal est divers, il varie d'homme à homme"; quoted in Jean Bourdeau, *Les maîtres de la pensée contemporaine* (Paris: Félix Alcan, 1907), 63.

18. Hermant went to Chicago to supervise construction of the French Pavilion at the Columbian Exposition, which he had designed. Also, he wrote one of the most perceptive views on American architecture of the period. See Jacques Hermant, "L'Art à l'exposition de Chicago," *Gazette des Beaux-Arts* (troisième période), 10 (1893):

237–53, 416–25, 441–61; and 11 (1894): 149–69. Quotation about Sullivan is on pp. 246–47.

19. Viollet-le-Duc, I: 485.

20. For Viollet-le-Duc's conception of *l'architecte savant* and *l'architecte dessinateur*, see ibid., I: 477–78; II: 55, 74–75, 112.

21. Ruskin, "Lamp of Truth," VI; Viollet-le-Duc, I: 18.

22. For Eidlitz, see mainly Biruta Erdmann, "Leopold Eidlitz's Architectural Theories and American Transcendentalism," (diss. University of Wisconsin-Madison, 1977). H. Allen Brooks, "Leopold Eidlitz (1823–1908)," (master's thesis, Yale University, 1955), is also useful. For Eidlitz's architecture, see Montgomery Schuyler, "A Great American Architect: Leopold Eidlitz," *Architectural Record* 24 (1908): 164–79; 277–92; and 365–78. For Eidlitz's involvement in the design of the Albany Capitol, see H.-R. Hitchcock, *The Architecture of H. H. Richardson and His Times*, rev. ed. (Cambridge, MA: MIT Press, 1961), 161–71.

23. In 1843, the year Eidlitz arrived in America, Horatio Greenough expanded some of Emerson's ideas in "American Architecture," *United States Magazine and Democratic Review* 13 (1843): 206–10; re-edited by Don Gifford, *The Literature of Architecture: The Evolution of Architectural Theory and Practice in Nineteenth-Century America* (New York: Dutton, 1966), 141–51. See also Greenough's *Form and Function: Remarks on Art, Design and Architecture*, ed. Harold A. Small (Berkeley: University of California Press, 1966). For the correspondence between Greenough and Emerson, see Nathalia Wright, "Ralph Waldo Emerson and Horatio Greenough," *Harvard Library Bulletin* 12 (1958): 91–116. Greenough was also a friend of the Reverend William Henry Furness, the father of Frank Furness, the Philadelphia architect in whose office Sullivan served an apprenticeship in 1873. The Reverend Furness had been, along with Emerson, a member of the 1836 Transcendentalist Group, and in that year he had published his *Remarks on the Four Gospels* to propose that Christianity should use a transcendentalist perspective to revise its notions on the historical Jesus. Moreover, the Reverend Furness had been a schoolmate of Emerson's at Boston's Latin School, and according to Perry Miller, *The Transcendentalists* (Cambridge: Harvard University Press, 1950), p. 124, Emerson's life-long and possibly only intimate friend. In 1870 the Reverend Furness presented a transcendentalist view of architecture at the fourth annual convention of the American Institute of Architects (quoted in Gifford, pp. 391–404). Thus, Transcendentalism was known in American architectural circles and had a degree of ideological influence on them.

24. John Root, whose opinions Sullivan held in high regard, considered that of all definitions of art, Eidlitz's was "the most nearly true." See John Wellborn Root, "Broad Art Criticism," *Inland Architect* 11 (1888): 2–6.

25. Leopold Eidlitz, *The Nature and Function of Art, More Especially of Architecture* (New York: Armstrong and Son, 1881), 57.

26. Ibid., 72, 196.

27. Sullivan, "Kindergarten Chats," in Louis H. Sullivan, *Kindergarten Chats and Other Writings*, ed. Isabel Athey (1947; repr. New York: Witenborn, 1968), 46.

28. Eidlitz, 222–23.

29. Ibid., 223, 92.

30. Ibid., 287.

31. *Kindergarten Chats*, 29–30.

32. Ibid., 49.

33. Herbert Spencer, *First Principles of a New System of Philosophy*, 2nd ed. (New York: Appleton, 1872), 538–59. Sullivan began reading Spencer while he was quite young; see Sherman Paul, *Louis Sullivan: An Architect in American Thought* (Englewood Cliffs: Prentice-Hall, 1962), 18.

34. Sullivan, "Essay on Inspiration," in Narciso G. Menocal, *Architecture as Nature: The Transcendentalist Idea of Louis Sullivan* (Madison, WI: University of Wisconsin Press, 1981), 166. In the last passage of "Inspiration," from which this quotation is taken, and perhaps clearer than in any other of his writings, Sullivan presented his belief that all that exists is but a part and an expression of a primordial and all-sustaining cosmic rhythm.

35. Sullivan, *The Autobiography of an Idea* (New York: Press of the American Institute of Architects, 1924), 313–14.

36. *Kindergarten Chats*, 206.

37. Eidlitz, 217–20. According to Arthur O. Lovejoy, *Essays in the History of Ideas* (Baltimore: Johns Hopkins Press, 1948), 153, as early as 1724 William Stukely had compared the interior of Gloucester Cathedral to "a walk of trees, whose touching heads are curiously imitated by the roof." This image was used subsequently by many novelists during the eighteenth and nineteenth centuries as well as by Sir James Hall, who in a paper presented to the Royal Society of Edinburgh on 6 April 1797, argued in favor of the timber origins of Gothic architecture. Hall published his argument later in his *Essay on the Origin, History and Principles of Gothic Architecture* (London: Murray, 1835). Thomas Hope, *An Historical Essay on Architecture* 2 vols. (London: Murray, 1835), also argued that Gothic buildings were like groves. Early examples of columns looking like trees appear in Friedrich Dauthe's reconstruction of the Nikolaikirche, Leipzig, 1784–97, in Schinkel's project of a Memorial to Queen Louise, 1810, and of course, in that textbook case, the kitchen of John Nash's Brighton Pavilion. For a view of the interior of the Nikolaikirche, see F. Landsberger, *Die Kunst der Goethezeit: Kunst and Kunstanschauung von 1750 bis 1830* (Leipzig: Insel, 1931), 167. Georg Germann, *Gothic Revival in Europe and Britain: Sources, Influences, and Ideas* (Cambridge, MA: MIT Press, 1973), gives a good account of many of these ideas and developments. In America, Ralph Waldo Emerson, "Thoughts on Art," *Dial* 1 (1841): 376, compared a Gothic church with a grove, and used that same text again in his essay "On Art." Emerson may have become familiar with the simile by reading Goethe.

38. *Kindergarten Chats*, 99.

39. Dimitri Tselos, "The Chicago Fair and the Myth of the 'Lost Cause,' " *Journal of the Society of Architectural Historians* 26 (1967): 263.

40. Sullivan told his friend Claude Bragdon that the Bayard Building was his best skyscraper. In turn, Bragdon reported this opinion of Sullivan's to Lewis Mumford, who published it in his *Roots of Contemporary Architecture*, 2nd ed. (1952; New York: Grove Press, 1959), 21.

41. The floor-to-ceiling heights of each story of the Bayard Building are as follows: first floor, 15 feet; second floor, 13 feet; third floor, 12 feet; fourth and fifth floors, 11 feet each; sixth through eleventh floors, 10 feet each; twelfth floor, 9 feet 6 inches; thirteenth floor; 14 feet six inches; see Sullivan, *The Bayard Building*, Real Estate Brochure (New York: Rost Printing and Publishing Company, n.d.), at New York, Avery Library.

42. For the influence of impressionist music and of symbolist poetry in Sullivan's esthetic thought of about 1906, see Menocal, *Architecture as Nature*, 128–29.

43. Sullivan, *Suggestions in Artistic Brick* (St. Louis: Hydraulic-Press Brick Company, c. 1910); reprinted as "Artistic Brick," in *Prairie School Review* 4 (1967): 24–26; this is the text I follow.

44. For the influence of French romantic rationalism on Sullivan, see Menocal, "The Bayard Building: French Paradox and American synthesis," *Sites* no. 13 (1985), 4–24, especially, 10–21. For French Romantic rationalism in general, see mainly Arthur Drexler, ed., *The Architecture of the École des Beaux-Arts* (New York: Museum of Modern Art, 1977); Robin Middleton, ed. *The Beaux-Arts and Nineteenth-Century French Architecture* (Cambridge, MA: MIT Press, 1982); Neil Levine, "Architectural Reasoning in the Age of Positivism: the Néo-Grec Idea of Henri Labrouste's Bibliothèque Sainte-Geneviève," (Ph.D. diss. Yale University, 1975); and David Van Zanten, "Félix Duban and the Buildings of the École des Beaux-Arts," *Journal of the Society of Architectural Historians* 37 (1978): 161–74.

45. "Artistic Brick," 24.

46. "The Tall Office Building Artistically Considered," *Kindergarten Chats*, 207–13.

47. "Artistic Brick," 24.

48. Ibid., 24. Viollet-le-Duc, I: 183–84.

49. Montgomery Schuyler, "The People's Savings Bank of Cedar Rapids, Iowa," *Architectural Record* 31 (1912): 44.

50. Besides appearing in the Cedar Rapids bank, Sullivan's severe style of 1910–14 is evident as well in other commissions of the period, such as the Bradley House, Madison, Wisconsin; the St. Paul's Methodist-Episcopal Church, Cedar Rapids, Iowa; and the Bennett House project, Owatonna, Minnesota.

51. "Ornament in Architecture," *Kindergarten Chats*, 187.

52. "The Young Man in Architecture," *Kindergarten Chats*, 220. Sullivan's abhorrence of architectural historicism is well-known, as is substantiated in many passages in his writings. It stemmed principally but not exclusively from the fact that he considered that relying stylistically on the architecture of the past was a "feudal"

act, as opposed to a "democratic" one as Whitman had defined the term in *Democratic Vistas*. Among Sullivan's writings, *Democracy: A Man-Search*, ed. Elaine Hedges (Detroit: Wayne State University Press, 1961), covers the subject best. For an analysis of *Democracy*, see Menocal, *Architecture as Nature*, 95–101.

53. Vischer remains untranslated and Sullivan had no German.

The Crystal Cathedral in Garden Grove, California and Chartres Cathedral, France: A Television Evangelist's Adaptation of Medieval Ideology

Jane Welch Williams

A YOUNG DUTCH REFORMED CHURCH PASTOR FROM CHICAGO, THE REVEREND Robert Schuller, preached his first sermon in Orange County, California, on a Sunday in March, 1955, standing on a snackbar rooftop in a drive-in theater and speaking to approximately 50 people in 30 cars. The charismatic Schuller founded his Garden Grove Community Church in the drive-in, and expanded his congregation rapidly. Twenty-five years later, Schuller dedicated his 18 million dollar dream cathedral in Garden Grove. To further celebrate this event, Schuller published *The Story of a Dream*, a brochure chronicling the saga of the little community church's growth in the years between 1955 and 1980.[1] The brochure, on sale in the cathedral bookstore, quickly sold out to tourists who flocked in tour buses to see the Crystal Cathedral.

By 1959, Schuller counted 507 in his congregation, and annual offerings of $83,046. In September of that year, he broke ground to build a new walk-in, drive-in church designed by Richard Neutra.[2] Schuller claimed the Parthenon as the model for Neutra's design of the first church on his new property in Garden Grove.[3] Completed in 1961, the building incorporated many of Schuller's innovative notions of sacred architecture: an open air pulpit from which he could speak to the drive-in crowd, fountains, and glass walls (Fig. 1).[4] But in a few years, he changed models. He had Neutra attach a nar-

1. Garden Grove Community Church, California, designed by Richard Neutra, dedicated in 1961.

row office building to the church called the Tower of Hope, following the medieval idea of church towers.[5] The 90-foot cross atop the office building symbolized the NEW HOPE Telephone Counseling service operated within the building, which offered free personal counseling (Fig. 2). Standing atop the 14-story building, the neon-lighted cross reaches 252 feet in the air, a worthy competitor to the Matterhorn at Disneyland, equally visible from the freeways nearby.[6] The Neutra tower, adjacent church, and service buildings had taken on the appearance of a modern-day monastic complex, with an adjacent cloister surrounded by cubicles for educational purposes. In 1969, Schuller, who now had a congregation of 4,301 and an annual offering of $523,000, purchased a 10-acre plot adjoining his growing church compound.[7] Then in 1975, Schuller inaugurated his most daring plan yet—the building of a "Crystal Cathedral," designed by none other than Philip Johnson, the architect par excellence in the service of international capitalism.[8] Schuller told Philip Johnson and his new partner John Burgee:

> You've got to come up with a design that will be so sensational, so striking, that when sophisticated, refined, cultured people see it, they will say "That has to be built. The human family must never be deprived of the joy of seeing it."[9]

Johnson and Burgee designed a pinched, four-pointed star plan encompassing 30,000 sq. ft. at its base (Fig. 9), and soaring upward irregularly from some views, symmetrically from others (Fig. 3, 5, 14, 15).[10] The glass envelope of the building, composed of 12,661 reportedly earthquake-proof reflective panels, is secured to steel pipe space trusses shored up by an independent steel bracing system—like a giant erector set. Each 2 x 5 foot glass panel is tempered to transmit only 20% of the sun's rays, having been treated with silicone sealant and set in an aluminum frame to which it is attached at only one point, thus allowing it flexibility to withstand pressure and vibration.[11] Against the inside northern flank of the building, an enormous organ encased in two wood structures rises in the center of the 185-foot chancel sheathed in imported marble. The main floor seating spreads out to either side of a long, narrow water fountain (Fig. 11). The balconies rise above the main floor on three sides like seating in a sports arena (Fig. 17).[12] The third major sound amplification system to be installed in the cathedral finally seems successful in overcoming the difficulties of sound reverberation caused by the glass walls.[13]

In 1978, with construction well-advanced, Schuller was faced with a lack of funds. He orchestrated a modern reenactment of the twelfth century Cult

2. The Tower of Hope, dedicated in 1968.

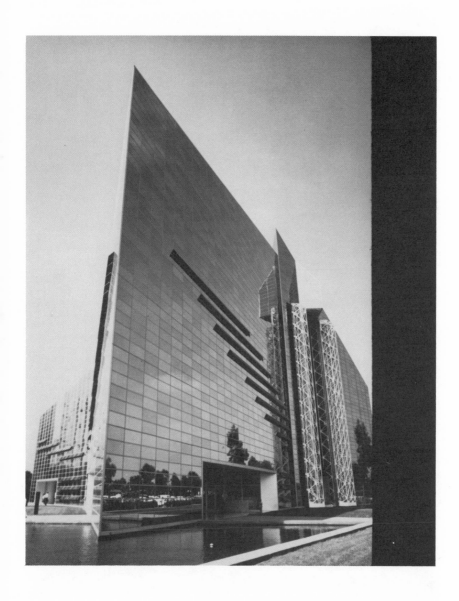

3. Crystal Cathedral, Garden Grove, California, designed by Philip Johnson and John Burgee, dedicated in 1980.

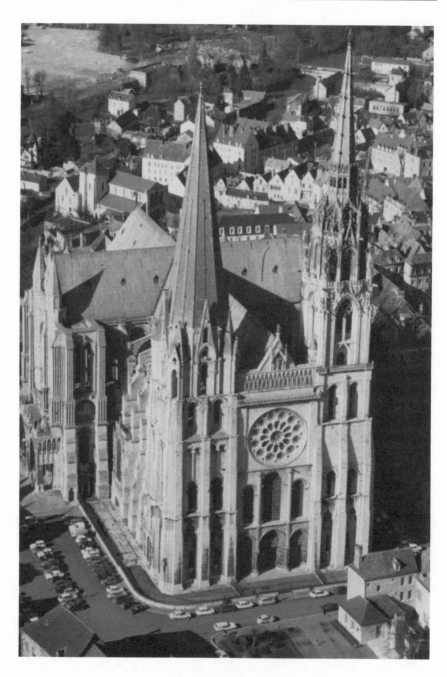

4. Chartres Cathedral, France, dedicated in 1260.

5. Crystal Cathedral illuminated at night.

6. Chartres Cathedral illuminated at night.

of Carts, urging people to deposit whatever money they could spare into wheelbarrows and cement mixers.[14] The so-called Cult of Carts occurred twice at Chartres, in 1144 and again in 1194, when people of all classes of society, but apparently primarily the poor serfs of the countryside, pulled carts by ropes over their backs to the construction site, spontaneously contributing and delivering materials necessary to continue the work. Like the Cult of Carts at Chartres, Schuller's reenactment served not only symbolically to broaden the base of support for the construction project, but, more importantly, provided a profoundly moving appeal to the super-rich for donations.[15] Schuller's prime-time religion had brought him star evangelist status, and even the *National Enquirer* listed a star-studded Hollywood following including John Wayne, Doris Day, Don Rickles, Jerry Lewis and his wife Patti, Rhonda Fleming, Glenn Ford, Dean Jones, and Joseph Campanella – worthy contributors, if not the elite Schuller had originally planned on soliciting.[16]

What is the art-historical prototype and historical antecedent of Reverend Robert Schuller's Crystal Cathedral? Chartres Cathedral, of course (Fig. 4, 6). Strange that the high-technology, high income counterpart of Chartres has risen in a World War II working class, bedroom community. Indeed, there are many ways in which Schuller's cathedral aspires to fulfill the beloved mythological misconceptions that have accreted to Chartres.

At first glance, nothing could be more opposite than Philip Johnson's and John Burgee's late twentieth century iconoclastic glass tent, composed of magnified crystal prisms, and the Gothic stone construction, designed and built by unknown architects and masons.[17] One might think the Gothic image of the Heavenly Jerusalem contrasts with the modern glass tent's openness to nature, only to realize that both claim to merge the heavenly and earthly spheres![18] Despite the differences in aesthetic idiom, both dominate their landscape and enclose enormous, useless space to symbolic purpose, claiming superregional, even universal significance for their ministry.[19] Both are pilgrimage centers and tourist attractions, more because of their aesthetic than their spiritual appeal (Fig. 5, 6).[20] And there are real, material similarities. Schuller and his architects openly spoke of seeking to emulate the scale of Gothic cathedrals like Chartres. The Crystal Cathedral is 415 feet long and 128 feet high; Chartres Cathedral is 422 feet long and 116 foot high.[21] Both dramatically attest to the highest technological advances of their age and both expose their support system as a part of their aesthetic appeal (Fig. 7, 8).

The Crystal Cathedral is what the architects of Chartres would have built, if they had known how – an entire building of glass.[22] The Crystal Cathedral

7. Interior view of the Crystal Cathedral showing the supporting pipe truss system and barely visible hanging mylar stars.

is Chartres Cathedral turned inside out. At Chartres, the real support for the structure is outside; from the inside, one cannot see what is really holding up the building. In the Crystal Cathedral, the support system is inside, obvious, an emphatic statement of design. There are aesthetic problems in both buildings which result from their exposed, repetitive support systems. Flyers on Chartres Cathedral and pipes in the Crystal Cathedral become clumsy

8. Exterior view of buttresses, Chartres Cathedral.

and crowded at corners. The flying buttresses at Chartres meet at 90-degree angles at the juncture of the transept with the church body, seeming to clash in a way that breaks the dark-light, void-solid rhythm. This happens in the Crystal Cathedral where three or four glass planes come together, causing the pipe supports to appear excessively clustered, breaking their repetitive rhythm. In both buildings, the system of supports ends abruptly, without an aesthetic resolution, like a voice that rises at the end of sentences. At Chartres, the nave buttressess stop against the mid-twelfth-century west front, jammed together as if they had collided at high speed. At the Crystal Cathedral, the pipe struts stop unceremoniously at the floor level, as if the erector set had just been set down on the cement slab.

Johnson and Burgee designed the building on the same basis of geometric expansion and variation that medieval architects employed. This is especially apparent in the geometric configuration and elaboration of the pipe truss system of the Crystal Cathedral.[23] And the plan of the Crystal Cathedral is uncannily similar to John James's reconstruction of the hypothetical geometry by which the first plan of Chartres was conceived (Fig. 9, 10).[24] Both building interiors have an inherent geometric coherence and grandiose proportion that cause the church furnishings within to seem out of place and discordant. At Chartres, the chairs placed in nervous rows in the nave and transepts seem foolishly tiny and insubstantial next to the giant stone columns of the nave arcade. The pulpit, the organ, and the eighteenth century high altar of marble all seem inappropriate, intrusive. But these foreign objects are at least veiled in pervading shadows. At the Crystal Cathedral, the disharmony of the interior furnishings is more disturbing, because daylight illuminates every part indiscriminately. The monochromatic greys of the International Style architecture clash with the colloquialisms of suburban American church furnishings. The organ built into huge blond wood casings almost totally destroys the architects' ethereal intentions (Fig. 11). Banks of wood-framed seating stand adjacent to the lattice wall of pipes, leaving an open space between the seating and the glass wall that appears both strange and dangerous. Little potted ferns dotting the edges of the raised seating wings seem incongruous and inappropriate next to the dynamic sweep of the pipe and glass walls. A huge Jumbotron television screen hangs menacingly over the wall next to the pulpit. In the unforgiving light, one's attention is distracted by the faulty surface of poured concrete slabs, the streaked glass, and dirty pipes. The platforms, wires, cameras, loud speakers, and other paraphernalia of television production remind one that this is a television stage. There is a loss of mystery in the twentieth-century antitype of the thirteenth-century type. Yet

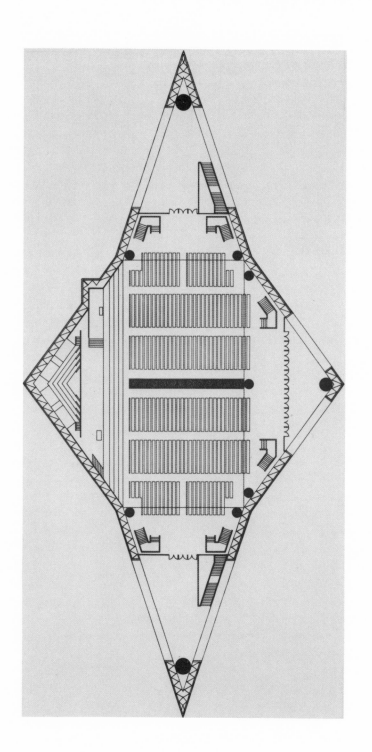

9. Crystal Cathedral, ground floor plan.

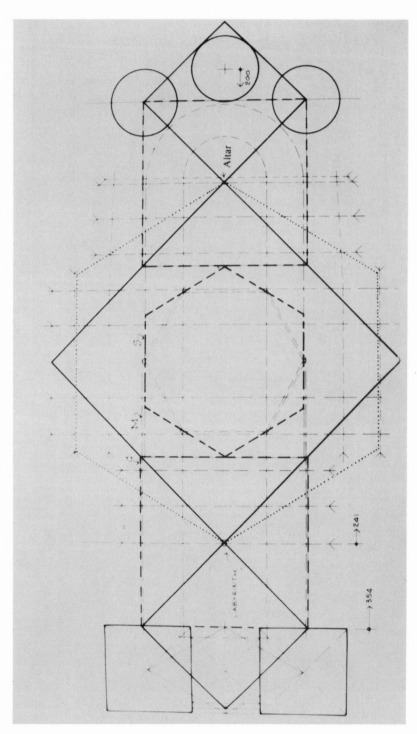

10. John James's postulated geometric basis for the first plan of Chartres Cathedral.

11. Interior view of the Crystal Cathedral chancel and organ.

both dwarf human presence with their soaring height, breaking the social dimension of everyday life to offer each individual an imaginary place in the eternal house of the Christian God. The two buildings are alike in their Gothic conception of symbolic space.

But stylistic comparison is not enough. Style is an expression of the aspirations of the patron projected by the artist: the significance of this partnership in style appears in ideology and economics as well as in architecture. In other words, art is a signifier of that which it does not represent explicitly. Reverend Schuller, with the eclectic mind of an evangelist, has elected to copy highly successful strategies from the past with the same nimbleness with which he has adjusted his ambitions to the exigences of the present. He hired Philip Johnson and John Burgee to build him a *cathedral*, although he has no claim to be a bishop with a proper diocese. The Crystal Cathedral is not simply an eclectic adaptation of Gothic manner to modern means; rather, it is primarily an ideological imitation based on the traditional modern notions of the power of faith in the Middle Ages and of the social basis of medieval cathedral construction epitomized by Chartres.

However, historians have misunderstood and falsified the history of Chartres Cathedral, which is repeated alike in guide books and in scholarly literature. I summarize this myth as follows:

> When the cathedral burned in 1194, all classes of society contributed to rebuild a palace for the Virgin. The cathedral bishop and canons, who were champions of liberty in the town, achieved peace within a formerly conflictive society and brought disparate societal groups together to the common goal. The cathedral windows represent the different people who contributed: kings, nobles, ecclesiastics, merchants, artisans, and farmers. Prosperous trade organizations in the town, whose products enjoyed widespread renown, donated 42 stained glass windows. They sold their fine merchandise at the cathedral fairs held in conjunction with the feasts of the Virgin, which brought merchants and pilgrims from all over France and beyond. Light, which according to medieval metaphysics, represented the splendor of godly perfection, enlivened the 176 stained glass windows of Chartres, and filled the interior with its heavenly glow. The town prospered and remained a great center of pilgrimage to the shrine of the Virgin.[25]

This story has evolved over the last two centuries, embellished by each generation of writers imbued with an idealistic notion of the Middle Ages and an unquestioning belief in the democratic benefits of the churchmen's progressive attitude. In this myth's most recent development, Otto von Simson expanded the account, emphasizing the new peaceful relations in the town, the mutually beneficial relationship between the trades and the cathedral, and the international renown of local products. In von Simson's elaboration of the nascent capitalistic circumstances surrounding the Gothic rebuilding of Chartres Cathedral, one can see the dominant ideology of his own time.[26] That he was successful in his enterprise, and that he correctly perceived the laudatory reception his effort would receive, is clear from the fact that his argument has lived on in subsequent literature.[27]

However, the medieval documents from Chartres reveal a very different picture. The canons at Chartres aggressively suppressed municipal organization in the thirteenth century, when the cathedral was built.[28] The local trades produced for immediate local consumption; their products were of inferior quality, seldom purchased outside of the region.[29] The Count of Chartres had jurisdiction over most of the town and the tradesmen. He appointed masters over the trades, in order to control their activities more easily and to extract his taxes.[30] The count's power grated against the canons' rights and privileges, causing increasing hostility. Most controversial was the canons' practice of taking selected tradesmen into their own service in the cathedral precinct and thus exempting them from the count's taxes.[31] When the count's tradesmen crossed over the boundaries of the cloister, into the service of the cathedral authorities, the count's ministers tried to continue extracting taxes from them. When refused payment, the count's officers either confiscated the adopted serfs' personal possessions or seized them by force, incarcerating and sometimes killing them. The cathedral officials invoked their justice over their serfs and the immunity of the cloister to regain their new serfs and the confiscated goods. The dispute between the count and the chapter over the adopted serfs had been actively fought out in this way at least since the mid-twelfth century.[32]

Since we know that many of these adopted serfs were tradesmen, it may be that the men shown in the trade windows at Chartres were actually the canons' serfs.[33] There is no documentation of the donation of any of the early thirteenth century windows in the cathedral,[34] and very little documentation of how the building was financed. The bishop and canons pledged a major portion of their income in 1194 to pay for the first three years of the building's reconstruction. But after that, their funds ran out.[35] The cathedral ecclesiastics must have pressed their economic exploitation of the town to its limit thereafter, especially in 1210, when the bishop prepared to go on the Albigensian crusade.[36] By John James's calculation, construction radically declined in volume due to lack of funds around 1210.[37] It is no coincidence that a collection of the Virgin of Chartres' new miracles was written around 1210; clearly, it was composed to inspire pilgrimage and donation to the cathedral.[38]

Apparently the townsmen's resentment had risen to such intensity that a minor incident in 1210 incited them to riot in the cathedral cloister. Urged on by the count's officers and joined by some of the canons' own serfs, they looted and ravaged the Dean's house, and some of the rioters died in the fighting.[39] By mid-thirteenth century, when the cathedral was essentially completed, social tension exploded again. Townsmen murdered a canon and several cathedral servants in the cloister, terrifying the canons and the bishop, who then fled the town for several years.[40] Pilgrimage fell off after the cathedral was rebuilt, and the town economy and population stagnated.[41]

Only in the twentieth century have tourists and the faithful flooded to the Gothic cathedral of Chartres. They find there the most completely preserved stained glass panorama of any medieval cathedral, and precious little light entering the windows—so little that scientists can barely measure it. The summer sunlight outside measures between 8,000 and 10,000 foot candles on a horizontal meter reading, while inside the cathedral, in some areas, there is no meter reading at all.[42]

In many ways, the Crystal Cathedral actually fulfills the idealistic and distorted view of Chartres currently extolled in French guidebooks. Reverend Schuller took up this elaborate falsification, like a blueprint. He suceeded in doing what the bishop and canons at Chartres only claimed to do; in a true demonstration of the power of faith, he built the Crystal Cathedral with the donations of his congregation, all $18 million of them.[43] In an admirable inversion of ideology and reality, instead of a strident, multichromatic gallery of alleged sponsors permanently extolled in the glass surround at Chartres (Fig. 13),[44] the Crystal Cathedral has each donor's name democratically stamped in identical fashion on tiny metal plaques attached to the 10,661 window frames (Fig. 12). More donors' names appear on little plaques attached to the cathedral's 4,000 seats, and others are engraved on 11,000 tiny hanging mylar stars (Fig. 7)—all barely visible.[45] Outside, marble plaques inserted in garden paths testify to continuing donations (Fig. 1).

While the Cathedral of Chartres never managed to establish a large international clientele in the Middle Ages, Reverend Schuller has succeeded in justifying a claim to universal ministry by television broadcasts from the cathedral to the United States and Canada and by satellite to Australia.[46] In addition to the 4,000 parishoners seated in the Cathedral at each service,

12. Name plates on window frames, Crystal Cathedral.

13. Kneeling donor, Chartres Cathedral window.

many brought in Cathedral buses from adjacent communities, and the capacity crowds listening from their own cars in the parking lot, his television audiences allegedly are now the largest church audience in the history of Christendom.[47]At 9:30 and 11:15 every Sunday morning, the 90-foot hanger doors on the Cathedral open at the push of a garage door opener, the fountains outside subside (Fig. 14), the Reverend steps in windblown robes to the edge of an imported marble parapet and, with arms raised to the skies, addresses the people in parked cars outside and the television audience beyond, saying: "This is the day that the Lord has made. Let us rejoice and be glad in it!" He rarely fails to extoll the light of faith that streams into the cathedral to fill the hearts of the faithful with hope.

Beyond conscious adaptation of medieval ideologies lie a number of striking parallels between this contemporary church in America and that of the French Gothic cathedral of Chartres, similarities of condition that speak of the survival and even exaggeration of medieval social forms in contemporary life. Like the medieval cathedral compound, the Garden Grove Crystal Cathedral is now surrounded by ancillary buildings that conduct the business of the cult. Chartres was a center of learning in the Middle Ages. Schuller recently announced on his television program his intention to begin raising funds for another multi-million dollar building on the Cathedral compound to house a training center for leadership. At Chartres, the canons celebrated Christmas by elaborating the liturgy with the addition of tropes, acclamations, and the *Laudes Regiae*, and by unveiling the altar which had been veiled during Advent.[48] Schuller puts on an annual Christmas liturgical drama, repeated nightly for weeks to audiences who pay for admission. The magnitude of this pageant is remarkable—recently, the cast included three camels, two donkeys, a ram, twelve sheep, and 390 people, in a show put on at a cost of $1,000,000 by the Executive Producer of Radio City Music Hall in New York City.[49] In 1984, Schuller inaugurated an equally spectacular Easter extravaganza.[50]

Schuller's practice of charging admission to specially staged cultural events and religious festivals at the Cathedral has caused him difficulties with the tax collectors. The legal fight between Reverend Schuller and local tax collectors who believe that many of the Cathedral activities are properly secular and subject to state and federal taxes recalls the medieval conflict at Chartres between the canons and the count's officers.[51] And just as the church today continues to be dependent on its exercise of sacred power to extract its income, so the secular government continues to try to exploit the ecclesiastical surplus for its own support.

14. Crystal Cathedral doors open to allow view of pulpit from parking lot.

Schuller unabashedly sells a plethora of Christian books, cards, records, tapes, posters, T-shirts, jewelry, figurines, and a myriad of tourist memorabilia and trinkets in his bookstore next to the cathedral in Garden Grove. The merchandise replicates remarkably that of the little stores surrounding the present-day Cathedral of Chartres. Tours of the Crystal Cathedral depart frequently from a visitor's center, again duplicating the accommodation for tourists at Chartres. The contemporary contradiction between altruism and economics is the same. In a recent television appeal for funds, Schuller called his television church an "inspirational national treasure that must be preserved." The words express the same ideology with which the French appeal for funds to preserve Chartres.

And the social contradiction between the medieval image and reality at Chartres and the contemporary image and reality at Garden Grove remains essentially the same. The windows of Chartres project an image of social cohesion and peaceful coexistence for the common good, while in actuality the townsmen rioted and killed in the cloister. In Garden Grove the congregation of well-fed and scrubbed families sing with confidence of their salvation while, just beyond, thousands of poverty-stricken unemployed crowd in the squalor of boatpeople ghettos and wetback slums.[52] The Crystal Cathedral, like the Cathedral of Chartres before it, is not renowned for its charitable works.[53] The ideology of the democratic economic foundation of the Crystal Cathedral is as far removed from reality as that of Chartres after all.

Despite these parallels, there are also striking differences between Chartres Cathedral and the Crystal Cathedral. Reverend Schuller meets personally with his congregation, who flock around him after every service—a practice the bishop of Chartres could not have risked.[54] Until recently, the only image in the whole compound was the statue of Christ as the Good Shepherd—one cannot fail to see a marked resemblance of this Christ to the good Reverend. At the statue's feet, a marble plaque commemorates his and his wife's donation to the church's Perpetual Endowment Fund with the inscription: "I have come so that they may live life more abundantly" (John 10:10). Each marble plaque inserted in the garden walkways represents a gift of $2,000, of which $400 paid for the marble and its engraving. The remaining $1,600 was placed into the fund, whose income provides for the maintenance of the Cathedral and its gardens. This is an interesting contrast to the sacred economy of the Middle Ages, in which endowments usually paid the clergy to pray regularly for the soul of the donor.[55]

Now, a new statue in Garden Grove embellishes the open space between the new and old church, a stone sculpture of Job struggling against symbolic

15. Job statue, Crystal Cathedral.

bindings; its inscription states: "When he has tried me, I shall come forth as gold" (Fig. 15). This inscription is indeed "the possibility thinker's" interpretation of Job 23:10, which actually reads "Et probavit me quasi aurum quod per ignem transit."[56] A major difference between Chartres and Schuller's cathedral is that, through hard-won responses from his flock, Schuller obtained the gold he needed for his dream. The primary economic basis for the reconstruction of Chartres was wheat production on diocesan land and income gained through the feudal network of obligations that the bishop and canons controlled.[57] Schuller has no such patrimony.

Another major difference between the two can be seen in their ministries today: Schuller's staff, well financed and ambitious, produces a plethora of organizations to serve every sector of their congregation, deluges the Sunday worshipper with brochures and literature to encourage participation, answers in excess of 20,000 letters a week by a highly advanced computer response system, and puts on a polished television show once a week.[58] Schuller himself has published and republished over 20 books on religion and the power of positive thinking. One of his latest, *The Power of Being Debt Free. How Eliminating the National Debt Could Radically Improve Your Standard of Living*, had clear political implications in the year of the Gramm-Rudmann law. His books are aggressively sold to the secular market by Thomas Nelson, who also markets Ronald Reagan's book against abortion.[59] Schuller's books emphasize the miracles possible for those who believe in themselves – God helps those who help themselves. How different from the emphasis at Chartres Cathedral on the miracles achieved by the Virgin for those who put their complete faith in Her. At Chartres today, limited funds and a small congregation are evident; the main cathedral publication is as concerned with new scholarship on the cathedral as it is with ministry.[60] There is an interesting contrast of ideologies here: at Chartres, literature encourages worship of the past and of the Virgin; at the Crystal Cathedral, printed messages, notices of programs, and the pastor's books encourage everyone to increase his or her income and self-esteem. One can see in this the contrast between royal and democratic ideology.

Until recently, there was another major difference. The bishop and canons of Chartres allied themselves with the Capetian kings, to their mutual benefit.[61] Schuller, on the other hand, had through most of his ministry carefully avoided any overt political alliance or controversy. He had consciously avoided issues of racism, politics, social or economic evils, which he felt caused confrontation that "generates a mental climate where redemptive dialogue . . . is impossible."[62] But now the striking link-up of American evangelists with the Republican party is alive in Garden Grove. The change started with the Reagan administration – first, in subtle ways, like inviting Donn Moomaw, Reagan's parish minister in California, to speak at the Crystal Cathedral.[63] Now, however, the advocacy is openly evident in keeping with the moral majority's new-found political success. In the bookstore, one can buy Reagan's books and records of Reagan reading the bible. Schuller has taken to discreetly assisting local Republican candidates.[64]

So we should ask, what is the social significance of Chartres in America today? Its contemporary ideological miscasting is a paradigm of successful ministry. Reverend Schuller has grasped the true reasons for this success, cheerfully combining medieval ideology with modern enhancements of tourism and evangelism, and with big business technology. He is so successful at it, that he even offers yearly courses on his methods to other evangelists. His formula is obvious – build a magnificent cathedral visible from afar on major thoroughfares, and send your message to the world by utilizing the highest technology available. The theology of light so eloquently and incorrectly attributed to Chartres can finally be turned on in Garden Grove, simply by pressing the television remote control (Fig. 16).

The world's first electronic church fulfills Walter Benjamin's prediction of the frightening possibilities of mass media art in modern society.[65] Thoroughly won over to Schuller's possibility thinking, his parishioners and presumably his television audience accept his thinly veiled political messages. He now preaches the importance of arms build-up and the sad necessity of war. The Crystal Cathedral's Gothic reenactment of dominion through its massive enclosure of useless space intimidates and muffles human presence (Fig. 17).[66] The Crystal Cathedral's authoritarian environment and Schuller's adaptation of medieval ideology reconcile his audience to compliance – as Tafuri commented, "free from the anxiety of choice."[67]

Monumentally scaled architecture continues to be a symbol of power in our society as it was in the Middle Ages. In Garden Grove, the Crystal Cathedral dwarfs the surrounding tract homes and trailer parks. But, recently, newly built high rise office buildings have caused the Crystal Cathedral itself to appear small in comparison. From the freeway, these symbols of corporate America render the Crystal Cathedral relatively insignificant, accurately portraying the relative power of business and religious interests today. This parting view from the freeway invokes the church's loss of dominance in modern society to corporate, secular enterprise.

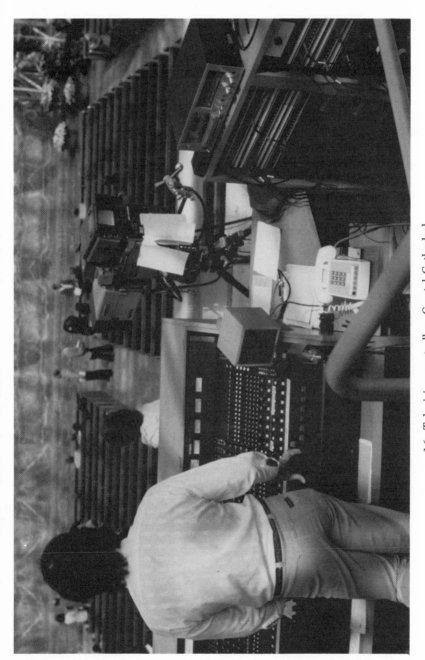

16. Television controller, Crystal Cathedral.

17. Interior view during Sunday service, Crystal Cathedral.

NOTES

1. *The Story of a Dream* was published and republished without any date or indication of writer, but presumably was first published in 1980 in honor of the Crystal Cathedral's completion. The Cathedral was dedicated on Sunday, September 14, 1980; see *Los Angeles Times*, 15 Sept. 1980, sec. 2, p. 5 (hereafter, *LA Times*). The early history of Robert Schuller's ministry in Garden Grove is chronicled in the first six pages of *The Story of a Dream*, accompanied by reproductions of old photographs, letters, and newspaper clippings. Schuller received extensive press coverage, both locally and nationally. The references cited in this article on his activities aim only to be representative, not exhaustive. I am indebted to O. K. Werckmeister, who patiently taught me the meaning of ideology, and to Holly Clayson, Tom Cummins, and Dieter Erbsmehl, who critiqued this work in its earlier stages.

2. *Story of a Dream*, 7.

3. Schuller had told Neutra: "Let it not be said that the most beautiful building ever built is the Parthenon." Quoted from John Pastier, "An Evangelist of Unusual Architectural Aspirations," *American Institute of Architects Journal* 68, 2 ser.: 49–50 (hereafter, *AIA*). For a further description and photographs of Neutra's work, see ibid., 50–53. Schuller more accurately described his new church as a "22-acre shopping center for Christ," "Profiles. Forms Under Light: Philip Johnson," *The New Yorker*, 23 May 1977, 44.

4. *Story of a Dream*, 9. For a description and photographs of Neutra's constructions on the site, see *AIA* (May 1979): 48–53. Outside, in the sanctuary pool designed by Neutra, 12 fountains symbolize the 12 apostles. *LA Times*, 17 May 1975, sec. 2, p. 1. The main auditorium is now used for a dining hall and meeting room.

5. *Story of a Dream*, 13–14. The symbolic nature of this construction is revealed by its lack of practicality: each floor is 2,000 square feet, very small for office accommodation, and is cut into by elevator, stairs, and toilets. *AIA* (May 1979): 51.

6. "A Bold Experiment in Modern Religion Arrives at a Milestone," *LA Times*, 17 March 1975, sec. 2, pp. 1, 8. Schuller's Tower of Hope is taller than Disneyland's Matterhorn and Anaheim Stadium's colossal A-frame scoreboard, competing for visibility from the Santa Ana and Garden Grove Freeways, *AIA* (May 1979): 51.

7. *The Story of a Dream*, 15.

8. The New Yorker's long "Profiles" article on Philip Johnson recounts how Mrs. Schuller called her husband's attention to Johnson's work; she had read an article in *Vogue* that featured photographs of Johnson's Fort Worth Water Garden. At first, the Schullers thought Johnson was a landscape architect, *The New Yorker*, 23 May 1977, 44. Johnson had never built a church before. He claimed to have been inspired by Victorian England's Crystal Palace and the Amphitheater of Epidaurus, Greece, S. C. Cowely, "Park and Pray," *Newsweek*, 1 May 1976, 103.

9. *The Robertson World of Construction* (Pittsburgh: H. H. Robertson Co., Spring, 1981), 7.

10. For views from all four sides, see Robert E. Fischer, "The Crystal Cathedral: Embodiment of Light and Nature," *Architectural Record* (Nov. 1980): 78 (hereafter, *Arch Rec*). For a description of the structural engineering, see *Engineering News-Record*, 3 Jan. 1980, 23, 25.

11. The reflective glass panels were supplied by Cupples Products Division of H. H. Robertson Co. For the technical details of the manufacture and installation of these panels, see *The Robertson World of Construction*, Spring 1981, 7. On the engineering of the tubular scaffolding, see *Engineering News-Record*, 3 Jan. 1980, 23, 25; see also Fischer, *Arch Rec* (Nov. 1980): 83. Reports vary on the actual amount of sunlight the glass cover allows to penetrate into the interior; according to Fischer, the glass allows 8% light and 10% solar transmission, ibid., 81.

12. The 185-foot chancel is made of imported Rosso Alicante marble, ibid., 81; also M. Jacqz, "California Design, California Crystal Gem," *Interiors* (Dec. 1980): 42. On the organs, see S. C. Cowley, "Park and Pray," *Newsweek*, 10 May 1976; also the anonymously written brochure, *The Crystal Cathedral Album* (Garden Grove, CA: Robert Schuller Ministries, 1984), 9.

13. The original system had been a disaster; see *LA Times*, 19 Feb. 1982, sec. 2, p. 1. The second system included electronic reinforcement for the sound projection provided by inconspicuous loud speakers mounted on chair backs – one loud speaker to every three or four people. The seat-distributed speakers were still not entirely satisfactory. Paul Goldberger found the new system "makes every voice sound as if it is coming from a movie sound track"; see his, "Philip Johnson's Crystal Cathedral," *On the Rise* (New York: Times Books, 1983), 185.

14. *The Story of a Dream*, 21.

15. Marcel J. Bulteau, *Monographie de la cathédrale de Chartres* (Chartres: Librairie R. Selleret, 1887), I, 87–93, 124–26 (hereafter *Monographie*). Martin Warnke reasoned that the romantic view which has been taken of this phenomenon has overrated its actual contribution to the construction. According to Martin Warnke, this was a way in which the serfs, ordinarily obligated to work, could lay partial claim to the building. The result of their effort so broadened the base of donation to the construction that it negated the obligation of the builder-patron to give partial claim for the building to major elite donors; see Martin Warnke, *Bau und Überbau. Soziologie der mittelalterlichen Architektur nach den Schriftquellen* (Frankfurt am Main: Syndikat, 1976), 42–45 (hereafter *Bau und Überbau*). One wonders if the obvious psychology behind Schuller's staging, to bring in larger contributions from the wealthy, was behind the supposedly spontaneous donations at Chartres as well.

16. Dick Saxty, *National Enquirer*, 8 March 1977.

17. Johnson first saw Chartres on a trip with his mother when he was 13 years old. In 1977, he said the three great architectural experiences of his life had been Chartres Cathedral, the Parthenon, and Ryonji Temple in Kyoto, *The New Yorker*, 23 May 1977, 47. Various other Gothic churches have been posited as Johnson's model. According to Robert E. Fischer, what Johnson "saw" in creating the design

was the Sainte Chapelle in Paris, where the enclosure is glass and structure seems to disappear; Fischer, *Arch Rec* (Nov. 1980): 80. There were other more recent architectural prototypes for Johnson's design, of which he was well aware. Johnson himself cited Norman Foster's Sainsbury Centre for the Visual Arts and Mies Van der Rohe's Friedrichstrasse office tower proposal in Berlin. Barbara Goldstein suggests a lesser known predecessor, the Crystal Chapel in Norman, Oklahoma; see Barbara Goldstein, "New Crystal Palace," *Progressive Architecture* (Dec. 1980): 78 (hereafter *Prog Arch*). On the unknown masons and architects of Chartres, see John James, *The Contractors of Chartres*, 2 vols. (Wyong: Mandorla Publications; London: Croom Helm Limited, 1981); hereafter, *Contractors*.

18. On the medieval understanding of the Gothic cathedral as the image of the Heavenly Jerusalem, see Laurence Hull Stookey, "The Gothic Cathedral as the Heavenly Jerusalem: Liturgical and Theological Sources," *Gesta* 8 (1969): 35–41. Schuller insisted on the glass fabric for his new church. Johnson said Schuller requested a space where the meeting with God could occur "in the presence of the sky and the surrounding world." Quoted from Manfredo Tafuri, "Subaqueous Cathedral," *Domus* (July/August 1980): 12. Remembering his years of preaching in the open air, Schuller said, "When you've worshipped in a drive-in as long as I have, you'll come to the conclusion that a roof that comes between your eyeball and the infinity of space limits your capacity for creative imagination," quoted from Fischer, *Arch Rec* (Nov. 1980): 78.

19. Warnke has analyzed the economic necessity for extra-regional financing of medieval construction, citing Chartres repeatedly, *Bau und Überbau*, 31, 35–39, 41, 55–57, 71–72.

20. The building immediately began to attract tourists. In the summer of 1981, approximately 1,000 tourists a day toured the building and the bookstore, *LA Times*, 19 Feb. 1982, sec. 2, p. 1. By 1983, tourists to Disneyland and Knott's Berry Farm also flocked to see the new architectural creation (and the home of the famous TV show); see Goldberger, *On the Rise*, 184.

21. *The Robertson World of Construction*, Spring 1981, 7. Johnson proclaimed that the Crystal Cathedral is higher, wider, and longer than Notre-Dame in Paris; see Manfredo Tafuri, *Domus* (July/August 1980): 12.

22. I am indebted to François Bucher for this analysis.

23. For diagrams of this geometric system, see Barbara Goldstein, "New Crystal Palace," *Progressive Architecture* (Dec. 1980): 80. For an analysis of the way medieval master masons used geometry to determine their designs, see John James's series of studies listed on p. 559 in Volume II of *Contractors*.

24. Ibid., I, 133–66, especially the hypothetical geometry on 59.

25. Before the mid–19th century, writers thought the present church was built by Fulbert. Around 1845 the discovery was made that the present church was built after a fire in 1194, *Monographie*, I: 99. A new set of explanations for the cathedral was required. Marcel Bulteau published the first new account of the cathedral's financ-

ing, based on one of the miracles related in a thirteenth-century text entitled *The Miracles of the Blessed Virgin Mary in the Church of Chartres*, in *Description de la cathédrale de Chartres* (Chartres: Garnier, 1850). Bulteau expanded the story in his *Monographie*, published in 1887. Subsequent writers repeated the story of the financing of the church. See, for example, Emile Mâle, *Notre-Dame de Chartres*, trans. Sarah Wilson (New York: Harper & Row Publishers, 1983), 65–67 (first edition in French published in 1948). Yves Delaporte's monograph on the windows similarly served as a basis for the tradition in subsequent literature that the town trades donated 42 windows; see Yves Delaporte and Etienne Houvet, *Les vitraux de la cathédrale de Chartres*, 4 vols. (Chartres: E. Houvet, 1926), hereafter, Delaporte, 1926.

26. Otto von Simson, *The Gothic Cathedral. Origins of Gothic Architecture and the Medieval Concept of Order* (New York: Harper & Row, 1964), 163–70, 177–78.

27. George Henderson, *Chartres* (Harmondsworth, Baltimore and Ringwood: Penguin Books, 1968), 68–74; Robert Branner, *Chartres Cathedral* (New York: W. W. Norton, 1969), 80–81.

28. This is apparent in the following excerpt from the thirteenth-century oath that the Chapter required their serfs to swear when they were granted manumission: ". . . you swear on the saints that you will not be part of a commune and that you will not be an organizer of a commune in the city of Chartres or anywhere else against the Chapter or against the church of Chartres. So you will do what you can to prevent it [a commune] from being formed and if it is formed, you will not be a part of it." Translated from quotation in Jean Baptist Souchet, *Histoire du diocèse et de la ville de Chartres* (Chartres: Imprimerie de Garnier, 1866), I: 547–50. The pope backed up the canons' prohibition of a commune; see Étienne de Lépinois and Lucien Merlet, *Cartulaire de Notre-Dame de Chartres* (Chartres: Garnier, 1865), I, nos. 126 and 128, hereafter *CND*.

29. André Chédeville, *Chartres et ses campagnes (XIe–XIIIe s.)* (Paris: Éditions Klincksieck, 1973), 448, 449, 452, 457, hereafter, Chédeville, 1973.

30. Reinhold Kaiser, *Bischofsherrschaft zwischen Königtum und Fürstenmacht* (Bonn: Rohrscheid, 1981), 421, hereafter, Kaiser, 1981. The surviving documents show the count and countess exercising this feudal power from the early twelfth century through the thirteenth. The count had already appointed a master over the tavern keepers in 1131; see René Merlet and Maurice Jusselin, *Cartulaire de la léproserie du Grand-Beaulieu* (Chartres: Imprimerie Ed. Garnier, 1909), no. 24. By 1291, the count still had the final right of appointment of the bakers' selected master; see Boutaric, *Actes du Parlement de Paris* (Paris: H. Plon, 1863), I: 422.

31. The bishop, canons, clerks, and provosts of the cathedral increased the number and usefulness of their serfs with men and women who had lived formerly in the jurisdiction of the count. In modern French literature, these domestic serfs are referred to as *avoués*, but they were not like *avoués* in other towns, who were specifically or exclusively armed protectors of the churchmen and their property. On the *avoués*, see especially *CND* I, cxxix–cxxx; also E. de Lépinois, *Histoire de Chartres*

(1854; rpt. Brussels: Editions Culture et Civilisation, 1976), I: 116–19, hereafter, Lépinois, 1976; A. Blondel, *Essai sur les institutions municipales de Chartres* (Paris: Impr. Durand, 1903), 26–27; Chédeville, 1973, 376–78; Kaiser, 1981, 420.

32. This repeated sequence of events is amply attested to in the deposition of 1194–95. Starting in July of 1194, and continuing until March of 1195, the Archbishop and Archdean of Sens inquired for the countess and for the chapter in order to ascertain what the custom had been concerning the *avoués*, and what had been so far determined by the previous arbitrators, the Archbishop of Reims and the Queen. Witnesses attested to fifty-one adopted serfs who had "crossed over" from service of the count to that of the cathedral; *CND* I: 229–43, no. 121. Nor did the papal legate's visit in 1194 or the Archbishop of Sens' ruling in 1195 end the urban power struggle; see *CND*, no. 123, 244, and also A. Thomas, ed., "Les miracles de Notre-Dame de Chartres," *Bibliothèque de l'École de Chartres* 42 (1881), 508–11, Miracle 1.

33. The occupations of thirteen of the adopted serfs were reported in the deposition of 1194–95. Nine of these were tradesmen: three potters, a barrel maker, a fuller, a changer, a woodworker, a shieldmaker, and an iron worker, *CND* I: 229–43, no. 121. Most of these trades may be seen in the trade windows. Furthermore, we know that the *avoués* engaged in selling wine, and making and selling wool— occupations which are also represented in the trade windows, *CND* I: 244, no. 123.

34. Delaporte, 1926, 8.

35. Thomas, ed., "Les Miracles de Notre-Dame de Chartres," 511.

36. Lépinois, 1976, 125.

37. John James, "What Price Cathedrals?," *Ancient Monuments Society Transactions* 19, 2nd ser. (London, 1972): 58.

38. On the date of the text, see Thomas, 506; and Jean le Marchant, *Miracles de Notre-Dame de Chartres*, ed. Pierre Kunstmann, Société Archéologique d'Eure-et-Loir, Bulletin, vol. 26 (Chartres: Imprimerie Durand, 1973), pt. 1: 1–12.

39. Hostilities had flared up earlier in the year, *CND* II, no. 193. In October, an altercation between one of the Dean's serfs and a townsman triggered the mob violence. The canons excommunicated the townspeople, and the king eventually fined the count's officers 3,000 pounds, *CND* II: 56–62, no. 203.

40. The chapter resided first at Mantes and later at Etampes. The king took 20 town burghers hostage and forced 200 members of all the trades, the agents of the count and the people to swear they would do no further harm to the chapter. For 1,000 pounds the canons purchased from the count the right to close the cloister. Pope Innocent IV granted the chapter permission to hold Matins at five in the morning because of the insecure conditions. Only after all these precautions did the chapter return; see: Lépinois, 1976, 139–43; *CND* II: no. 315, no. 317, no. 324; *Gallia Christiana* (Paris: V. Palme, 1744), VIII: no. 96, col. 367; no. 97, col. 367–68; no. 98, col. 368; no. 99, col. 368–69.

41. See Chédeville's summation of his findings, 505–29.

42. James Rosser Johnson, *The Radiance of Chartres* (New York: Random House, 1964), 10. For a reinterpretation of the dim light in early Gothic cathedrals, see John Gage, "Gothic Glass: Two aspects of a Dionysian Aesthetic," *Art History* vol. 5 (London, 1982): 36–58.

43. The price seems to have crept up. In September, 1980, Schuller claimed the building would cost $16 million, *LA Times*, 13 Sept. 1980, sec. 1A, p. 3. In 1981, a cost of $20 million appears in the press, *LA Times*, 9 Dec. 1981, sec. 1, p. 1.

44. According to Delaporte, donors appear in 116 windows of Chartres Cathedral: 44 kings, princes and lords, 42 artisans, 16 ecclesiastics, 14 others not strictly members of the three aforementioned classes. Delaporte, 1926, 6–7.

45. *Prog Arch*, Dec. 1980, 78.

46. Schuller's program is called "The Hour of Power." Mocking this title and Schuller's "Tower of Hope," popular critics conflate the two by nick-naming Johnson and Burgee's post-modern AT&T building in New York City the "Tower of Power."

47. In 1977, Schuller's TV audience was estimated at 3 million, *The New Yorker*, 23 May 1977, 43. Yet Schuller's TV rating slipped for awhile. In 1982, Schuller's "Hour of Power" audience declined to an estimated 2 million people on 188 radio stations in the United States, *LA Times*, 15 Dec. 1982, sec. 6, p. 1. But in 1984, his program reached 3.5 million people weekly on 192 radio stations; *The Crystal Cathedral Album* (Garden Grove: Robert Schuller Ministries, 1984), 12. In a televised sermon on Feb. 23, 1986, Schuller said Arbitron had recently reported that his program had 6.3% of the audience, top market share compared with other religious broadcasts.

48. Yves Delaporte, *L'ordinaire Chartrain du XIIIe siècle* (Chartres: Société Archéologique d'Eure-et-Loir, 1953), 85, 86, hereafter, Delaporte, 1953.

49. *LA Times*, 9 Dec. 1981, sec. 1, pp. 1, 3, 19. That year, Schuller titled the show "The Glory of Christmas, a Living Nativity." The Times article reported the show cost one million dollars to produce. In the spirit of things, producer Bob Jani (from Radio City Music Hall) attributed the pageant's idea to St. Francis of Assisi, who, after a pilgrimage to Bethlehem, set up a crib with straw at Christmas in Greccio, Italy, and reenacted the nativity. One wonders what St. Francis would have to say about Jani's 40-foot-tall crèche, enlivened by seven suspended subteen angels with nine-foot wing spans, and backed by a 75-foot curtain and 656 light bulbs. Tickets for 40 performances ranged from $6.50 to $12.50, available through Ticketron.

50. *LA Times*, 31 March 1984, sec. 1A, p. 6. Seats for the 1986 Easter performances ranged from $14 to $18.

51. In an article entitled "The Tax Man Shatters the Dreams of Concerts in Crystal Cathedral," the *LA Times* reported on December 15, 1982, that state tax officials considered many of the Crystal Cathedral attractions too commercial to be tax exempt. Schuller had to drop his plans for a 1982–83 concert schedule in the Cathedral, which included eight classical and popular music attractions, from the Prague Sym-

phony Orchestra to Robert Goulet, and the Fifth Dimension. Schuller said he was in the "process of desecularizing" the concerts. But state officials were at that time still reviewing earlier concert appearances by Victor Borge, Fred Waring, and Lawrence Welk, and the renting of space for meetings such as psychological counseling and weight-control classes. The state officials were eyeing greedily Schuller's near $30 million revenues, which had been totally tax-free; see Herman Wong, *LA Times*, 15 Dec. 1982, sec. 4, pp. 1 and 6. The state eventually charged Schuller's church $473,185 in property taxes for 1979 to 1982. Subsequently, however, Schuller managed to obtain a reappraisal of the property value, and compelled the state to refund $247,922, *NY Times*, 28 Sept. 1984, sec. A, p. 16.

52. In 1983, an *LA Times* article zeroed in on Buena Clinton, a 39-acre apartment complex 3 miles from the Crystal Cathedral. The project was dashed up by speculators on a former bean field at the very same time that Schuller constructed Neutra's drive-in church. The apartments were the largest such project in Orange County at the time. Their cheap construction deteriorated rapidly, and their cheap rent brought poor tenants who had to accept faulty wiring, crumbling walls, rotting stairways, blocked-up plumbing, and rodent infestation. Prostitutes and junkies roamed the streets. Slum property owners succeeded in preventing building maintenance enforcement. Local governmental officials justified the situation by claiming that improvements would raise rental costs, leaving 4,500 residents homeless, many illegal aliens unable to pay higher rents, see *LA Times*, 2 Oct. 1983, sec. 1, pp. 1, 3, 24, 26.

53. There is a noticeable lack of mention of charitable activities in the Chartres documents, although one can assume that ritual charities were conducted by the cathedral clergy. A notation in the thirteenth Ordinary that charity should not be given during a Lenten procession implies that the chapter dispensed charity during some festive processions, Delaporte, 1953, 98. The Hôtel Dieu or Aumone de Nôtre Dame, adjacent to the cathedral, was not primarily funded by the cathedral. It was founded by the Countess Berthe in 819, and rebuilt by a knight after the fire of 1134. It was staffed by monks and nuns, but administered by the chapter of the cathedral. The Hôtel was enriched primarily by royalty, nobility, and lesser lords (Lépinois, 1976, I: 332–38). The Crystal Cathedral has concentrated its charitable efforts on far away Chiapas, Mexico, where it has undertaken to establish a medical facility (*The Story of a Dream*, 25). As in the case of medieval documents from Chartres, one simply does not find much mention of charitable activities either on the television program or in the Cathedral's public relations literature.

54. The bishop of Chartres had a protected passageway between his palace and the eastern end of the cathedral. Jan van der Meulen has posited the existence of a whole series of protective bridges that originally connected the cathedral to ancillary buildings; see his "Angrenzende Bauwerke der Kathedrale von Chartres," *Jahrbuch der Berliner Museen* 16 (1974): 5–45. John James found no wear on the thresholds of some of the doors to these passageways. Perhaps some of them were

seldom put to the use for which they were originally intended; see James, *Contractors*, I, chap. 4, n. 4, 5, 7, 8, and 44, and photographs 54, 56, 68.

55. "Perpetuity of faith . . . silently speaks through the centuries," Crystal Cathedral brochure, no date.

56. The *Glossa Ordinaria* interprets the passage to mean that even when exhausted through tribulations and withdrawn from life, Job was augmented by merit, *PL* 113. 819. Schuller has been dubbed a "possibility thinker" because of his theology of success through possibility thinking, which he expounds persistently in his sermons and in his books, whose titles frequently feature this message: *Move Ahead through Possibility Thinking, Peace of Mind Through Possibility Thinking, The Greatest Possibility Thinker That Ever Lived*. According to Schuller, the way to achieve success is to think of desirable possibilities and to work hard toward them, with self-confidence and faith in God's power to help.

57. See Chédeville's excellent chapter, with charts of the chapter's grain production; "L'exploitation du sol," Chédeville, 1973, 161–245. The canons' enormous receipts of wheat were recorded in the 1300 *Polypticon, CND* II: 279–429.

58. In a long article (1976) that mixed humor with frank admiration, the *Wall Street Journal* gave Schuller's business acumen front page coverage in 1976. At this time, Schuller had installed an elaborate computer system to answer the flood of letters he was receiving: William M. Abrams, "Religion Inc. Possibility Thinking and Shrewd Marketing Pay Off for a Preacher," *Wall Street Journal*, 16 Aug. 1976, sec. E, pp. 1 and 12, hereafter, *WSJ*.

59. Paula Span, "Robert Schuller: The Best-Selling Televangelist," *WSJ*, 3 May 1984, sec. E, p. 26.

60. *Notre-Dame de Chartres*, a quarterly publication averaging 20 pages.

61. The king exercised his opportunity to affect the choice of new bishops. After the bishop's consecration, he did fealty to the king and kingdom, and then received the regalia from the king, who had held it during the episcopal interregnum; see Robert L. Benson, *The Bishop Elect* (Princeton: Princeton University Press, 1968), 170–73, 365–67. The king frequently judged the controversies which the bishop and chapter brought before him in their favor, and he performed his royal military duty by commanding the protection of the church of Chartres. The two Gothic builder bishops, Bishop Renaud de Mouçon and Bishop Gauthier, supported the kings in their wars. Bishop Renaud was a close relative of the king, and Bishop Gauthier was a confidant of Queen Blanche; see L. Delisle, *Catalogue des Actes de Philippe Auguste* (Paris: A. Durane, 1856), nos. 409, 800, 1020; *CND* 249, nos. 164; Lépinois, 1976, I: 106, 113; *Gallia Christiana*, VIII, col. 1152.

62. *LA Times*, 17 March 1975, sec. 2, p. 8.

63. The Reverend Donn Moomaw, of the Bel Air Presbyterian Church, then pastor to President and Mrs. Ronald Reagan, who offered the Invocation at the Presidential inauguration in January, 1981, was the featured guest at the Crystal Cathedral on August 9, 1981; *LA Times*, 8 Aug. 1981, sec. 1, p. 31.

64. On October 25, 1981, Schuller hosted John and Donna Crean, and dramatically announced that they had previously donated one million dollars to the new cathedral, but had asked that their gift remain anonymous. Now, they had decided to donate a large ranch in the nearby foothills to the cathedral, and Schuller persuaded them to accept the congregations' acclaim and gratitude publicly. At the same time, the Creans' son was running against seventeen opponents to represent the Republican party in the upcoming election of the 43rd Congressional district, *WSJ*, 6 July 1982, sec. E, p. 14.

65. Walter Benjamin, "The Work of Art in the Age of Mechanical Reproduction," *Illuminations*, trans. Harry Zohn (New York: Schocken Books, 1976), 217–51.

66. Reviewers of Johnson's architectural design of the Crystal Cathedral in the United States were generally complimentary. Not so, the European critics. Ernst Hubeli commented that Johnson's intention to build a neutral space had become instead a Gothic power demonstration, which binds to it the association of a repressive society. Ernst Hubeli, "Vernunfts- und gefühlsmässig out," *Aktuelles Bauen* 16 (1980): 7–13. Manfredo Tafuri saw the building as a subaqueous construction of congealed quotations, filled with stupefied marine fauna. Manfredo Tafuri, "Subaqueous Cathedral," *Domus* (July/August 1980): 8–15. Johnson's "glass machine," according to Tafuri, is "indifferent to the images mirrored in it[;] it flaunts its passivity with respect to their insignificance." Ibid., 12.

67. Ibid.

Index

Index

EDITORS' NOTE: The editors would like to acknowledge with thanks the special assistance of Ms. Deborah Mitchell in the preparation of this Index.

mRts

meδieυαl & Renαissαnce texts & stuδies
is the publishing program of the
Center for Medieval and Early Renaissance Studies
at the State University of New York at Binghamton.

mRts emphasizes books that are needed —
texts, translations, and major research tools.

mRts aims to publish the highest quality scholarship
in attractive and durable format at modest cost.